Practiced Citizenship

Practiced Citizenship

Women, Gender, and the State in Modern France

Edited by Nimisha Barton and Richard S. Hopkins

Foreword by Johnson Kent Wright | Afterword by Elinor A. Accampo

University of Nebraska Press | Lincoln and London

Library of Congress Cataloging-in-Publication Data
Names: Barton, Nimisha, editor. | Hopkins, Richard S., 1961– editor.
Title: Practiced citizenship: women, gender, and the state in modern France / edited by Nimisha Barton, Richard S. Hopkins.
Description: Lincoln: University of Nebraska Press, 2019. | Includes index.
Identifiers: LCCN 2018027872
ISBN 9781496206664 (paperback)
ISBN 9781496212450 (epub)
ISBN 9781496212467 (mobi)
Subjects: LCSH: Women—France—Social conditions—20th century. | Women's rights—France—History—20th century. | Sex role—France—History—20th century. | Women—Political activity—France—History—20th century. | BISAC: HISTORY / Europe / France. | POLITICAL SCIENCE / History & Theory. | SOCIAL SCIENCE / Women's Studies.
Classification: LCC HQ1613 .P73 2019 | DDC 320.082/0944—dc23 LC record available at https://lccn.loc.gov/2018027872

Set in Lyon Text by E. Cuddy.

For Rachel

Contents

Illustrations

Foreword

JOHNSON KENT WRIGHT

No doubt every book is a "labor of love" for its author—or for its editors and contributors, as the case may be. But the timeworn phrase takes on a special meaning in this instance, for reasons that require some explanation. The earliest versions of the essays in *Practiced Citizenship* were first presented at a one-day conference in April 2014, honoring the historian Rachel G. Fuchs on the occasion of her retirement from Arizona State University. There is nothing unusual about saluting academic retirement in this fashion. But the conference was in fact uncommon in every respect. Although it was organized by three of Rachel's colleagues at ASU, it was staged without institutional support or external funding of any kind. Those who attended—current and former students of Rachel's and longtime colleagues and collaborators, traveling from locations across North America and Europe—made their way to Tempe on their own. There they paid tribute to their friend and mentor, not with conventional homages but simply by sharing reports on their own current historical research. No one who was present that Saturday will forget the astonishing array of topics and images that passed by, as if glimpsed in some dizzying historical kaleidoscope: *blanchisseuses* laboring on the banks of the Seine; fond depictions of the Restoration's "royal family"; nuns humiliated by a public *fessée*; murderous wives and teenage toughs hauled before the bar; diseased children suffering in hospital; feminist novelists and lawyers defending indigents and immigrants or protesting the "white" slave trade; women miners in the Ruhr and Silesia, converts to Catholicism in French North America; and, above all, that small herd of cattle flummoxed by a "ha-ha." The cornucopic display of work in progress honored and delighted Rachel far more than any number of ordinary tributes would have done. Unforgettable too was her affecting expression of gratitude at the end of the proceedings, alluding to a difficult patch in relations with her home institution: "You made sure that I ended my career here on a positive note; that was important to you, as it was important to me, and thanks to you, I *have* ended it on a positive note."

What a career it had been. Rachel was born in Staten Island in 1939, and her initial work at Boston University, inspired by family roots in Belarus, was in Russian history. By the time she had launched her family and returned to graduate study, she had switched to French social history, completing a Ph.D. at Indiana University with the late Bill Cohen in 1980. She took the job at ASU in 1983, and after that there was no stopping her. Her first book, *Abandoned Children: Foundlings and Child Welfare in Nineteenth-Century France*, came out in 1984, followed by *Poor and Pregnant in Paris: Strategies for Survival in the Nineteenth Century* (1992), *Gender and Poverty in Nineteenth-Century Europe* (2005), and the award-winning *Contested Paternity: Constructing Families in Modern France* (2008).[1] Founded on meticulous archival research, combining a sociologist's understanding of societal structures with a psychologist's insight into individual choices, this was a body of work that made Rachel one of the world's foremost authorities on the history of the modern family. That was more than enough to earn her the deep respect of her colleagues and students. But their profound and abiding affection owed much as well to her unmatched record of service to the profession in general and to the field of French history in particular. An enthusiastic teacher and tireless promoter of her graduate students, Rachel relished the kind of committee work avoided by most of the rest of us. She rarely said no to a *folie raisonnable*, twice hosting the annual meeting of the Society for French Historical Studies at ASU and devoting an enormous amount of her energies in the years just before her retirement to coediting the journal *French Historical Studies*. As everyone who worked with her knows, Rachel brought to all these collective labors a zestful *joie de vivre* and *joie de travailler ensemble* all her own.

There was no sign of those joys abating or of Rachel's slowing down with retirement. If anything, relinquishing the journal and stepping away from ASU permitted a fresh release of professional energies. The conference in spring 2014 was followed by research trips to France, as Rachel turned her attention to not one but two unfinished writing projects, with tantalizing working titles: "The Angel-Makers of Mission Street: Abortion and Community in Late Nineteenth-Century Paris" and "Crossing Boundaries: Families in Vichy France." Meanwhile, and not surprisingly, Rachel missed students intensely. This was one of the reasons she accepted an invitation to teach at the Citadel in Charleston in the fall of 2016—no doubt enjoying the honor and the improbability of serving as the General Mark W. Clark Distinguished Visiting Chair of History. The cadets, it is safe to say, got a little more in the way of family history in their class on World War II than they were probably used to. While in Charleston, however, fate intervened, cruelly. Having just returned there in mid-October, after evacuation owing to Hurricane Matthew, Rachel suffered a massive stroke and never regained consciousness. She passed away two days later, with her husband, Norman, and her children, Mindy and Daniel, at her side. For those who knew her, her death is still difficult to accept or even conceive. She had one of those personalities, brimming with vitality and buoyancy, with an apparently effortless capacity for making new friends while clinging to the old, that made her sudden disappearance all the more shocking and painful.

Rachel's premature departure naturally affected work on this volume, which was already well underway by then. Its editors and contributors had keenly looked forward not just to dedicating *Practiced Citizenship* to her but to placing the book in her hands. Can there be any doubt about the intense pleasure and pride with which she would have received it? At the conference in 2014, the question arose whether the participants might be said to represent a distinctively "Fuchsite" school or approach to the social history of modern France and French families. That Rachel firmly rejected. The sheer variety of historical topics, and means of capturing them, on display that day in Tempe obviously precluded any such notion. Besides, Rachel was the first to insist that her own historical research and writing was never a one-woman show, but depended on that of a whole cohort of like-minded practitioners. For just that reason, however, Nimisha Barton and Richard Hopkins are surely right to suggest that *Practiced Citizenship* ought to be regarded as a kind of companion volume or even sequel to *Gender and the Politics of Social Reform in France*, the collection of essays that Rachel edited with Elinor Accampo and Mary Lynn Stuart in 1995—long a touchstone in the field, of which she was justly proud.[2] But if Rachel would have welcomed that suggestion, what would she have made of the title itself and the editors' critical use of T. H. Marshall's famous analysis of the development of "citizenship" in modern history—corrected, of course, for its astigmatism in regard to gender?

It is true that these ideas played no role in putting together the original conference and scarcely figured in the discussion inspired by the presentations. All the same, one might hazard the guess that not only would Rachel have approved of *Practiced Citizenship* as title and organizing theme, but it might even have persuaded her of the existence of a specifically "Fuchsite" approach to history after all. Barton and Hopkins's introduction and Elinor Accampo's incisive retrospective analysis both demonstrate how apt Marshall's scheme is for tying together the various contributions to the volume—that is, once the true role of individual political praxis in propelling modern citizenship forward has been restored to it. What the essays together suggest is something far closer to the way in which female self-emancipation has actually been won in the modern world, in France and elsewhere, with generations of wives, mothers, sisters, and daughters taking initiative, so to speak: acting as citizens in the street, the press, in courtrooms, and in committee rooms, long before they were actually able to do so at the ballot box. But readers and admirers of Rachel will also recognize how appropriate the idea of "practiced citizenship" is for capturing the essence of her own historical work—and a lot of her personality too. What attracted her attention most of all, as a historian, from *Abandoned Children* to *Contested Paternity*, was a very specific kind of historical actor: ordinary men and, above all, women who, at a crucial turning point in their lives, decided to take matters into their own hands. As for her own outlook, Rachel always accurately described herself as a "political animal," in not just the Aristotelian but also the Schmittian sense of the term. As it happens, one of France's greatest living philosophers recently published a profound meditation on the idea and reality of citizenship, from antiquity to the present.[3] Concluding with a plea to "democratize democracy," Etienne Balibar argues that the essential act of citizenship in the West has always been neither "participation" nor "resistance" but rather "insurrection." A similar understanding of the term can certainly be sensed in Rachel's work as a historian and in the way she lived her life. It is difficult to imagine a more fitting tribute to her memory than *Practiced Citizenship*.

Notes

1. Rachel G. Fuchs, *Abandoned Children: Foundlings and Child Welfare in Nineteenth-Century France* (Albany: State University of New York Press, 1984); *Poor and Pregnant in Paris: Strategies for Survival in the Nineteenth Century* (New Brunswick NJ: Rutgers University Press, 1992); *Gender and Poverty in Nineteenth-Century Europe* (Cambridge, UK: Cambridge University Press, 2005): *Contested Paternity: Constructing Families in Modern France* (Baltimore: Johns Hopkins University Press, 2008).
2. Elinor A. Accampo, Rachel G. Fuchs, and Mary Lynn Stuart, eds., *Gender and the Politics of Social Reform in France, 1870-1914* (Baltimore: Johns Hopkins University Press, 1995). See also now Rachel G. Fuchs and Anne R. Epstein, eds., *Gender and Citizenship in Historical and Transnational Perspective* (London: Palgrave Macmillan, 2016).
3. Etienne Balibar, *Citizenship*, trans. Thomas Scott-Railton (Malden MA: Polity, 2015).

Introduction

NIMISHA BARTON AND RICHARD S. HOPKINS

For over fifty years, scholars have grappled with the model of citizenship first forwarded by the British sociologist T. H. Marshall. According to his schema, the attainment of full citizenship in modern nation-states proceeded in three consecutive stages: from civil rights (i.e., the right to work and make contracts) to political rights (i.e., the right to vote) to social rights (i.e., the right to a certain minimum standard of living guaranteed by social legislation).[1] The shortcomings of this model as it pertained to women seemed clear to feminist scholars early on. As the political theorist Carole Pateman demonstrated, the modern social contract undergirding nation-states was from the start premised on an implicit "sexual contract." According to Pateman, the birth of modern democracy necessarily entailed the total political erasure of women.[2] Indeed this is what many historians of the French Revolution have demonstrated and declared.[3] That women in France did not gain suffrage until a century and a half after the Revolution would appear to confirm these readings.

Yet through the concept of "the social" historians since the 1990s have succeeded in reexamining and ultimately complicating both Marshall's typology and early feminist readings of women's total exclusion from the body politic and the national community. For this generation of scholars, "the social" denoted the nineteenth-century reimagining of the liberal republic's engagement with the citizen through the social realm, a domain considered distinct from both political and economic spaces.[4] While scholarly accounts initially focused on the shifting (male) citizen's relationship to the state as a political and economic subject, eventually they came to interrogate how the state's newfound interest in the social invested women with great importance, in spite of their lack of formal political rights.[5] As Denise Riley and Joshua Cole demonstrated in particular, the social domain was an object of inquiry and a site of objectification by state planners, social scientists, doctors, and others who were looking for pathologies in the working classes to explain their propensity to violence, revolt, and insurrection of all varieties. As Riley explains, their inquiries into the social led to an expanded interest in families, specifically "familial standards" of "health, education, hygiene, fertility, demography, chastity and fecundity." Against the background of an alarming "crisis of depopulation" in late nineteenth-century France, families emerged as a seemingly depoliticized object of study, an essential building block of society that could rally many to its noble cause. And, as Riley put it, "the heart of the family [was] inexorably the woman."[6]

In their pathbreaking book, *Gender and the Politics of Social Reform*, Elinor A. Accampo, Rachel G. Fuchs, and Mary Lynn Stewart used the rhetoric and actions of Third Republican statesmen in France to illustrate the centrality of women and families to that corner of the social realm in which the state was most interested in the late nineteenth and early twentieth centuries: namely, the health and welfare of the declining French population. In a frightening era of depopulation, these scholars argued, women became central to the national project of increasing the quality and quantity of the French population and thus integral to the crafting of the welfare state. Populationist and familialist fears crystallized in a bevy of maternalist and family-centered welfare laws intended to shore up families by protecting and providing for women. Throughout, the particular culture of republicanism in France rallied both men and women to the cult of republican motherhood, an indispensable construct of the French nation.[7] In the end Accampo, Fuchs, and Stewart shed new light on the evolution of women's citizenship, claiming that social rights rooted in republican notions of womanhood came early and fast for women in France even while political rights would continue to lag behind. The seeming inconsistency resulted from the "gendered thinking" of Third Republican statesmen who sought "not only to create a version of republican motherhood to serve the family and the state, but also to use women to tame working-class men."[8]

Gender and the Politics of Social Reform was pivotal in demonstrating women's centrality to the social from the perspective of middle-class men, who sought to redefine womanhood, harness women's reproductive capacities, and engage in nation-state building with an eye to women's gendered service to the state. Building on that significant scholarly contribution, this volume seeks to tell the complicated story of how the newfound realm of the social—from the social legislation it produced to the very activist space it furnished—also provided a space *for women* to maneuver, exert power, and achieve their own ends.[9] In order to demonstrate the significance of women's deeds and words in the public realm, the volume engages with recent scholarship on social citizenship that tends to highlight how citizenship is lived, practiced, and deployed by historical subjects who nevertheless lack the formal status of citizenship. Through an emphasis on citizenship as practice, these essays demonstrate how gender normativity and the constraints placed on women as a result nevertheless created opportunities for a renegotiation of the social—and sexual—contract. In the process this volume offers a rereading and reinterpretation of well-trod historiographical terrain on women, gender, and citizenship in modern France. Most significant, however, the volume suggests how a return to the social may prove a fruitful avenue of inquiry to explore citizenship cultures and practices and how scholars might reconsider citizenship for marginalized groups through this creative new framework, as indeed many have already begun to do.[10]

According to traditional historical narratives, the French Revolution and the legal codification of patriarchal norms under the Napoleonic Code (1804) and later the Civil Code (1815) cast a shadow over women's autonomy, agency, and exercise of citizenship in nineteenth- and twentieth-century France. Scholarly consensus regards the Civil Code as an authoritarian and paternalistic legal document enshrining male power within the household at the head of the family and male control over women within the confines of marriage. Essentially the Civil Code shaped the private lives of men and women by codifying patriarchy in ways that reflected in miniature the larger inscription of patriarchal gender norms in the newfound polity, more broadly.

Further circumscription of women's lives and citizenship continued in the first half of the nineteenth century, with political and religious arguments about women's rights that relied on sexual difference. Whether in the utopian socialist vision of "the feminine," which called for women's emancipation, or in the traditionalist Catholic and conservative construction of republican motherhood, essentialist arguments served to relegate most French women to the domestic sphere, while at the same time giving rise to socialist and liberal feminist movements in opposition.[11] When women transgressed the domestic sphere and rose as militants during the Commune to challenge the ideologies that oppressed them, critics and supporters of the uprising alike used the language of domesticity and women's essential nature to deem the *communardes* "unnatural," dangerous, and uncontrolled women.[12]

The crisis of depopulation that appeared with full force in the 1880s further brought women—and women's bodies—under patriarchal state and social control. As women assumed greater importance in the effort to successfully repopulate France, the disciplinary state apparatus disincentivized nonprocreative behavior, especially after the "hecatomb" of the First World War. Despite the legend of *les années folles*—a hedonistic period that conjures up images of a scantily clad and gyrating Josephine Baker, jazz nightclubs, and the tomboyish *garçonne*—the post-World War I specter of a "civilization without sexes" was frightening to many contemporaries and experienced by some Frenchwomen as a deeply conservative time.[13] Indeed France passed the most conservative reproductive legislation in Europe after the war, the centerpiece of which was a 1920 law outlawing abortion, prosecuting abortion doctors and their clients harshly, and even punishing purveyors of contraceptive propaganda.[14] Moreover the demands of repopulation presented immense obstacles to the French feminist struggle, compelling women to adopt familialist claims to advance their campaigns for legal and political equality.[15] Many scholars see these factors as together responsible for the tardiness of women's suffrage in France, secured only in 1944, and by extension, as confirmation of Pateman's thesis.

Yet in the past two decades a chorus of feminist rereadings of these narratives has opened up fresh perspectives that constitute the new theoretical grounding for the contributors to this volume. To start, many historians have begun to question the extent to which the French Revolution severed women from political, economic, and associational life. These scholars tend to shift our gaze from the letter of the law to the manner in which the law was lived, practiced, and "maneuvered" in daily life.[16] As the nineteenth century wore on, both middle-class and working-class women made strides that cannot be adequately understood when viewed exclusively through the lens of formal political enfranchisement and legal modes of participation. For instance, feminist rereadings even within the field of French feminism have led to surprising and creative interpretations that contradict what was once considered orthodoxy in the field. Although the history of feminism in France was once reduced to an either/or choice between the assertion of abstract individualism (in the Anglo-Saxon model) or the adoption of relational or familial feminism (in the French model), in her groundbreaking 1984 article, Karen Offen demonstrated how French feminists "subvert[ed] the sexual system from within" by claiming republican motherhood to advance claims for suffrage, thus demonstrating what she calls their "political astuteness."[17] Moreover recent works have opened wide the meaning, aesthetics, and practices that composed *fin-de-siècle* feminist politics and subjectivities, successfully reimagining what it meant to repurpose existing political, social, and culture tools to women's advantage.[18]

In addition to positing an expanded definition of feminist action and resistance, scholars have also demonstrated how middle-class women in France, as elsewhere throughout Europe, proved themselves to be active participants in, leaders of, and architects of a vibrant associational life centered predominantly on philanthropic works, regardless of formal feminist self-identification. In *Blessed Motherhood, Bitter Fruit*, Accampo explored the contradictions that nineteenth-century feminists embodied through her study of Nelly Roussel, who, as a

French wife and mother of three, represented the ideal of the "eternal feminine" while simultaneously touring the French countryside to proselytize about the importance of birth control.[19] Influenced by Catholic traditions or aristocratic notions of noblesse oblige (both of which figured women's civic participation as nurturing and healing to the body politic), these women's attentions were devoted above all to alleviating the heavy burdens placed on working-class women, children, and families. Their mandate grew increasingly pressing as the nineteenth century blurred into the twentieth and an alarming "crisis of depopulation" gripped the French state and society.

By the 1880s populationism drastically changed the terms on which women of all classes would participate with the state and French society. Male politicians, statesmen, philanthropists, and others greeted the maternalist welfare activities of middle-class Frenchwomen with enthusiasm, bankrolling many of their philanthropic activities that sought to increase the quantity and quality of the French population. As the nineteenth century wore on, the patriarchal thrust of the Napoleonic Code, which inscribed men as the head of families and husbands as masters of wives, slowly eroded as feminist activists protested the Code's restrictions on divorce and paternity suits. Meanwhile, as Fuchs demonstrates in *Contested Paternity*, "activist judges" sided with women against men who would "seduce," impregnate, and desert them.[20] With increasing success, working-class women in France brought even middle-class men to justice, drastically reversing both class and gender relations of power that previously would have seemed unthinkable. Consequently scholars have traced a wave of social legislation at the end of the nineteenth century and into the twentieth that further chipped away at male privilege.[21]

In short, while previous scholarship emphasized the continuity of repression and disenfranchisement of women in France, recent scholarship in the field has instead begun to trace a broader shift toward paternalist state intervention in the realm of the social, particularly where women, children, and families were concerned, that in fact *undermined* male privilege. This new body of scholarship suggests that while women were denied many formal rights, the social domain nevertheless provided many opportunities for engagement and negotiation with as well as resistance to political, economic, social, cultural, and other structural constraints. In other words, whereas historians once observed only the constraints placed on women by the gendered expectations of normative female behavior and especially republican motherhood, they now examine the ways in which these norms necessarily invited challenge and resistance and, on occasion, even upended the existing political, economic, and social order.

In the face of mounting evidence, many scholars have turned both Marshall's typology of citizenship and early feminist readings of women's total political exclusion on their head, proposing instead that women in France were in fact beneficiaries of social rights prior to either political or economic rights of citizenship. Of course the exercise of their social rights was contingent on a gendered and sexualized embodiment of their reproductive selves. That is, they enjoyed the prerogatives of social citizenship in their capacity as mothers and wives—a variety of citizenship mediated through their bodies.[22] Women who transgressed these boundaries—by choosing not to marry or bear children or by choosing to use contraception—endured social ostracism, at best, legal punishment, at worst.[23] Although less often acknowledged, men who transgressed these boundaries were also increasingly ostracized by the late nineteenth and early twentieth centuries, when populationist and pronatalist sentiment demanded that all citizens—men and women—do their reproductive duty to ensure the future of France.[24]

Thus, while acknowledging the at times severe political and legal limits placed on women from the birth of democracy in 1789 until women's suffrage following World War II, this collection of essays nevertheless speaks to revisionist interpretations of women's and gender history in France that traces the state's growing "embrace" of women over the course of two centuries. Though it would not be codified into law until 1944, and further legal battles would seek to secure women's rights until the 1960s,[25] these contributions nevertheless highlight the creative possibilities that appeared at moments of political rupture and rebirth in the course of history as well as the everyday ways in which political, economic, and social citizenship were shaped, manufactured, and practiced in daily life.[26] In other words, this volume addresses women's *exclusion from* and *participation in* the social realm through the prism of their own words and deeds. Put simply, though they were formally excluded from the body politic in some ways (i.e., female suffrage), they emerged as beneficiaries of the state in other ways (i.e., welfare benefits).

As scholars have amply demonstrated, legal limitations founded on traditional gender norms presented very real obstacles to women's exercise of citizenship and access to political, economic, and civil rights. Yet these same repressive constructs prompted women to locate alternative ways to carve out personal and political power. In order to engage with the political life of the nation and to improve their lives and the lives of their children, women in France sought to influence both national and international policy by creating activist networks at home, throughout Europe, in the empire, and even farther afield. In the process they managed to redefine the meanings of citizenship even in the absence of actual political rights. This volume traces those complex power negotiations in which women often deployed normative gendered categories in order to exercise a type of citizenship that was increasingly disposed to help women out of a strong populationist ethos. The contributors to this book employ creative interpretive frameworks and analyze new archival sources to reshape our scholarly conceptions of gender, citizenship, and the modern French state.

Chronologically the chapters span the modern period, starting with the French Revolution and continuing up to the Vichy period. Methodologically the chapters tend toward social history, revolving around practice and lived experience, though several (Jarvis, Thompson, and Pedersen) feature fresh readings of visual and literary texts to examine how the debate over women's activism and changing gender roles played out on cultural terrain. Thematically the chapters move from considerations of gender and the family in the realm of revolutionary and restoration politics toward working-class French and immigrant women's interactions with state and quasi-state actors and infrastructures in the late nineteenth and twentieth century. The final contributions move the narrative from working-class women's maneuvering of the social domain as constructed through familialist laws and institutions to middle-class women's maneuvering of the social domain through the pursuit of national and international social reform efforts on behalf of all women. Together they suggest how the social realm furnished women with new tools, strategies, and opportunities while simultaneously acknowledging that the very strictness of reinvigorated traditional gender roles accompanying populationism compelled them to do so. In other words, the contributions honor individual agency even—indeed especially—within the confines of limitations.

Katie Jarvis opens the collection by rethinking the narrative of women as a priori excluded from modern political citizenship. In an analysis of the rich visual imagery attending an early act of women's revolutionary violence in 1791, Jarvis argues for a modern version of citizenship that was not immediately gendered male, that created space for revolutionary women to enact anticlerical forms of citizenship on behalf of the budding nation. In the end, Jarvis concludes, "the Dames [revolutionary market women] advanced a form of embodied citizenship in which individuals contributed to the body politic through their social relationships." This contribution sets the scene for the rest of the volume by introducing the concept of citizenship as formed in the crucible of revolution and the legacies that women in the nineteenth and twentieth centuries would inherit.

Just as ideas about family, maternity, and the justness of gendered punishment informed the revolutionaries' response to female violence and women's place in the body politic, Victoria E. Thompson's chapter continues to interrogate how social relationships—specifically the family—structured political life and legitimacy in postrevolutionary France. She focuses especially on representations of the Bourbon family during the Restoration that posited the royal family as both a social institution and a metaphor for state and society. During the Restoration, Thompson argues, citizenship was still a relatively new and unstable concept and, in depictions of Marie-Thérèse, "diverse models of feminine belonging to the nation ... were still in play in the early nineteenth century." Significantly, Thompson concludes, "rather than seeing the family as a unit that constrained women to domestic roles, the example of Marie-Thérèse demonstrates how family belonging could also provide women with novel ways of exercising civic participation."

Utilizing social historical approaches, Nimisha Barton and Stephanie McBride-Schreiner next demonstrate how motherhood provided working-class French and immigrant women with ways to exercise their power vis-à-vis state officials. Through analyses of police and hospital records, respectively, their chapters complement one another by demonstrating how women lay claim to resources to, as Barton writes, "effectively and imaginatively get what they needed in order to ensure their survival." Both contributions are attentive to the mobilization of gendered social identities: working-class mothers on the one hand, middle-class men on the other. According to Barton, "That French and immigrant wives, widows, and mothers possessed and performed social identities that the state valued, incentivized, and amply rewarded during this period is key to their success but does not undermine their successes nor the savviness of their strategies."

Although immigrant and working-class women were more stymied than most by the limits to formal citizenship placed on them by all-male legislators and politicians, middle-class French women in particular were able to reimagine the terms of their civic participation in France, as Jean Elisabeth Pedersen, Eliza Earle Ferguson, Cheryl A. Koos, and Sara L. Kimble show. These four chapters thus shift our gaze to middle-class female reformers who, in spite of their lack of formal political rights, nevertheless engaged in various forms of activism that sought to improve the lot of many, particularly working-class women and children.

In her analysis of what she terms "the social novel," Pedersen's argument is firmly in line with recent interpretations forwarded most notably by Lynn Hunt regarding the revolutionary potential of novels to help men and women access the interiority of others and thus sympathize with the plight of those less fortunate than themselves.[27] Through the "imagined empathy" elicited by three social novels, Pedersen demonstrates how female authors engaged in social reform efforts through literature and fiction rather than the emerging statistical sciences upon which the social is commonly believed to be founded. She points to the significance of women's literary production in women's activist struggles, commonly overlooked in favor of formal political (read: male) participation in reform. Describing a combination of what she calls "authorship and activism," Pedersen also restores women to the literary tradition of social novelists that otherwise tend to exclude them in favor of more well-known male authors, such as Victor Hugo and Charles Dickens. Perhaps unsurprisingly, unlike male authors who located the social reform impulse for tragic women within the breasts of chivalrous men, female authors "identified the cause of social reform with the efforts and achievements of female characters."

Some enterprising women also involved themselves in international, imperial, and transnational social justice struggles, as the contributions of Ferguson and Kimble make clear. Turning from social reform on the domestic front to the international struggle for human rights on the world stage, Ferguson's chapter examines the role of upper-class philanthropic women leaders who were active in turn-of-the-century movements against white slavery across the continent. Ferguson analyzes the climate of gender and sexual panic surrounding not just Frenchwomen but French girls (*jeunes filles*) that proved fertile ground in which middle-class women's voluntary associations flourished. Availing themselves of (and perhaps even "exploiting," as Ferguson puts it) the current legal and political climate intended to protect seemingly vulnerable young women, elite *bourgeoises* successfully shaped international laws such as the Convention relative à la répression de la traite des blanches, lack of formal political rights notwithstanding. Though Ferguson is quick to highlight that women could only ever "persuade," never "compel" statesmen to do what they wished, her argument nevertheless illustrates that women engaged in the social realms with creativity and determination.

Because both Pedersen and Ferguson analyze the words and deeds of middle-class Frenchwomen, the bourgeois politics of morality and respectability always loomed in the background. Behind much of the do-gooding impulse of these female reformers were gendered fears about (im)morality, sexuality, and the nation. These fears heightened the farther right along the political spectrum one went, which is the subject of Koos's chapter. Koos analyzes conservative Catholic women who engaged in the public sphere in order to uplift women and children and demonstrates that women's activism led them to causes both liberatory and oppressive. According to Koos, middle-class organizations run by conservative Frenchwomen focused on restrictive gender roles, especially women's obligations to children and families, with terrible consequence. As Koos argues, their associational activities "helped to create the ideological climate for the transition to the Vichy Regime and contributed to its early popularity and acceptance." In this sense Koos lays bare the central question of this volume: Did women, by adopting traditional gender hierarchies rather than challenging them, enhance the scope of creative possibility for women or "further reinforc[e] women's structural political marginalization at a crucial moment in France's history"? As it turns out, the answer might be, frustratingly, both.

Kimble broadens our perspective with a transnational history of how feminists in France and the United States used international bodies to force the issue of women's suffrage onto the national agenda back home. Specifically she examines "the value these early feminists placed on international law as a means to redress the imbalance of power between men and women." Kimble's contribution thus opens up new avenues of transnational scholarly inquiry, arguing, "By seeking the international as the site for legal change and subsequent enforcement, these feminist activists questioned the value of the nation-state as the final authority to resolve problems of inequality in citizenship." Like Ferguson, Kimble shows how "the national context of Third Republic France became a proving ground for women's activism in emerging transnational civil society."

In a thought-provoking synthesis, Elinor A. Accampo furthers the discussion of women, gender, and citizenship with an emphasis on the limitations to practiced citizenship that these authors elucidate. Her insightful observations suggest that future directions for this line of scholarship, pushing us to examine the extent to which social rights for women advanced the cause of women's rights and, more broadly still, the interests of women as autonomous beings. Her contribution to this conversation reminds us precisely what makes women, gender, and citizenship an exciting and fruitful ground for continued scholarly inquiry.

In this introduction we laid out the scholarly conversation on women, gender, and citizenship in France as it has evolved in the past three decades. We have surveyed feminist readings of women's citizenship in France that tend to characterize theirs as a debased form of citizenship whose main features were formal political, economic, and civic disenfranchisement. By contrast, the contributors to this volume demonstrate how the political and legal culture of modern France evolved over the course of the nineteenth and twentieth century in ways that tended to bring women into the social and cultural life of the nation as well as the state and civil spheres rather than further exclude them. Through an analysis of women's participation in the social realm, we suggest how citizenship was lived, practiced, and deployed by women in France. This volume thus demonstrates how gender normativity and the constraints placed on women as a result nevertheless created opportunities for a renegotiation of the social contract.

Of note, this volume is not about exceptional women who worked concertedly and self-consciously to undermine patriarchal customs, norms, and laws.[28] Rather it concerns women who lived more ordinary lives, who were less exceptional, and who, in many instances, ascribed to certain traditional gender norms. What is surprising, however, is the way they knowingly worked these gender codes to get what they needed from the French state and society. Though they rarely acted out of a self-conscious desire to subvert norms, the ways they knowingly inhabited gendered norms and behavior and deployed them to their own benefit makes them perhaps more revealing than their nonconformist sisters. In the end, the strictest gender hierarchies allow—indeed impel—the ongoing search for creative ways to subvert the existing order through daily practice in everyday life.

Significantly this volume also challenges the existing transnational scholarly conversation about citizenship, which often centers on laws, discourses, and ideologies of those in power. In that sense citizenship has often been imagined by scholars prescriptively and, by extension, proscriptively. It is as practice and participation in the civic and associational life of the nation—that is, through the social—that the contributors to this volume understand citizenship. Citizenship entails more than edicts from on high mandating and even legislating certain forms of embodied behavior. Rather it is a lived experience created from below and responding to conditions "on the ground." Therefore the contributions to this volume suggest that the field collectively reexamine the meanings—and limits—of formal citizenship as a category of historical analysis that has been profoundly shaped by the so-called linguistic turn and its concomitant overemphasis on discourse, rhetoric, and ideology.[29] Instead this volume emphasizes the importance of practice in the making of *both* gender and citizenship. As such, it invites scholars working in the transnational fields of women's and gender history as well as citizenship studies to reimagine citizenship as produced not from on high nor resisted from below; rather we encourage scholars to reconsider citizenship as manufactured through informal, everyday experiences, as deployed by savvy historical actors who shape the civic life of the nation through daily practice, constraints notwithstanding.

Notes

1. T. H. Marshall, *Citizenship and Social Class, and Other Essays* (Cambridge, UK: Cambridge University Press, 1950).
2. Carole Pateman, *The Sexual Contract* (Cambridge, UK: Polity Press, 1988).
3. Joan B. Landes, *Women and the Public Sphere in the Age of the French Revolution* (Ithaca NY: Cornell University Press, 1988); Joan Wallach Scott, *Only Paradoxes to Offer: French Feminists and the Rights of Man* (Cambridge MA: Harvard University Press, 1996); Dominique Godineau, *The Women of Paris and Their French Revolution* (Berkeley: University of California Press, 1998); Françoise Gaspard et al., *Au pouvoir, citoyennes! Liberté, egalité, parité* (Paris: Seuil, 1992); Charles Sowerwine, "Revising the Sexual Contract: Women's Citizenship and Republicanism in France, 1789–1944," in *Confronting Modernity in Fin-de-Siècle France: Bodies, Minds, and Gender,*

ed. Christopher E. Forth and Elinor A. Accampo (Basingstoke, UK: Palgrave Macmillan, 2010).

4. Jacques Donzelot, *L'invention du social: Essai sur le déclin des passions politiques* (Paris: Seuil, 1994).

5. Denise Riley, *Am I That Name? Feminism and the Category of "Women" in History* (Minneapolis: University of Minnesota Press, 1988); Joshua Cole, *The Power of Large Numbers: Population, Politics, and Gender in Nineteenth-Century France* (Ithaca NY: Cornell University Press, 2000). See also François Ewald, *L'Etat providence* (Paris: B. Grasset, 1996); Mary Poovey, *Making a Social Body: British Cultural Formation, 1830-1864* (Chicago: University of Chicago Press, 1995); Judith F. Stone, *The Search for Social Peace: Reform Legislation in France, 1890-1914* (Albany: State University of New York Press, 1985). For Germany, see George Steinmetz, *Regulating the Social: The Welfare State and Local Politics in Imperial Germany* (Princeton NJ: Princeton University Press, 1993. For a transatlantic perspective see Daniel T. Rodgers, *Atlantic Crossings: Social Politics in a Progressive Age* (Cambridge MA: Harvard University Press, 2009.

6. Riley, *Am I That Name?*, 50.

7. Elinor A. Accampo, Rachel G. Fuchs, and Mary Lynn Stewart, eds., *Gender and the Politics of Social Reform in France, 1870-1914* (Baltimore: Johns Hopkins University Press, 1995). See also Philip G. Nord, "The Welfare State in France, 1870-1914," *French Historical Studies* 18, no. 3 (1994): 821–38; Elisa Camiscioli, *Reproducing the French Race: Immigration, Intimacy, and Embodiment in the Early Twentieth Century* (Durham NC: Duke University Press, 2009).

8. Elinor A. Accampo, "Gender, Social Policy, and the Formation of the Third Republic: An Introduction," in Accampo et al., *Gender and the Politics of Social Reform*, 21–22.

9. As Accampo wrote, "Women did often resist efforts to regulate their lives, sometimes by protesting protective labor legislation, other times by manipulating the system to their own ends and in fact permanently bending the system itself" ("Gender, Social Policy, and the Formation of the Third Republic," 22).

10. For example see Andrea Mansker, *Sex, Honor, and Citizenship in Early Third Republic France* (Basingstoke, UK: Palgrave Macmillan, 2011); Elizabeth Heath, *Wine, Sugar, and the Making of Modern France: Global Economic Crisis and the Racialization of French Citizenship, 1870-1910* (Cambridge, UK: Cambridge University Press, 2014); Catherine Raissiguier, *Reinventing the Republic: Gender, Migration, and Citizenship in France* (Stanford CA:

Stanford University Press, 2010); Minayo Nasiali, *Native to the Republic: Empire, Social Citizenship, and Everyday Life in Marseille Since 1945* (Ithaca NY: Cornell University Press, 2016).

11. Claire Goldberg Moses and Leslie W. Rabine, *Feminism, Socialism, and French Romanticism* (Bloomington: Indiana University Press, 1993); Jean Elisabeth Pedersen, *Legislating the French Family: Feminism, Theater and Republican Politics, 1870–1920* (New Brunswick NJ: Rutgers University Press, 2003); Whitney Walton, *Eve's Proud Descendants: Four Women Writers and Republican Politics in Nineteenth-Century France* (Stanford CA: Stanford University Press, 2000).

12. Carolyn J. Eichner, *Surmounting the Barricades: Women in the Paris Commune* (Bloomington: Indiana University Press, 2004); Gay L. Gullickson, *Unruly Women of Paris: Images of the Commune* (Ithaca NY: Cornell University Press, 1996).

13. On the climate of gender and sexual conservatism after World War I, see Mary Louise Roberts, *Civilization without Sexes: Reconstructing Gender in Postwar France, 1917–1927* (Chicago: University of Chicago Press, 1994).

14. Angus McLaren, *Sexuality and Social Order: The Debate over the Fertility of Women and Workers in France, 1770–1920* (New York: Holmes & Meier, 1983).

15. Karen Offen, "Depopulation, Nationalism, and Feminism in Fin-de-Siècle France," *American Historical Review* 89, no. 3 (1984): 648–76; Elisa Camiscioli, *Reproducing the French Race: Immigration, Intimacy, and Embodiment in the Early Twentieth Century* (Durham NC: Duke University Press, 2009), chap. 5.

16. For instance, Jennifer Ngaire Heuer shows that women in France managed to successfully position themselves as citizens vis-à-vis the state in order to forward their claims. See *The Family and the Nation: Gender and Citizenship in Revolutionary France, 1789–1830* (Ithaca NY: Cornell University Press, 2005).

17. Offen, "Depopulation, Nationalism, and Feminism."

18. Elinor A. Accampo, *Blessed Motherhood, Bitter Fruit: Nelly Roussel and the Politics of Female Pain in Third Republic France* (Baltimore: Johns Hopkins University Press, 2006); Mary Louise Roberts, *Disruptive Acts: The New Woman in Fin-de-Siècle France* (Chicago: University of Chicago Press, 2005); and on female honor codes, Mansker, *Sex, Honor, and Citizenship*.

19. Accampo paints Roussel as a feminist full of contradictions: "Though Roussel nuanced her rhetoric, her end goal was subversive and radical" (*Blessed Motherhood*, 47). She further argues that "defying categorization, Roussel always evoked opposites" (100).

20. Rachel G. Fuchs, *Contested Paternity: Constructing Families in Modern France* (Baltimore: Johns Hopkins University Press, 2008). See also Pedersen, *Legislating the French Family*; Mansker, *Sex, Honor, and Citizenship*, chap. 3.

21. Accampo, "Gender, Social Policy, and the Formation of the Third Republic"; Emmanuelle Saada, *Empire's Children: Race, Filiation, and Citizenship in the French Colonies*, trans. Arthur Goldhammer (Chicago: University of Chicago Press, 2012), 148–52; Ivan Jablonka, *Ni père ni mère: Histoire des enfants de l'Assistance Publique, 1874–1939* (Paris: Seuil, 2006); Sylvia Schafer, *Children in Moral Danger and the Problem of Government in Third Republic France* (Princeton NJ: Princeton University Press, 1997).

22. Laura Levine Frader, *Breadwinners and Citizens: Gender in the Making of the French Social Model* (Durham NC: Duke University Press, 2008); Camiscioli, *Reproducing the French Race*.

23. Françoise Thébaud, *Quand nos grand-mères donnaient la vie: La maternité en France dans l'entre-deux-guerres* (Lyon: Presses universitaires de Lyon, 1986); Roberts, *Civilization without Sexes*; Jean-Yves Le Naour and Catherine Valenti, eds., *Histoire de l'avortement: XIXe-XXe siècle* (Paris: Seuil, 2003).

24. Some scholars have recently begun examining these dynamics. See Judith Surkis, *Sexing the Citizen: Morality and Masculinity in France, 1870–1920* (Ithaca NY: Cornell University Press, 2006); Kristen Stromberg Childers, *Fathers, Families, and the State in France, 1914-1945* (Ithaca NY: Cornell University Press, 2003); Geoff Read, *The Republic of Men: Gender and the Political Parties in Interwar France* (Baton Rouge: Louisiana State University Press, 2014). There may even have been revolutionary antecedents. See Suzanne Desan, *The Family on Trial in Revolutionary France* (Berkeley: University of California Press, 2004); Claire Cage, *Unnatural Frenchmen: The Politics of Priestly Celibacy and Marriage, 1720-1815* (Charlottesville: University of Virginia Press, 2015). And, as Bruno Perreau has recently demonstrated, adoption and citizenship are extraordinarily bound up in modern France through the emphasis on the heterosexual nuclear family and the successful performance of traditional gender roles that it entails. Bruno Perreau, *The Politics of Adoption: Gender and the Making of French Citizenship*, trans. Deke Dusinberre (Cambridge MA: MIT Press, 2014).

25. Camille Robcis, *The Law of Kinship: Anthropology, Psychoanalysis and the Family in France* (Ithaca NY: Cornell University Press, 2013).

26. Heath, *Wine, Sugar*; Nasiali, *Native to the Republic*; Raissiguier, *Reinventing the Republic*.

27. Lynn Hunt, *Inventing Human Rights* (New York: Norton, 2008).

28. Nelly Roussel is just one example of these extraordinary women. See Accampo, *Blessed Motherhood*. Recent reinterpretations of French feminism also posit new, creative modes of feminist acts and behaviors. See, for example, Roberts, *Disruptive Acts*.

29. See Judith Surkis, "When Was the Linguistic Turn? A Genealogy," *American Historical Review* 117, no. 3 (2012): 700–722.

1

"Patriotic Discipline"

Cloistered Behinds, Public Judgment, and
Female Violence in Revolutionary Paris

KATIE JARVIS

Two years into the French Revolution, just days before Holy Week of
April 1791, the mood in Paris was far from peacefully contemplative.
As Easter approached, rumors flew that counterrevolutionary nuns
were colluding with priests who had refused to swear their loyalty
to the Constitution. Journals painted pictures of "aristocrat-nuns"
secretly attending "good" Masses with these refractory priests.[1] Editors reported that the priests' sermons brazenly compared the counterrevolution to Christ, the government assemblies to tyrants, and the
Revolution to Hell.[2] However insulting this was to the nation, things
truly exploded when the disgruntled nuns spanked their pupils for
confessing to a pro-revolutionary priest. Unluckily for the nuns, their
pupils happened to be the children of tenacious market women called
the Dames des Halles.[3]

The backlash would be remembered for "posterity" as one giddy
witness put it.[4] Fed up, the Dames des Halles literally took matters
into their own hands and submitted the nuns to their own "correction." The market women dragged the counterrevolutionary nuns
out of their cloistered convents into public streets. Swiftly lifting the
nuns' skirts, the Dames struck the nuns' bare rears with bunches of
straw and brooms.[5] As the nuns prayed to endure the trial, the Dames
exposed the nun's naked bottoms to the public gaze. The Dames boldly
continued their rounds over two days to several counterrevolutionary

convents throughout the capital. Most Parisians shared the Dames' anger. They worried that rebellious priests and nuns would undermine new religious reforms called the Civil Constitution of the Clergy. This controversial legislation subordinated the Catholic Church to the nation. As Parisians cheered on the Dames from the sidelines, they defended revolutionary reform.

The spanking spree generated numerous pamphlets and images that offer rich commentary on what the authors termed "patriotic discipline." In the aftermath the general public took delight in what one artist described as the "good lessons" that the "female citizens" gave to nuns who aided "fanatic priests." Most newspapers, pamphlets, and images satirically depicted the event but praised the market women's attack. The accounts burst with gendered tropes colored by sexual overtones. Citing an oft-repeated statistic, one watercolor proudly reported the Dames' accomplishment of "621 buttocks spanked; Total 310 and a half asses" since, as another pamphlet thankfully explained, "the Treasurer of the Miramionnes order only had one buttock."[6]

The revolutionaries' endorsement of this collective violence among women stands in stark contrast to the deputies' condemnation of violent confrontations among women two years later. In 1793 officials lambasted fights that spilled out across the city's markets between the Dames des Halles and a women's political club. The two groups disputed price controls and patriotic clothing with their fists.[7] The National Convention famously asserted that these massive brawls stemmed from women's irrationality, and, following this Rousseauian discourse, the deputies claimed women were unsuited for political participation. The National Convention then banned women's political clubs, which effectively blocked women from full citizenship until 1944. Led by Joan Landes, Joan Scott, Geneviève Fraisse, and Carole Pateman, scholars have built an enduring narrative of female citizenship across the longue durée based upon the gendered overtones of the deputies' 1793 ban.[8] Modern French citizenship, they maintain, was inherently bifurcated by sex from the outset.

In contrast, by probing the Dames' violence in 1791 and other revolutionaries' reactions to it, this chapter overturns the notion that the revolutionaries immediately envisioned citizenship as masculine. During the nun spankings, no male or female revolutionaries blamed mass violence on natural feminine disorder. Far from condemning the Dames' assault on counterrevolutionary nuns as manifesting feminine deficiencies, public opinion celebrated the market women's violent attack as civic activism and explicitly championed the Dames as exemplary female citizens. The unexpected cleavage between the applause of 1791 and the ban of 1793 disrupts our historical starting block for modern female citizenship. How, then, did the revolutionaries conceptualize the relationship among gender, violence, and women's political action in 1791?

This chapter focuses on the slaps that echoed across the capital to ask two key questions: First, how did artists and pamphleteers use gender as a common key for portraying, judging, and re-disseminating the violence? I argue that the revolutionaries seized gendered tropes to denounce the nuns' moral and political failings. Writers spread rumors of convent lust and artists drew battered nuns in titillating poses to denounce them as counterrevolutionary plotters. For Parisian consumers, this well-worn imagery amounted to more than a sexual critique. Authors and illustrators relied on Parisians' understanding of gendered stereotypes to convey additional messages. They channeled their religious and political grievances across the nuns' beaten rears. Their tactics bring us to a second pivotal question: Why did male and female revolutionaries justify this collective violence among women in 1791? I argue that state officials could not condemn the Dames' attacks because the market women defended religious reform while thrashing the nuns. The Dames did not undercut their political legitimacy by lashing out at the vowed women. On the contrary, they strengthened it. The convent clashes suggest that the relationship between gender and violence was much more contingent than the deputies later maintained in 1793. The discrepancy reveals that the relationship between gender and citizenship remained uncertain in the formative stages of modern democracy. It forces us to reconsider the narrative arc that posits gender as the initial prerequisite for revolutionary citizenship.

The Counterrevolution in the Cloister

The revolutionaries began to overhaul their relationship between the Church and the state in 1789, but the centuries-old alliance between cross and crown created a political minefield. Four months after the fall of the Bastille, the deputies nationalized Church property as a way to generate revenue for the national debt. But in 1790 the deputies drastically wrested power from the Church by passing the Civil Constitution of the Clergy. In a series of volatile laws, the Legislative Assembly decreed that priests would become civil servants elected by parishioners, responsible to the nation, and paid by the state.[9] In the late winter of 1791 the deputies required priests to take an oath "to the Nation, to the Law, and to the King, and to uphold with all their power the Constitution decreed by the National Assembly,'" and, in the same breath, to "watch carefully over the parish faithful who are entrusted to [them]."[10] It became impossible to pledge equal allegiance to the revolutionary government and to St. Peter's seat in Rome. French clerics personally chose sides. All but seven French bishops refused the oath, and only half of parish priests accepted the stipulations on their collars.[11] Revolutionaries considered nonjuring priests to be dangerous cadres of counterrevolutionaries who could sway the hearts and minds of their parishioners. Likewise patriotic newspapers warned that nuns and monks who sympathized with rebellious priests swelled the ranks of counterrevolutionary agents who plotted inside the nation.

Parisians reached into a deep arsenal of Old Regime anticlericalism to attack refractory priests and their nun and monk allies in the winter of 1790–91. For over two centuries the French had attacked clerics as undersexed or oversexed to buck their authority in local and national politics. Now the French redeployed these techniques with a vengeance to protect the Civil Constitution of the Clergy. Since the mid-eighteenth century, critics had increasingly questioned the virtues of celibate life. Priests failed to live up to the ideal Enlightenment father who served the public good by raising a family.[12] Celibacy likewise robbed nuns of the opportunity to fulfill their highest gendered calling as mothers who raised moral children.[13] Revolutionary propagandists seized these themes to portray "the celibate clergy as a nation within the nation" whose sexual and political loyalty lay with Rome and the counterrevolution.[14]

But if revolutionaries chastised clerical celibacy, they feared the erotic relations of religious men and women in cloistered spaces even more. Sexual deviance had long formed the backbone of anticlerical sentiment. Pornographic novels portrayed "'unnatural' sexual practices that resulted from claustration."[15] Court cases in which clerics sadistically abused their pupils fed public anxieties. Personal memoirs led the French to imagine that the sexually unimaginable hid in dark convent cells. Moreover, as Mita Choudhury has argued, Enlightenment and revolutionary writers wavered between portraying the convent as a sexual playground and as a place of unjust imprisonment. Aristocratic families could consolidate their inheritances by cloistering unlucky children in convents and monasteries.[16] In the explosive atmosphere of the Civil Constitution of the Clergy, revolutionaries imagined nonjuring priests and nuns as robbers of children's liberty as well as spiritual, sexual, and political seducers.

Exposing the Counterrevolution:
The Parisian Spanking Sprees

The deputies had ridden roughshod over priests who challenged their authority since they instituted the oath in 1790, but anticlerical anxieties peaked just before April 1791. Provocative plays such as *The Capuchins*, *The Nun Despite Herself*, and *The Priests' School* bubbled with dissimulating priests, debauched nuns, and innocent children incarcerated by their families. For example, *The Cloistered Victims*, performed at the Théâtre de la Nation, wove the tale of a young girl whose fanatical mother throws her into a convent. There the nonjuring priest and treacherous mother superior abuse the innocent girl. She remains locked away until a juring priest, the revolutionary mayor, and the National Guard free her, much to the delight of theatergoers. The dismayed editor of the *Journal général de France* noted, "The spectators never fail, at every performance, to cry against the [counterrevolutionary] religious characters."[17] Parisians theatrically rehearsed opening the counterrevolutionary cloisters before the market women invaded the real cloisters nine days later.

In early April the mounting tensions between nonjuring priests and Parisian revolutionaries came to a head as municipal officials replaced refractory clerics with juring, elected ones. On April 3 Jean-Baptiste-Joseph Gobel assumed his post as the new bishop of Paris.[18] When the revolutionaries installed Gobel to lead the capital's faithful, they rejected the pope's bishop, confirmed their split with Rome, and entrusted religious morality to the state. The next day National Guardsmen escorted elected priests to their congregations throughout the capital.[19] Père Duchesne, a leftist pamphlet character of the popular classes, had high hopes that the new clerics would be "more human, more charitable than the old ones." He abrasively offered lunacy certificates for asylum lockup "to the former Archbishop of Paris [and] to all the other Bishops, Priests, and to all the skullcapped john-fuckers who have not taken their oath."[20] Patriotic citizens, the government, and their juring priests hoped to have thrown away the metaphorical key.

However, on April 4 rumors flew that the refractory clergy and counterrevolutionary nuns were plotting their next move. Parisians even speculated that scorned priests stuffed barrels of gunpowder into the church basement of Saint-Roch. The neighborhood grew so nervous that the National Guard had to search the dark caverns to disprove the paranoia. In this contentious environment, Antoine-Eléonor-Léon Leclerc de Juigné, the former archbishop of Paris, issued an incendiary ordinance against the Civil Constitution of the Clergy. On April 5 reports surfaced that nonjuring priests responded by rallying at the Sorbonne and that, together, "they declared the new Bishops elected by the People *intruders*." Newspapers incensed readers by reporting that three juring priests retracted their oaths during the meeting. In the course of one week the revolutionaries realized that their ecclesiastical system could unravel.[21]

The revolutionaries suspected that hostile nuns would hide and support these rebellious priests. Nuns who staffed schools and hospitals did not have to take the oath. And Parisians feared the refractory clergy would work through them. Refashioning anticlerical traditions, Parisians hypothesized that the nuns' confessors seduced them into being counterrevolutionary agents.[22] The revolutionaries suspected that "shameful monks" and "beguines, who were like submissive women imitating their lovers," engaged in debaucheries while plotting behind cloister grilles.[23] The day after the rumored assembly of rebellious priests, a leftist pamphlet under the name of Mère Duchêne, the wife of the fictive Père Duchesne, explicitly attacked the nuns of St. Anne. She maintained the nuns "jumped with rage on the [revolutionary] catechisms" when their "wise" students wanted to welcome their new juring priest. In a passage filled with foresight, the fictitious Mère Duchêne eerily warned the nuns, "Behold the people who are running[,] they are going to bring you reason, they are going to thrash you . . . in order to make you learn to shut yourselves away in your sphere."[24]

Over the following two days, from April 6 to 8, Mère Duchêne's threats became a reality as the massive spanking spree rocked the capital. Saint-Roch became a hotbed once again. The market women had previously demanded that nuns there admit the elected priest and educate their children with the reformed catechism. The nuns, however, repelled their new priest and his National Guard escort with insults. They also refused to teach their pupils spiritual lessons that supported the Civil Constitution of the Clergy. After these final affronts, "the citizen mommies rushed [the convent] armed with switches" and took matters into their own hands.[25]

The Dames des Halles raced across the city to at least eight of sixty Parisian convents to patriotically "discipline" the scrambling nuns.[26] Although the revolutionaries accused all nuns of similar sins, pamphleteers who reproduced the event assigned each order a particular counterrevolutionary specialty. The writer of *Song on the Whipped Asses: Historical Detail on the Communities of Grey Sisters*, one of the least sensational pamphlets, accused the sisters at Saint Nicolas-des-Champs of turning away their juring priest and menacing the crowd with threats of cannons behind convent walls. The market women responded to these nuns by wielding bundles of sticks on their behinds. In contrast, the revolutionaries charged the Filles de Sainte Marie with spiritual and political plotting in the form of sexual collusion. The public first suspected that the order harbored nonjuring priests when they hosted twenty-two masses instead of the usual six. Parisians concluded that, in the arms of these welcoming nuns, "the refractory priests found all sensual satisfaction." On the other side of the Seine, the market women from the Place Maubert found a refractory priest and his seminarians hiding inside the convent of the Miramionnes.[27] Because of the order's large pensions, the pamphleteer concluded that the Miramionnes attracted "some Priests, Monks & Abbots who knew well how to make them taste the joys of Paradise."[28] The Miramionnes' wealth did not spare them from the Dames' slaps either. For two days the Dames reddened rears across the capital, from Saint Sulpice in the southwest to Saint Martin des Champs in the north and the Trinitaires de la Roquette in the eastern Faubourg Saint Antoine.

Amid whistling blows and clattering clogs, the Dames physically delineated two clear rivals: counterrevolutionary religious persons faithful to Rome and citizen supporters of the Civil Constitution of the Clergy. Yet the two sides in the nuns affair stretched beyond factional politics. On a fundamental level the market women and the nuns engaged in a battle between two competing discourses of "good" and "evil." One account reported that a "Dame-Citizen" shouted that the nuns had "dared" to choose the "house of God" for their mischievous activities.[29] Revolutionary pamphleteers painted the Dames' busy hands as the earthly hands of God, who "wants to punish" nuns.[30] Ensuing articles frequently called the spankings "Patriotic Discipline" or "Corrected Fanaticism." Thus the Dames punished the nuns' ideological misbehavior just as the nuns would punish their children. One spiritually indignant journalist huffed that the "fanaticism" of these Roman supporters especially had no place in the upcoming "holy week."[31]

The Dames strategically turned their focused violence into a communal activity by chasing the nuns into the "open streets." During the beatings the convent door became the threshold between private, plotting enemy and transparent, patriotic citizens. Thus when the "Dames de la Halle opened up the cloisters," they enabled other citizens to judge the errant women.[32] In addition, a nun's veil was a portable cloister: wearing her order's clothing materialized her vows.[33] Consequently the Dames ripped away nuns' private allegiances by deranging their clothing. When one pamphleteer wrote that some of the nuns' bottoms saw the air for the first time in twenty-six years, he implied that the Dames brought religious, political, and sexual loyalties out of a long-standing bastion of secrecy.[34]

By assaulting the nuns in the streets, the Dames invited fellow Parisians to legitimize the attack through their collective gaze. Although the Dames alone struck the nuns, they incorporated spectators into the popular judgment by "making them see" the nuns.[35] The *List of All the Religious Sisters and Sanctimonious Women Who Had Been Whipped by the Dames of the Markets* playfully described this dynamic: "It was truly a very pleasing spectacle, to see each one of these good lively women of the markets seize one of these sweet things, pull aside their skirts, and expose to the air their delicate posteriors on which, with their robust hands, our ladies applied redoubled strikes, the air resounded with the correction that these bigots had deserved. . . . All the citizens of the capital applauded."[36] The editor of the newspaper *La Chronique de Paris* confirmed that all witnesses denounced the nuns. "No part of the people," he insisted, "is duped by their [the nuns'] hypocrisy."[37]

The market women sent a decisive message. Mere days after the Dames spanked the nuns, the National Assembly passed a law that all educators, religious or not, must take the civic oath "to be faithful to the nation, to the law and king, and to maintain with all [their] power the Constitution."[38] On April 15 seven hundred male and female teachers of poor children speedily lined up at the Commune to comply.[39] By beating the nuns the Dames had pushed education into the state's moral domain and strengthened the Civil Constitution of the Clergy.

Representing the Violence

The nuns had no time to nurse their wounds before enterprising pamphleteers, engravers, and journalists pounced on their humiliation. By reproducing the conflict in image and word, they added a second round of spectators to the public tribunal. Splashed about in several newspapers and pamphlets, and represented in at least four published drawings, the Dames' intervention left more than bodily marks. Texts and caricatures strategically employed scatological, sexual, and gendered themes to vindicate the Dames and denigrate the nuns. On the one hand, writers played on gendered deviations to signal the nuns' moral and political failings. On the other hand, artists relied on gendered tropes to tap into well-worn visual symbols. Citizens easily recognized these gendered markers to interpret their political messages.

In the days following the assaults, patriotic citizens devoured popular representations on the Pont Neuf and at the Palais Royal.[40] A few sympathetic to the nuns' religious cause protested that these images and accounts disgraced the nuns again. One defender complained that the Dames "exposed, half-nude, the poor recluses to the vilest and the most enthusiastic libertines of the capital."[41] However, hawkers overwhelmingly cried titles that praised the Dames. This section analyzes this favorable corpus of texts and images.

Publishers maximized their audience market by printing pictures of the spanking spree. Between one half and one third of French citizens were illiterate.[42] Presses catered to this need by selling over six hundred distinct caricatures from 1789 to 1792.[43] According to the historian Antoine de Baecque, visual caricature was the mainstay in the "commerce of laughter and political denunciation."[44] Anticlerical images in particular spiked when the National Assembly nationalized Church land in 1789.[45] As for "patriotic spankings," the historian Annie Duprat has found twenty distinct caricatures during the Revolution, four of which depict the nuns affair.[46] Printers reproduced these four images in different sizes, in contrapositive, with added color, or combined with captions to produce a dynamic canvas for political critique.

The four distinct drawings of the "patriotic discipline" feature the Dames thrashing the nuns in essentially the same pose (fig. 1). The details of the figures and the background vary, but the bodily positioning is identical: a market woman raises a bundle of sticks behind her head ready to strike the bare rear of a nun. The nun is doubled over, often with hands clasped in prayer. This distinctive configuration of bodies created a crucial visual legend for interpreting the violence:

1. *La Discipline patriotique ou le Fanatisme corrigée: Epoque arrivée dans la semaine de la Passion 1791, par les Dames de la Halle*. Etching. 15x21.5cm. BnF Qb-370 T.20, Folio 39, De Vinck 3495.

it simultaneously cast the nuns as misbehaving children, as "legitimate" victims of domestic violence, as laughingstocks with delusions of saintly scourging, and as sexual deviants whose libertine practices were exposed in the streets.

The images and accounts multiplied because they sold well. Since the revolutionaries freed the press, few regulations prevented authors from poaching one another's ideas or trying "to win readers by employing the same title and style."[47] Not only did the writers and artists copy one another's successes to gain a financial edge, but relaxed censorship increased the range of material that could be openly sold.[48] When a royalist editor confronted a hawker for shouting sensational headlines, the colporteur coolly replied, "What do I care? My journal has to sell."[49] Police threats regarding "obscene books and images" did not derail the sale of material covering the nuns' uncovering.[50] Royalist Jacques-Marie Boyer de Nîmes described how the image *The Miraculous Event*, which parodied a bare-bottomed nun's hopes for martyrdom by giving it a malicious halo, spread like wildfire on "all the quays and all the streets."[51]

Yet the printers of "smut" did not hold a monopoly on depicting the Dames' spanking spree. Journalists juxtaposed tongue-in-cheek accounts with serious reports to further humiliate the nuns, especially with regard to sexual dimensions. The journalist Gorsas, who ran a spanking image in his paper, also printed an erratum explaining that the treasurer of the Miramionnes contacted him and offered to prove that she did in fact have two buttocks. He asserted that he would amend the final count in his newspaper without requiring demonstrative evidence.[52] Even Baudouin, the prolific and official printer for the National Assembly, printed *Great Detailed Description concerning the Religious Men and Women Who Have Been Whipped by the Dames de la Halle at Paris*.[53] One could have easily interpreted Baudouin's government title as a subtle endorsement by the Assembly. The "patriotic discipline" blurred the lines among genres as writers, artists, printers, and publishers all sought to profit from the dramatic event.

Pamphleteers, like their visual counterparts, denounced the nuns and validated the Dames' slaps in biting satire. They mockingly drew on legal overtones to banish the nuns to the margins of civil society. One pamphleteer explained that "this vengeance [of the people]" was "very useful, in as much as it acts when the law has no force."[54] The journal *Les Révolutions de France* assumed a wry sense of officiality to report that "the Dames des Halles . . . held a National session at [the convents of] the Miramionnes, the Daughters of Sainte-Marie, and among the multitude of the Moustiers. Everything happened with great order. Each one was whipped in her own turn."[55] By likening the Dames' judgment to a session of the National Assembly, presenting the chaos as legislative proceedings, and casting their punishments as a measured exercise, the accounts colored the Dames' violence with a scathing sense of civic legitimacy.

Other pamphlets punned on procedural order by naming their pamphlets a "list" of various sorts. Lists of different people, such as revolutionary deputies, were common during the Revolution. But since critics accused nuns and priests of sexual crimes, pamphleteers may also have been echoing the *List of All the Priests Found in Flagrante Delicto with the Prostitutes of Paris under the Old Regime*, which had recently made public the very real list of around one thousand clerics tracked by Parisian police.[56] However, many of the details in the lists of nuns were "unfounded," as evidenced by literary names for some victims, such as "Cunégonde."[57] This reference alluded to Voltaire's *Candide*, in which the Grand Inquisitor sexually exploited Cunégonde and the old woman character lost a buttock. The referential loop of satire and reality became an infinity knot.

Writers and artists did not hesitate to sexualize their satire. Merely drawing chaste nuns' naked lower halves was enough to inscribe their bodies with a voyeuristic stigma. And since the nuns' virginity was supposed to reflect their spiritual purity, the revolutionaries usurped the nuns' moral authority through gendered inversions. During the eighteenth century the French believed that feminine sensibility and moral authority was encoded on a woman's face.[58] Consequently artists undermined the nuns' feminine virtue by analyzing their character and counterrevolutionary intentions from their behinds. Artists provided nearly full views of the nuns' rears but only partially revealed facial profiles. And writers riffed on the nuns' feminine sensibility by cleverly mixing vocabulary for "buttocks" and "face." One Mère Duchêne pamphlet warned the misbehaving nuns, "Mère Duchêne has a good arm. . . . You will not need blush for your cheeks; I have the secret for giving color to persons who lack it."[59]

Pamphleteers and artists humiliated the nuns as oversexed and undersexed, often simultaneously. During the Revolution one third of images depicting grotesque bodies highlighted "the 'dirty parts' of anatomy (stomach, buttocks, genitals)." Written accounts and images likewise played with scatological themes to link "bodily monstrosity" to "political deviance."[60] Revolutionaries presented the nuns' rears as too public yet too covered, too sexualized yet too sterilized. The *List of Aristocratic and Anticonstitutional Asses* rejoiced in this topsy-turvy fluidity. The pamphlet proclaimed that heads had been at the center of the Revolution, but, "yes, who would have ever thought that ASSES would dare put themselves at the fore of the fatherland, & would want their turn to figure into history."[61] The author goes to great lengths to describe the physical appearance of each group's exposed behinds. He categorically describes the "truly beautiful perspective" of the Miramionnes' rears, the Récolettes' "pumpkins of Moses," the ugly, blackened, and fouled buttocks of the Sisters of Saint-Sulpice, Saint-Laurent, Sainte-Margueritte, la Magdeleine, and Saint-Germain-l'Auxerrois, and warns that the deceptively tanned and fleshy bottoms of the Filles du Calvaire could be mistaken as patriotic rears, but, alas, they too are soiled. The pamphlet suggests that some rears would repel readers, and others would entice them, but that all 621 buttocks were equally guilty in their excessive or deficient sexuality.

In a similar fashion, representations played with the tenuous connection between female sexuality and patriotic motherhood. The nuns' rash treatment of the Dames' children and their deviant celibacy symbolized a broader yet deeply personal threat they posed to French families. Artists picked up on this fulcrum of gendered legitimacy to endorse the Dames' strikes. Instead of portraying the wronged children, artists only alluded to them via the Dames' maternal breasts and the nuns' barren rears. In other words, artists symbolically incorporated the children in the central sites of reproduction and physical violence. This is apparent in an etching entitled *Corrected Fanaticism or Patriotic Discipline* (fig. 2). A Dame spanks a nun who is ironically praying before a cross marked "obedience to the Law." Trampled underfoot are three leaflets: "Bull of [Pope] Pius VI," "The Handling of Monseigneur the Archbishop of Paris," and "Actes d. Apo . . ." (presumably the royalist newspaper *Actes des Apôtres*). These papers serve as the only masculine presence in absentia. The domineering Dame has forced the nun into a submissive position. The sister is bent over; her praying hands and tucked elbows protect her flanks as she implores God. The market woman's breasts hang out of her dress in close proximity to the nun's exposed rear. Like allegorical, if erotically charged, revolutionary symbols, the Dame's bare breasts hint at her "natural" rage as a mother against those who have poisoned her children. In this image and other variations, the Dame's fertile, reproductive parts sharply contrast with the nun's sterile lower half.[62] The "citizen mommies" feed familial and political life; the nun can produce only fecal matter.[63]

2. *La Fanatisme corrigée ou la Dicipline [sic] patriotique*. Paris: Chez Villeneuve, 1791. Etching. 14.5x11cm. BnF Reserve Fol QB-201 (124).

Of course female breasts acted as mutable symbols in the spanking depictions. They represented maternal duties as well as potentially subversive sexuality. With regard to the nuns, these two options alternatively rendered them undersexed and oversexed. Old Regime images unabashedly portrayed wet nurses of both peasant and aristocratic stock with exposed breasts to feed their charges.[64] On their heels the revolutionaries deployed the female breast to glorify citizen-mothers in simple portraits, revolutionary festivals, and caricatures. A 1790 engraving perfectly captures the political valiance: a nursing woman gazes lovingly into the face of her child, whose tricolored bonnet snuggles into her bare bosom.[65] Infertile breasts in revolutionary caricatures, in contrast, signaled female shortcomings and thus twin moral and political deviancy. For example, in a caricature condemning the king's pro-pope aunts, the engraver spotlights the women's sharp, elongated, and wizened breasts. They look sick when compared to the ideal revolutionary "roundness," suggesting that their maternal deficiencies correspond to their political sentiments.[66] From a sexual perspective, naked breasts could imply a woman's promiscuity and moral depravity. In obscene propaganda that depicted homosexual relations, artists exposed chests to signal "decadence" between two women. In such scenes, artists usually critiqued *both* parties.[67] However, in the 1791 spanking images, artists did not appear to taint the bare-breasted Dames with homosexual overtones because they did not depict two "guilty" parties. Instead making public the sexual shades of the women's privates provides a titillating element. Uncovered breasts and bare rears ultimately provide a sharp contrast between patriotic sexuality and its cloistered antithesis.

However, revolutionary artists faced a particular challenge with the spanking pose: counterrevolutionaries could potentially glorify the nuns as martyrs. Most citizens prayed before religious iconography at home or in church, which habituated them to interpret scenes through spiritual symbolism. Portrayals of Catholic martyrs glorified their physical sufferings rather than derided their mangled bodies.[68] Most important, martyrs' violent victimhood echoed Christ's "ultimate act of sacrifice."[69] In his March 1791 letter to French priests, the pope encouraged such sacrificial resistance by asserting, "The violence must augment the courage and fidelity of true Christians [against the Civil Constitution of the Clergy]."[70] Finally, Parisians could mistakenly conflate portrayals of the nuns' spankings with a penitential movement that shook the city earlier in the century, when fanatical women called "convulsionaries" asked others to beat them with sticks in order to be "saved" by God.[71]

3. *Fait miraculeux arrivé à Paris l'an de salut de 1791*, le six avril, 1791. Etching. 25.5x30cm. BnF De Vinck 3497.

To disarm readings of spiritual sacrifice, artists parodied them, evoking signs of prayers like clasped hands, skyward glances, and prayer cushions to mock sympathizers. The etching *The Miraculous Event Which Happened in Paris April 6, the Year of Grace 1791* (fig. 3) depicts several Dames armed with switches who punish a bare-bottomed nun kneeling on a prie-dieu while other citizens gather around.[72] The print pokes fun at the sisters' delusions of martyrdom by enshrining one nun's naked rear in a blinding halo of light. St. Benoît-Joseph Labre, known for his self-flagellation and made a saint by the pope two months earlier, descends from heaven carrying the monarchical fleur-de-lis and the papal proclamation condemning the revolutionary oath. The saint places a floral crown upon the nun's beaming "saint behind," as the accompanying poem describes it. One of the Dames is taken aback by the saint emerging from the clouds; another Dame falls on her knees praying; the one wielding the switch appears unmoved; but most important for communal judgment, one spectator is using a spy glass for a better look at it all. The voyeuristic detail is intentionally humorous and alludes to prurient interest in the violent thrashing, but it drives home the most important point: the Dames *publicly* punished the nuns to signal a collective, sovereign judgment, which would overshadow any of the nuns' claims of a higher sacrifice.[73] Royalist Boyer de Nîmes boiled with indignation at the "monstrous" scene. He sputtered that the etching "threw ['ridicule'] on those who pushed Christian heroism to the point of not fearing martyrdom."[74]

Besides flagging the nuns' sexual humiliation and undercutting their potential martyrdom, the whipping poses and their gendered descriptions deployed another powerful theme: domestic violence.[75] Since the French considered women, like children, to be under the control and jurisdiction of the male head of household, husbands could legally beat their wives.[76] According to the literary scholar Mary Trouille, "the limitations [of wife-beating] lay in the severity . . . and the motivation, which should be to ensure obedience and good behavior."[77] For women's crimes of adultery, this translated into public whipping in the sixteenth century, whereas, by the mid-eighteenth century, husbands could send an adulterous wife to a convent.[78] Gestures to domestic violence abound in the nun spanking images. In these "correction" scenes, the Dames des Halles assert themselves as substitute husbands for these "brides of Christ." The Dames' dominating stance with raised sticks and the nuns' submissive position replicate stereotypical images of domestic violence drawn over previous centuries. *The Chastised Woman*, an engraving likely from the sixteenth century, depicts the exact same pose but in nonsatirical form. A woman is kneeling with hands clasped together. Her bare bottom is exposed to her husband, who lifts a bundle of sticks to bring down upon his target (fig. 4).[79]

In addition to this visual configuration, several accounts and captions ambiguously described the Dames as wielding *verges* against the nuns' naked rears. The word meant "switch," but it could also imply "penis."[80] *Le Courrier de Paris* used the word to mock one reader who complained that libertines plotted the spankings. The newspaper

4. *La Femme châtiée*. Paris: Imprimerie Guiraudet et Jouast, sixteenth or seventeenth century. Engraving. BnF Oa 22 (235).

satirized his objection that there were "women armed with *verges*" who "stripped" the nuns.[81] *Les Révolutions de Paris* similarly defended the Dames' actions by characterizing them as "some strikes of *verges* given aptly and very decently to the nuns who let the sacred fire of patriotism extinguish within them."[82] Thus the journalists portrayed the Dames as extending male authority to taint the nuns' past chastity, stigmatize their current exposure, and issue a patriarchal punishment. An adulterous wife could violate her marriage vow to her husband, whereas the nuns had undermined the oath of the Civil Constitution of the Clergy. Therefore, when read through domestic violence tropes, the Dames and their *verges* corrected the husbandless nuns on behalf of the nation.[83] Thus the nuns doubly failed in their highest gendered calling: as mothers and as wives.

The double meaning of the Dames' *verges* also highlighted the semi-pornographic undertones of the images. Choudhury notes that in libertine literature of the eighteenth century, "every convent has its store of dildos" that nuns shared with their students.[84] Spiritual, sexual, and, in the case of the 1791 spankings, political miseducation of convent pupils supposedly went hand in hand. In Old Regime erotic novels like *Venus in the Cloister* (1683), confessors spiritually misdirected and sexually manipulated nuns, fanatical nuns became priests' eager apprentices or helpless victims, and convent pupils received corrupt lessons from both.[85] As the result of this anticlerical heritage, the revolutionaries believed that joint sexual and spiritual seduction, rather than erroneous intellectual instruction, caused spiritual error. Depicting the Dames using *verges* rather than their bare hands also blurred the boundaries between infantile spanking and penitential whipping. This element recalled the lewd sadomasochism of the court cases and libertine literature in which penitential acts served as a cover for sexual abuse. For example, in the 1748 erotic novel *Thérèse philosophe*, which takes inspiration from a famous court case, a libertine priest lashes his young female penitents and sexually assaults them after they pass out.[86] Thus the obscene spiritual-sexual association lying beneath the surface of the 1791 caricatures served as a double attack: it insinuated the nuns' rumored physical depravity and disqualified them from teaching children, and it made the nuns a proxy for condemning the nonjuring priests who appeared as their spiritual and sexual partners.

Although rare, some written narratives assert that the Dames des Halles spanked refractory priests and monks during their patriotic tour of the convents. There are no visuals illustrating this female-on-male aggression. But authors who included these allegations similarly played off of domestic violence themes to condemn the priests. In Old Regime scenes in which wives beat husbands, husbands receiving the "correction" were portrayed as weak and unnatural men. These men were unfit to lead their household.[87] With the domestic punishing roles reversed, communities humiliated men and subjected them to charivari-like shaming. After the 1791 spanking spree, the writer Louis-Sébastien Mercier hinted at refractory clerics' carnivalesque failure. He described how "the women were armed with *verges*" and dominated the scene. They whipped "some skullcapped men and women possessed by the counter-revolution demon" while "the [spectator] men laughed at the grimaces of the flagellated goblins."[88] Not only did these written scenes suggest that refractory priests were unable to lead their flocks, but their lashes by *verges* also suggested their sexual impotence despite their presumed debauchery.

When images traced out nuns' naked behinds, a Dame's bare breast, or bunches of *verges*, revolutionary artists sexually charged the scene. However, most illustrations protected the Dames against lewd accusations. Unlike libelous images that scandalized the secret sexuality of the "boudoir," the Dame's public attack meant that sexual overtones became a conduit for the critique rather than the focus of the critique.[89] On the whole the accounts and images stress that the majority of the *direct* contact occurred between the Dames des Halles and the nuns. Physically separating male and female actors was crucial. Propagandists highlighted this divide to sell their representations as principled voyeurism: sexual organs condemned the victims, but spectators' isolation freed them from moral complicity in the indecent exposure. Thus the images blurred Rabelaisian delight in bodily excesses with elements of bourgeois propriety to simultaneously titillate and critique. The Dames' "small correction on women by women," as one paper called it, relied heavily on a sense of performance that encouraged spectators of both sexes to judge the beating through their collective gaze.[90]

Denouncing Disorder and Vindicating Violence among Women

Unlike spectators who reveled in the spanking, the police and the Department of Paris were not amused. The new administration butted up against a particularly thorny problem. On the one hand, the demonstrators reinforced the government's newly elected priests and the attacks protected the vulnerable Civil Constitution of the Clergy. If officials denounced the Dames' patriotic slaps, they would defend refractory clerics by default. On the other hand, the nascent Department of Paris desperately sought to reestablish its policing authority in the capital. How could the administration condemn the popular acts of violence while commending the Dames' patriotic intentions?

Peuchet, the chief of police, needed to carefully reconcile the state's competing interests in the nuns affair. He issued a public statement to try to calm the commotion. Peuchet reminded Parisians that "indifference to public force" was "a forgetfulness of duties prescribed by law." But he shifted blame to sensational pamphleteers, libelous journalists, crass artists, and political rabble-rousers who misled citizens into confusing "freedom with the power to disobey the laws of the State." Although the government and popular societies had condemned the violence, "no cause has yet been indicated; one has not identified any instruments used in ignorance or maliciousness to mislead the people."[91] In his linguistic acrobatics, Peuchet avoided faulting any citizens or inadvertently defending counterrevolutionary nuns. Yet he simultaneously denounced the violence.

So why, despite all of these gendered elements, did the revolutionaries not condemn the violence as stemming from feminine disorder? Despite being the only other moment of mass violence between groups of women, 1791 shared none of the 1793 conclusions concerning women's irrational passions. I have found no mention of women's "natural" propensity toward emotional chaos during the nuns affair. In fact ten days after the spankings, one pamphlet called directly on "all our gay lassies of the Halles and markets" to incite *new* violence to prevent refractory clergy from staging a massacre rumored for Good Friday.

At the most basic level it appears that the revolutionaries did not want to jettison the favorable political effects of the Dames' spanking spree by attacking female violence. Ironically the relationship between gender and religion discouraged the revolutionaries from condemning the Dames' violence as gendered chaos. As evidenced by the nuns' betrayal, the revolutionaries feared that women were especially susceptible to refractory clergy's spiritual seduction.[92] The revolutionaries also needed to show that French mothers offered "natural" morals that were more virtuous than those dictated by a foreign spiritual leader. From this perspective celibacy did not confer female virtue; it could undermine it. To gloss over the rough edges of the attack journalists praised the Dames as "mothers of citizen families."[93] Pamphleteers insisted that the "female citizens" would educate children without "lying" in the future, thereby correcting problems of "centuries" past.[94] Moreover, by conducting their "patriotic discipline" without male guidance, the Dames seemed to prove that the revolutionaries' maternal ideals could triumph over Catholic "female superstition."[95] In order to draw moral legitimacy from women's support of the Civil Constitution of the Clergy, the revolutionaries had to grant legitimacy to Parisian women's violence.[96]

Conclusion

Two years later, in 1793, the market women brawled with the local women's political club with very different results. In contrast to the patriotic praise the Dames received for spanking the nuns in 1791, the Jacobin deputies recoiled from the Dames' 1793 street fights by banning female political clubs. The deputies mostly condemned this later violence in terms of destructive gendered disorder. On the surface, the ban appeared to be a distinct backlash against violence rooted in women's nature. However, as the historian Stuart Carroll has argued, "violence is . . . a cultural category, whose idiom, meaning and discourse, will depend on the context."[97] And the 1791 attacks reveal how rapidly the context for gendered violence vacillated during the Revolution.

Male and female revolutionaries did not uniformly denounce violence among women. According to Micah Alpaugh, in 1791 only 16 of 117 Parisian street demonstrations involved physical assaults.[98] Although the spankings spree is unusually intense by these 1791 standards, revolutionaries actually *celebrated* the Dames' violent attacks. In addition the market women alone slapped the nuns. In other instances of crowd activism, revolutionary women often "began the movement," encouraged men to join, or acted as cultural buffers to mitigate physical conflict.[99] Yet in April 1791 male spectators remained on the sidelines, and the only peacekeepers that arrived were male National Guardsmen.

Due to these exceptional elements, the Dames' attack deviates from the usual historiographical narrative of women and violence in the Revolution, where all roads lead to the 1793 ban. In his study, for example, Jean-Clément Martin argues that "outside a very limited militant milieu, one searches in vain for positive images of violent revolutionary women. The gender [of the actors] clearly determines how violence was judged during the epoch."[100] However, the Dames do not fit into this narrative in 1791. And Dominique Godineau similarly observes, "As for those who search to denigrate a political movement, they often underline feminine violence in order to symbolize the savagery, the 'destructive madness,' the malfunction of the entire target group."[101] But this too was not the case in 1791. Revolutionary illustrators and propagandists feted the Dames as heroines who taught counterrevolutionary nuns forceful lessons. We know that Parisians ate up these images and accounts because they multiplied at an impressive rate. Godineau justly points out that the sexual overtones infused these spanking caricatures with carnivalesque flavors. She argues that the heavily gendered tropes moralized the message and entertained the viewer, but she also maintains that the satire ultimately rubbed off on the Dames and belittled their actions. However, when we couple the imagery with written accounts and officials' carefully worded reactions, we see that this laughter does not entirely deride the Dames' female violence or brush aside their political intent.[102]

This chapter has argued that the relationship among gender, violence, and women's political action was more fluid than the 1793 conflicts and our historiographical narratives suggest. In 1791 male and female revolutionaries deployed gendered themes to critique the nuns and support the Dames. The Dames' demonstration was powerful *precisely because* its public display of gendered violence provided a common canvas for communal judgment. Writers and artists effectively seized gendered signposts to guide public opinion on the violence. In word and image they humiliated the nuns, dispelled ideas of false martyrdom, invoked domestic violence themes, and charged recalcitrant clergy with sexual transgressions. Yet no one blamed the violence on natural feminine disorder. Officials did not portray the spanking spree as the inevitable product of quarrels among women, as a symptom of inherent female irrationality, or as the result of troublesome political interference by women. Instead officials blamed the violence on rabble-rousing propagandists and vindicated the Dames' patriotic intentions. Thus in 1791 violence among women created a model for female activism rather than nullifying it.

The Dames' initiatives against the nuns and the public's approval compels us to reconsider the notion of citizenship in its embryonic stages.[103] The revolutionaries conceptualized civic membership in various veins before it formally hardened into institutional components such as voting, participating in political societies, or serving in the militia. In 1791 the Dames advanced a form of embodied citizenship in which individuals contributed to the body politic through their social relationships. By practicing citizenship as lived experience, the Dames and other revolutionaries could not transcend their gendered bodies, but they could use gender to creatively maneuver in politics.[104] Thus the Dames forged their own visions of nascent citizenship in the early Revolution.

Scrutinizing the ways in which the revolutionaries applauded the market women's "corrections" on the nuns makes it clear that gender, violence, and citizenship were not locked in a causal trio at the birth of modern citizenship. Despite the deputies' 1793 claims to the contrary, female violence operated on a spectrum of acceptability whose boundaries were mutable, dynamic, and, above all, contingent. In 1791 the revolutionaries deployed well-worn tropes of gender, maternity, and sexuality to critique counterrevolutionary women without condemning the violent strikes of patriotic female citizens. Gender and violence intertwined during the Revolution, but modern citizenship was not encoded with a set configuration between the two.

Notes

The author thanks Rachel Fuchs, Suzanne Desan, and the audience members at the 2014 Arizona State University and Society for French Historical Studies conferences for sharing their insights. This work was funded in part by the Baylor University Office of the Vice Provost for Research and the Fulbright Commission Franco-Américaine.

1. George Granville Levenson-Gower Sutherland, "April 15, 1791," in *The Despatches of Earl Gower*, ed. Oscar Browning (London: C. J. Clay and Son, Cambridge University Press Warehouse, 1885), 79; Antoine-Joseph Gorsas, *Le Courrier de Paris dans les 83 Départements*, April 6, 1791, 138–39, Bibliothèque nationale de France (hereafter BnF) Lc2 161.

2. Gorsas, *Le Courrier*, April 3, 1791, 138.

3. Louis-Marie Prudhomme, *Les Révolutions de Paris*, no. 92, April 9–16, 1791, BnF Lc2 171.

4. *Liste des Culs Aristocrates et Anti-Constitutionnels, qui ont été fouettés hier au soir à tour de bras, par les Dames de la Halle, et du Faubourg Saint-Antoine* (Paris: Imprimerie Patriotique, 1791), 3, BnF Lb39 5505.

5. *Liste de toutes les sœurs & dévotes qui ont été fouettées par les Dames de Marchés des différents Quartiers de Paris* (Paris: L'imprimerie de Tremblay, 1791), 2–4, 8, BnF Ld4 7148.

6. *La discipline Patriotique ou le Fanatisme Corrigée*, 1791, etching, 15x21.5cm, BnF Qb 370 (20)-FT 4.

7. Katie Jarvis, "Politics in the Marketplace: The Popular Activism and the Cultural Representation of the Dames des Halles during the French Revolution," PhD diss., University of Wisconsin, Madison, 2014, 359–90.

8. Joan Landes, *Women and the Public Sphere in the Age of the French Revolution* (Ithaca NY: Cornell University Press, 1988); Joan Scott, *Only Paradoxes to Offer: French Feminists and the Rights of Man* (Cambridge MA: Harvard University Press, 1996); Geneviève Fraisse, *Muse de la Raison: La démocratie exclusive et la différence des sexes* (Aix-en-Provence: Alinéa, 1989); Carole Pateman, *The Sexual Contract* (Stanford CA: Stanford University Press, 1988).

9. Timothy Tackett, *Priest and Parish in Eighteenth-Century France* (Princeton NJ: Princeton University Press, 1977), 272–75.

10. Lucien Misermont, *Serment à la constitution civile du clergé: Le Serment civique et quelques documents inédits des archives vaticanes* (Paris: Librairie Victor LeCoffre, 1917), 31.

11. Suzanne Desan, *Reclaiming the Sacred: Lay Religion and Popular Politics in Revolutionary France* (Ithaca NY: Cornell University Press, 1990), 6.

12. E. Claire Cage, *Unnatural Frenchmen: The Politics of Priestly Celibacy and Marriage, 1720-1815* (Charlottesville: University of Virginia Press, 2015), 5.

13. Mita Choudhury, *Convents and Nuns in Eighteenth-Century French Politics and Culture* (Ithaca NY: Cornell University Press, 2004), 5.

14. Cage, *Unnatural Frenchmen*, 65.

15. Cage, *Unnatural Frenchmen*, 54.

16. Choudhury, *Convents and Nuns*, 6,19.

17. *Journal général de France*, no. 107, April 17, 1791, 428.

18. Claude-François Beaulieu, *Journal du Soir*, no. 84, March 25, 1791, 3, BnF Lc2 415.

19. *Gazette nationale ou le Moniteur universel*, April 5, 1791, 387.

20. Jacques-René Hébert, *Je suis le véritable père Duchesne, foutre*, no. 46, April 3, 1791, 1, BnF Lc2 508.

21. *Journal général*, no. 94, April 4, 1791, 375–76 and no. 95, April 5, 1791, 380.

22. Jacques-Marie Boyer de Nîmes, *Histoire des Caricatures de la Révolte des Français* (Paris: Imprimerie du *Journal du Peuple*, 1792), 257, BnF La32 29 (1).

23. Louis-Sébastien Mercier, *Annales patriotiques et littéraires de la France, et affaires politiques de l'Europe*, no. 555, April 10, 1791, 1274, BnF Lc2 249.

24. *Douzième Lettre Bougrement Patriotique de la Mère Duchêne* (Paris: Chez Huilhemat, 1791), 8, BnF NUMM 56702.

25. Mercier, *Annales patriotiques*, no. 552, April 7, 1791, 1261–62.

26. Boyer de Nîmes, *Histoire des Caricatures*, 224; *Journal général*, no. 100, April 10, 1791, 399; *Chanson sur les culs fouettés: Détail historique des communautés de sœurs grises* (Paris: De l'Imprim. de Labarre, 1791), 1, BnF Ld4 6997.

27. *Chanson sur les culs fouettés*, 1–6. For the locations of churches and religious orders during the Revolution, see P. Pisani, *L'église de Paris et la Révolution*, vol. 1 (Paris: Alphonse Picard et Fils, 1908), 310–23.

28. *Chanson sur les culs fouettés*, 1–6.

29. *Liste des Culs Aristocrates et Anti-Constitutionnels*, 6.

30. *Chanson sur les culs fouettés*, 3.

31. Gorsas, *Le Courrier*, April 3, 1791, 137.

32. Camille Desmoulins, *Révolutions de France et de Brabant* (Paris: Imprimeries du Cercle Social, 1791), no. 73, April 1791, 354, BnF NUMP 13712.

33. Nicole Pellegrin, "Habiller la norme sous l'Ancien régime. Les vêtements de religion féminins dans et hors clôture: Créations, (dés)habillages et habitus," paper presented at Séminaire Genre et classes populaires, Paris, June 25, 2015.

34. *Liste des Culs Aristocrates et Anti-Constitutionnels*, 5.

35. *Liste des Culs Aristocrates et Anti-Constitutionnels*, 5–6.

36. *Liste de toutes les sœurs & dévotes qui ont été fouettées*, 3.

37. *La Chronique de Paris*, no. 99, April 9, 1791, BnF Lc2 218.

38. A. de Beauchamp, ed., *Recueil des lois et règlements sur l'enseignement supérieur*, vol. 1, *1789-1914* (Paris: Typographie de Delalain Frères, 1880), 7; Misermont, *Serment à la constitution civile du clergé*, 29.

39. *La Chronique de Paris*, no. 106, April 16, 1791.

40. *Journal général*, no. 100, April 10, 1791, 399.

41. Gorsas, *Le Courrier*, April 10, 1791, 154.

42. Rolf Reichardt, "Prints: Images of the Bastille," in *The French Revolution: Recent Debates and New Controversies*, ed. Gary Kates (London: Routledge, 1998), 224.

43. Antoine de Baecque, *La Caricature Révolutionnaire* (Paris: Presses du CNRS, 1988), 14.

44. de Baecque, *La Caricature Révolutionnaire*, 18.

45. de Baecque, *La Caricature Révolutionnaire*, 35.

46. Annie Duprat, "'La trésorière des Miramionnes n'avait qu'une fesse...,'" *Annales historiques de la Révolution française* 361 (2010): 53.

47. Jeremy D. Popkin, "Journals: The New Face of News," in *Revolution in Print: The Press in France, 1775-1800*, ed. Robert Darnton and Daniel Roche (Berkeley: University of California Press, 1989), 150.

48. de Baecque, *La Caricature Révolutionnaire*, 19.

49. *L'Anti-Marat, Ouvrage périodique par une société de gens de lettres* (Paris: 1791), 2, BnF Lc2 540.

50. *Gazette nationale*, April 11, 1791, 415.

51. Boyer de Nîmes, *Histoire des Caricatures*, 223.

52. Gorsas, *Le Courrier*, April 12, 1791, 186–87.

53. Bibliothèque Historique de la Ville de Paris 31598 (no. 2), *Grand détail concernant les dévots et les dévotes qui ont été fouettés par les dames de la Halle à Paris* (Paris, Baudouin).

54. *Liste de toutes les sœurs & dévotes qui ont été fouettées*, 1.

55. Desmoulins, *Révolutions de France*, no. 73, 355.

56. Cage, *Unnatural Frenchmen*, 68–69.

57. *Journal général*, no. 100, April 10, 1791, 399.

58. On the cultural importance of physiognomy, see Michael Kwass, "Big Hair: A Wig History of Consumption in Eighteenth-Century France," *American Historical Review* 111 (2006): 631–59.

59. *Quatorzième Lettre Bougrement Patriotique de la Mère Duchêne* (Paris: Chez Huilhemat, 1791), 5, BnF NUMM 56702.

60. de Baecque, *La Caricature Révolutionnaire*, 41.

61. *Liste des Culs Aristocrates et Anti-Constitutionnels*, 2.

62. See also *Discipline patriotique*, 1791, etching, 16.5x11cm, BnF Qb 201 (214).

63. *La Discipline patriotique*, BnF Qb 370 (20)-FT 4.

64. See David, *Nourrice*, etching, BnF MFILM R-5680, and etching, BnF MFILM R-5679.

65. Etching, around 1790, BnF MFILM R-5683.

66. de Baecque, *La Caricature Révolutionnaire*, 110.

67. Lynn Hunt, "Pornography and the French Revolution," in *The Invention of Pornography: Obscenity and the Origins of Modernity, 1500-1800*, ed. Lynn Hunt (New York: Zone Books, 1993), 308.

68. de Baecque, *La Caricature Révolutionnaire*, 44.

69. Stuart Carroll, introduction in *Cultures of Violence: Interpersonal Violence in Historical Perspective*, ed. Stuart Carroll (New York: Palgrave MacMillan, 2007), 1.

70. *Journal Général*, no. 82, March 23, 1791, and no. 83, March 24, 1791.

71. Arlette Farge, "Proximités pensables et inégalités flagrantes: Paris, XVIIIe siècle," in *De la Violence et des Femmes*, ed. Cécile Dauphin and Arlette Farge (Paris: Editions Albin Michel, 1997), 88.

72. Duprat, "'La trésorière des Miramionnes," 62.

73. Lynn Hunt describes how pornographic images, as opposed to libertine texts after 1789, made "the reader both a voyeur and a moral judge" ("Pornography and the French Revolution," 325).

74. Boyer de Nîmes, *Histoire des Caricatures*, 222.

75. Thanks to Natalie Zemon Davis for suggesting I investigate the pictorial background of domestic abuse.

76. Mary Trouille, *Wife Abuse in Eighteenth-Century France* (Oxford : Voltaire Foundation, 2007), 19-20.

77. Trouille, *Wife Abuse*, 15.

78. Trouille, *Wife Abuse*, 18.

79. For a similar domestic violence scene see Le Pautre, *Corrige, si tu peux, par un discours honeste*, 1676, BnF Oa 22 (235).

80. *Dictionnaire de l'Académie française*, 4th edition (1762) Project ARTFL, http://artfl-project.uchicago.edu/content/dictionnaires-dautrefois.

81. Gorsas, *Le Courrier*, April 10, 1791.

82. Prudhomme, *Les Révolutions de Paris*, no. 92, April 9-16, 1791.

83. For more on "unruly women," see Natalie Zemon Davis, "Women on Top," in *Society and Culture in Early Modern France* (Stanford CA: Stanford University Press, 1975), 131-51.

84. Choudhury, *Convents and Nuns*, 146-47.

85. Choudhury, *Convents and Nuns*, 142.

86. Cage, *Unnatural Frenchmen*, 54-58.

87. I have found only one revolutionary image in the Bibliothèque national de France's electronic holdings: a woman, who is an allegory for the Constitution, spanking a man's bare rear. *Il n'a qu'à venir il sera traité de la sorte*, 1791-92, etching, 31.5x39.5cm, BnF MFILM M-100523. For examples of

prerevolutionary domestic violence scenes in which the wife is the disciplinarian, see *La Femme quy fouette son mari* (around 1670) and *L'école des mary* (XVIIe siècle) in *La Guerre des Sexes: Les Albums du cabinet des estampes* (Paris: Albin Michel, 1984), 83.

88. Mercier, *Annales patriotiques*, no. 555, April 10, 1791, 1274.

89. de Baecque, *La Caricature Révolutionnaire*, 188.

90. Prudhomme, *Les Révolutions de Paris*, no. 92, April 9–16, 1791.

91. *Gazette nationale ou le Moniteur universel*, April 14, 1791, 427.

92. Choudhury, *Convents and Nuns*, 182. On counterrevolutionary Catholic women in the countryside, see Desan, *Reclaiming the Sacred*; Olwen Hufton, "In Search of Counter-Revolutionary Women," in Kates, *The French Revolution*, 302–33.

93. Boyer de Nîmes, *Histoire des Caricatures*, 223

94. *Liste de toutes les sœurs & dévotes qui ont été fouettées*, 2.

95. Suzanne Desan demonstrates how, in Year II, the Jacobins became torn between "the articular moral and emotional ability of women to win over the hearts of men and children for the Republic" and potentially Catholic "female superstition." Suzanne Desan, "The Family as Cultural Battleground: Religion vs. Republic under the Terror," in *The French Revolution and the Creation of Modern Political Culture*, vol. 4, ed. Keith M. Baker (Oxford: Permagon, 1994), 184.

96. According to Stuart Carroll, "the boundaries of legitimate and illegitimate violence" are one of the most important factors in discerning how "violence is culturally specific" (introduction, 9). In Arno Mayer's schema of political violence, we can consider the nuns affair "violence of foundation, which sets up and anchors a new order of legitimacy." Arno Mayer, *The Furies: Violence and Terror in the French and Russian Revolutions* (Princeton NJ: Princeton University Press, 2000), 75.

97. Carroll, introduction, 12.

98. Micah Alpaugh, *Non-Violence and the French Revolution: Political demonstrations in Paris, 1787-1795* (Cambridge, UK: Cambridge University Press, 2015), 3, 5.

99. Dominique Godineau, "Citoyennes, boutefeux et furies de guillotine," in Dauphin and Farge, *De la Violence et des Femmes*, 38; Alpaugh, *Non-Violence and the French Revolution*, 71.

100. Jean-Clément Martin, "De la violence des femmes pendant la période révolutionnaire: Un paradoxe persistant," in *Penser la violence des femmes*, ed. Coline Cardi and Geneviève Pruvost (Paris: La Découverte, 2012), 95.

101. Dominique Godineau, introduction in *Penser la violence des femmes* (Paris: La Découverte, 2012), 73.

102. Dominique Godineau, "Femmes et violence dans l'espace politique révolutionnaire," *Historical Reflections/Réflexions Historiques* 29, no. 3 (2003): 564.

103. Anne Verjus has explored how standards of individual autonomy and the familial unit applied to both men and women who were denied voting rights. Anne Verjus, *Le Cens de la famille: Les femmes et le vote, 1789–1848* (Paris: Editions Berlin, 2002).

104. For example, Annie Smart has analyzed the feminine "home as a realm for civic experience and values." Annie Smart, *Citoyennes: Women and the Ideal of Citizenship in Eighteenth-Century France* (Newark: University of Delaware Press, 2011), 3.

2

Restoring the Royal Family

Marie-Thérèse and the Family
Politics of the Early Restoration

VICTORIA E. THOMPSON

Portraits of several kings adorned the walls of the salon of 1814. There was Jean-Jacques Le Barbier's Henri IV, under whose aegis Louis XVIII had entered the capital in March 1814; Saint Louis by the same artist; Charles Meynier's Louis XIV and his king of Corinth; and François Gérard's Louis XVIII himself.[1] Francis I was the subject of Anicet-Charles-Gabriel Lemonnier's *François Ier recevant la La Sainte Famille de Raphaël*. Set in the sixteenth-century court of Francis I at Fontaine-bleau, the painting depicts the king "in the middle of his family," contemplating a painting of the holy family by Raphaël. In this painting within the painting, Mary lifts the baby Jesus into her arms as Joseph watches over her shoulder. While Mary gazes into her baby's eyes, Saint Elizabeth looks lovingly at her own son, Saint John the Baptist.[2] The canvas is in the mid-ground of the painting, left of center. The composition and lighting draw the eye to Francis, sitting in the center. To his right we see a group of men: courtiers, artists, and men of letters. To his left we see the women of the court and the family. Prominently placed in front of the canvas so that her head is between Mary's knees and Jesus's body is a woman, her arm outstretched toward a young boy. According to Christine Le Bozec, she is the duchesse d'Angoulême, Louise de Savoy, mother of Francis I.[3] Lemonnier's painting shows the French royal family establishing its legitimacy through a comparison to the holy family. The maternal figure, in the overlapping images of

Mary and Louise, serves as a focal point for a display of familial affection. She also connects the world of politics and the world of family, ensuring continuity between the two just as Louise de Savoy, duchesse d'Angoulême, ensured the future of the monarchy as regent during the military campaigns of Francis I. Another duchesse d'Angoulême, Marie-Thérèse, daughter of Louis XVI and Marie-Antoinette, would play a similarly significant role in the family politics of the Restoration.

Although originally destined for Josephine's art collection at Malmaison, Lemonnier's painting *La Sainte Famille* unwittingly captured the family dynamics of the restored Bourbon monarchy so well that it likely served as inspiration for a print in which Louis XVIII and his family gaze at a painting of Louis XVI and his family.[4] These two images serve as entry points into an analysis of the complicated and ultimately unsuccessful efforts of the restored Bourbons to cement their position as "first family" of France. Both images illustrate how one family referred to another to shore up its legitimacy. In the case of Louis XVIII and his "august family," the "holy" family of Louis XVI served as the legitimating counterpart to the odd assortment of Bourbons who crossed the channel in the spring of 1814.

Scholars have recognized the symbolic importance of Louis XVI and other Bourbon kings in Restoration politics.[5] As a relatively unknown king, Louis XVIII needed to establish his claim to legitimate rule in a country for which having a Bourbon monarch was no longer a given. He also had to reassure the French that he did not wish to return to the political system of the Old Regime. In this effort his own family was of crucial importance. In need of establishing a royal legitimacy based neither on divine right nor on bonds of patronage and obligation, the government and supporters of Louis XVIII emphasized affective ties as the glue that connected the monarch to his subjects. As others have argued, attempts were made early on to depict Louis XVIII as a "good father" to his people.[6]

Yet to be a good father to the people of France also entailed cultivating an image of a good father within his own family. As Martin Wrede and Christine Weil note, the "styling of the king as *pater familias* of an entire nation henceforth required, to be credible, a corresponding development in the private sphere."[7] In texts, images, and public appearances the royal family appeared as a modern family, with a good father at its head and an appropriate distinction between the sexes.[8] However, reliance on family politics contributed to the monarchy's failure in allaying fears of a return to the Old Regime, in part because the focus on the family of Louis XVIII rendered its central female figure, Marie-Thérèse, crucially important. At a time when both gender roles and conceptions of the family were unstable, Marie-Thérèse incarnated a variety of female types. Some of these—the devoted daughter and "mother"—would become normative for women in positions of political leadership by the mid-nineteenth century. Others, such as the politically powerful "queen" or courageous heroine, were more unsettling. The family politics of the early Restoration illustrate the political importance of the family, both real and imagined, as France continued its long and difficult transition toward a stable parliamentary system. In considering the variety of female roles attributed to Marie-Thérèse, we come to appreciate the diverse models of feminine belonging to the nation that were still in play in the early nineteenth century.

Family Bonds and French Politics

In the second half of the eighteenth century, French intellectuals turned to the family in order to rethink social and political bonds. During these years traditional social hierarchies based on legal privilege came under pressure as new elites from the world of finance rose to positions of prominence. Concerns over social confusion and self-interest led to a privileging of the family as an alternate model of society, one in which bonds of affection prompted individuals to act for the benefit of others.[9] The nuclear family was also used to critique royal authority. Jean-Jacques Rousseau admonished rulers that love was a more effective tool than fear, illustrating this principle through his depictions of affective relationships among family members. With his fictional couples Julie and Wolmar and Sophie and Emile, Rousseau portrayed relationships based on affection as the essential foundation for a well-functioning civil society. In the 1780s Marie-Antoinette and Louis XVI attempted to portray themselves as good parents. Marie-Antoinette's "deepening passion for motherhood" was translated into paintings of the queen as mother.[10] For his part, Louis XVI broke with royal tradition by not taking a mistress, and his modest hobbies made him a model of a new type of "father" to his people.[11] But in attempting to embrace new familial values, the monarchs contravened courtly etiquette and tradition, making many enemies. In the political and economic crisis of the late 1780s, these enemies were only too willing to portray the royal couple, and especially Marie-Antoinette, as cold-hearted and duplicitous. From the October days of 1789 until their executions in 1793, the king and queen were criticized and dehumanized.[12] While revolutionaries glorified families, particularly mothers, in festivals and with maternal iconography, the republic, as a political system based on fraternity, did not have at its head a "first" family that could model appropriate social bonds.

Nonetheless the "centrality of narratives about the family to the constitution of all forms of authority" meant that the family garnered much attention after 1789, as state and society were transformed.[13] As Lynn Hunt has shown, French men and women reimagined social and political bonds through stories of good and bad fathers, bad and absent mothers, orphaned sons and dutiful daughters. Conceiving the nation as a family writ large, revolutionaries extolled the bonds of affection that united people through their own free will rather than by means of coercion. The Enlightenment critique of despotism had included an attack on the unrestrained authority of fathers, and during the Revolution legislators diminished the power of fathers and conferred individual rights upon all family members. The politicization of the family as a model for society became increasingly pronounced as revolutionary politics heated up and legislators reformed family law.[14] As the family bore more symbolic weight as a model for society and polity, it also became more fragile; real families were torn apart during the Revolution as members were executed, emigrated, or went to war, while legal changes transformed the roles and responsibilities of family members toward each other.[15]

In the aftermath of the Terror, fear of social disorder and concerns over illegitimate children and property rights favored a shift toward a rehabilitated father figure, one with greater authority over other family members. The Civil Code of 1804 restored paternal authority within a family in which gender roles were clearly defined. As Rachel Fuchs states, the authors of the Civil Code envisioned a very specific sort of family: "In their ideal patriarchal marriage, each person would be in his and her proper role."[16] However, despite the passage of the Civil Code, as Suzanne Desan asserts, reforms in family law during the Revolution and empire meant that "no one . . . could take the makeup of the family and the sacrifice of individuals [to the family unit] as givens." The family as a social institution and as a metaphor for state and society would remain "a site of political and social contestation" well into the nineteenth century.[17] The Civil Code restricted women's political, legal, and economic rights, but it could not entirely contain the messy reality of postrevolutionary French social and political life. Thus in the courts, as Fuchs has shown, women deprived of the right to file paternity claims employed alternative strategies to force fathers to take responsibility for their children, strategies that judges supported despite their violation of paternal authority as enshrined in the Civil Code.[18] And while the Civil Code attempted to define women's rights and duties, several competing models of women's civic participation still existed. While historians have tended to focus on key moments, such as the closure of women's clubs in 1793, to argue that women's roles became restricted to the purely domestic sphere over the course of the Revolution, women continued to exercise civic participation in the early nineteenth century. Under Napoleon, women played an important role in civic festivals; during the empire and Restoration elite women exercised leadership at court, in salons, and as members of political networks.[19]

Were these women citizens? Not if we define citizenship as the ability to vote and hold political office. However, recent scholarship asks us to reconsider what we mean by citizenship through its reconceptualization of motherhood as a form of civic participation.[20] Before the Revolution, as Mira Morgenstern has argued, measured love (rather than passion) among family members was necessary if male children were to grow up to be citizens able to participate virtuously in public life.[21] It was mothers who provided the necessary example of such love. Thus, as Jennifer Popiel notes, Rousseau's ideal family did not oppose the realm of the family or the domestic with that of politics; the second was dependent upon the first, as a good society could not exist without good families.[22] The family, centered in the home, or what Annie Smart has described as the "civic intimate sphere," was a space for the formation of future citizens as well as an arena in which women could exercise a form of citizenship by performing actions dedicated to improving the public good.[23] As Margaret Darrow has shown, after the Revolution aristocrats made the choice to contribute to the public good by embracing domesticity.[24] While earlier scholars saw motherhood as a justification for women's exclusion, this scholarship demonstrates how women used motherhood to create civic identities for themselves.

During the Restoration citizenship was still a relatively new and unstable concept. At the end of the seventeenth century a citizen was someone who possessed specific legal privileges by virtue of inhabiting a city. Over the course of the eighteenth century the term became more ubiquitous and capacious, connoting vague membership in a kingdom, a fatherland (*patrie*), and/or a nation. The term was contested throughout the Revolution, marked by a "permanent ambiguity between the idea of an active participation in the political community of citizens and an assigned belonging to the new nation."[25] The instability of the concept of citizenship and the fragility of the family posed challenges to political leaders such as Louis XVIII who sought to use the family to shore up their legitimacy. At the same time, and despite the passage of the Civil Code, this instability and fragility meant that women exercised a variety of civic roles. Marie-Thérèse had more opportunities than most women to play a role in the fate of the nation, yet the prints and texts that celebrated the many different types of womanhood that she incarnated suggest a measure of acceptance for diverse models of femininity in the early years of the Restoration.

Une fête de famille

The day after Louis XVIII returned to Paris as king, May 4, 1814, he stood on the balcony of the Tuileries palace, trying to silence the crowd cheering *Vive le Roi!* When he finally succeeded, he said, "Don't call me your King anymore, call me your father." The crowd cheered even louder, as cries of *Vive notre père!* rang out across the Tuileries garden. This anecdote was reported by the author of the new royalist periodical *L'ami de la religion et du Roi.* The author felt that these "truly paternal words" were especially important to share with readers outside of Paris, since they proved that in Louis XVIII, the French had a king "who loves us, and who has a stake in us loving him."[26]

L'ami de la religion et du Roi was the "foremost Catholic [news]paper" in Restoration France and a strong supporter of the Bourbons.[27] For its cofounder and editor Michel Picot, family affection was the most important social bond.[28] Picot repeatedly evoked familial affection to demonstrate the legitimacy of the Bourbons as rulers and to depict the nature of bonds that linked one citizen to another. Louis XVIII was a good father not only because he loved his subjects but also because he presented himself as a family man, whose affection for others served as a counterweight to the social and political hierarchies of the Restoration. Thus, on the afternoon of May 4 crowds outside the Tuileries palace repeatedly called for the king to show himself, and he, along with other members of the royal family, repeatedly acquiesced. At one point his younger brother the comte d'Artois (the future Charles X) joined him on the balcony, took the king's hand, and kissed it. Louis XVIII responded by taking his brother in his arms. Writing about this moment, Picot enthused, "At this sign of fraternal amity, with these effusions of such a touching sentiment, the crowd could no longer contain its joy; enthusiasm was at its peak." A king who let his love for his brother overcome royal protocol was a king, Picot implied, who felt for, and thus would care for, his fellow man, regardless of rank. This ability to feel made him a good leader, since his affection for his family was mirrored by his affection for the French. "His arms," Picot wrote, "are opened to receive us, and his eyes are filled with tears of tenderness."[29]

The family played an important role in Restoration politics. As the sentimentalism of the prerevolutionary period became the foundation for the domestic ideology of the postrevolutionary period, strong family bonds that united family members under the leadership of a benevolent yet firm father were desired in both private and public life. Conservatives attempted to restore and encourage hierarchical relationships within the family as a bulwark against excessive individualism and social disorder.[30] Educating the French about relationships among members of the royal family was also important. As the daughter of Louis XVI, Marie-Thérèse provided continuity from one monarch to the other. The comte d'Artois was the immediate successor to the throne, while hopes for future heirs lay in the marriage of the duc d'Angoulême and Marie-Thérèse and, later, in the marriage of the duc de Berry. However, in 1814 most French men and women were not very familiar with the royal family.[31] Because the legitimacy of the Bourbon monarchy was not a given in 1814, the strong emphasis placed by supporters of the regime on the family members of Louis XVIII was unprecedented.[32] Indeed even before returning to France, Louis XVIII realized the crucial importance of family ties. When his niece Marie-Thérèse was freed from prison in December 1795, Louis worked tirelessly to convince her to marry her cousin and his nephew, the duc d'Angoulême.[33] After Marie-Thérèse joined him in exile, he urged her to publish the memoir she had written in prison to gain sympathy for the royal family. And although Louis and his wife, Marie-Joséphine of Savoy, were barely on speaking terms, he forced her to join him in England to shore up his image as a family man. Louis XVIII thus worked hard to assemble his various family members—his wife, who died in 1810; his niece Marie-Thérèse; his brother the comte d'Artois; and his nephews, the ducs d'Angoulême and de Berry—in England in preparation for returning to France.[34] When he entered Paris, he made sure his family surrounded him, and the family regularly appeared in public together.

While Natalie Scholz argues that a display of "sentimental" affection among royal family members was valued only after the assassination of the duc de Berry in 1820, when it was deployed to attenuate political divisions, Picot's exultations show us that from the very beginning the royal family was depicted as a loving unit.[35] Attention to the ways in which relationships among different family members were depicted allows us to better understand the complex ways such relationships were used to communicate a variety of political messages, including the delicate relationship between the past and the present. Royal propaganda thus focused on demonstrating continuity between the families of Louis XVI and Louis XVIII, while also articulating gendered differences meant to balance the necessity of remembering the past with a desire to move toward a brighter future.

Royal propaganda repeatedly placed Louis XVIII and his family within a larger family that included that of Louis XVI. In the early years of the Restoration, numerous published works seeking to familiarize the French with the royal family focused on Louis XVI, yet in recounting his childhood they also explained the former king's relationship to his two younger brothers, one of whom was Louis XVIII. Prints also illustrated these family ties. Some were meant to illustrate the Bourbon line, descending from Henri IV to Louis XVIII. Others connected the family of Louis XVIII with the family of Louis XVI.

Reminding the French of the family ties between Louis XVI and Louis XVIII educated the French about the Bourbons. It also established expectations of what it meant to be ruled by a king. When Louis XVIII returned to Paris, a king had not ruled the country for almost twenty-two years. In the interim much ink had been used to describe the worst and the best traits of monarchy. It was therefore crucial that Louis XVIII and his supporters establish a framework for thinking about his rule, and revisiting the life of Louis XVI allowed them to do so. An 1816 poem illustrated this. Imagining what Louis XVI might have said on the eve of his execution, the author portrayed the former king as someone who had tried to improve France: "The errors, the abuses of preceding reigns / Undermined the effects of my beneficent plans."[36] The theme of Louis XVI as an unsuccessful reformer, foiled by his kindness and moderation, runs throughout these works and set an agenda for Louis XVIII. Louis XVIII had already made clear his willingness to embrace reform with his 1805 and 1813 declarations, which promised moderation.[37] In addition the attribution of clemency to Louis XVI was meant to reassure the French that, like his brother, Louis XVIII would not be vindictive toward his enemies. To make this argument without blaming the French, authors such as René de Chateaubriand contrasted the "tyrant" Napoleon with Louis XVI. For Chateaubriand, it was Louis's repeated assurances that he forgave his enemies that established him as the "true king, the French king, the legitimate king, the father and the head of the country!"[38] By extension, Louis XVIII, who as the former king's brother was raised in the same family and thus (according to these accounts) instilled with the same virtues, was the legitimate ruler of France.

While prints and written texts established the legitimacy of Louis XVIII as monarch through family imagery, situating him within the family of Louis XVI, his own family, and the family of the French, they also revealed the delicate line the regime and its supporters walked between a painful and potentially divisive past and a presumably brighter, unified future. The work of Sheryl Kroen and Emmanuel Fureix illustrates the paradox faced, and cultivated by, Louis XVIII. On the one hand, as Kroen has demonstrated, the regime followed a "politics of *oubli*," or forgetting, that was meant to bring warring factions of opinion together and erase signs of the past that could serve as rallying points for those opposed to the monarchy.[39] On the other hand, Fureix has highlighted the importance of commemorating victims of the Revolution, especially the royal family, as a means to "channel" competing memories and reinforce the continuity of the Bourbon dynasty.[40] Forgetting and remembering were important ways the Restoration monarchy attempted to control the legacy of the Revolution, but these dual policies led to constant tension. *L'ami de la religion et du Roi*, for example, repeatedly evoked memory only to call for a need to forget. Thus in describing the entry of the king in 1814, Picot recalled "the sad and terrible scenes that occurred" in Paris since Louis XVIII had left the city in 1791. Immediately afterward, he asked, "But why turn back to these morbid ideas?," recommending instead thanking Louis XVIII for "throwing a veil over the past."[41] Similarly funerary sermons for Louis XVI, held throughout the country in 1814, asked mourners to dry their tears and rejoice: "France, my dear Fatherland [*Patrie*], console yourself, cease your sighs and your sobs, your sad widowhood is finished; the tender Lily of the Bourbons flowers again on the Throne, with a new luster. You see in your midst [*dans ton sein*] all the members of this great family, that was so dear to you. . . . They bring you the immortal Testament of Louis XVI, peace, forgiveness, love, happiness."[42]

Although, as in this example, the entire family of Louis XVIII was meant to be a source of consolation in its willingness to forgive, the monarchy could not afford to forget the past. Since his execution in 1793, the martyrdom of Louis XVI and his family was the centerpiece of royalist discourse. Royalists explained the hardships of the Revolution as punishment for the death of the king and saw the Restoration as a blessing brought about by Louis's willingness to die for the sins of his subjects. The death of the king also served as a warning against regicide. The restored monarchy thus needed to strike a balance between remembering and forgetting. Louis XVIII was a monarch who could "dry the tears" of the French, allowing them to forget past divisions and, as the architect Jean-Bernard Roger put it, "abandon [their] mourning."[43] The suffering of so many during the Revolution, including the royal family, made the happiness of the family of Louis XVIII a poignant sign that France could put its troubled past behind it. Louis XVIII was not shy in making this connection. At a dinner given by the city of Paris to celebrate the Saint-Louis, the king gathered his family around him as he spoke to the assembled notables. As reported by Picot, he told them, "I had the greatest urgency to find myself reunited to my great family; but I had to wait until I could be surrounded by this one here (*gesturing, in the most noble and touching manner, to the Princes that surrounded him*); they were my consolation in my adversity, and still today they are my happiness."[44]

By contrast, Marie-Thérèse served as a constant reminder of the suffering of the Revolution. The duchesse d'Angoulême was frequently portrayed in mourning for members of her family, perhaps nowhere more dramatically than during funeral masses for her parents. In May 1814, as in subsequent masses, she appeared "in high mourning, with a black veil that covered her almost entirely." Hélène Becquet argues that the figure of Marie-Thérèse in mourning was central to royalist discourse, an aide-mémoire for those who might be tempted to forget their obligation to ask forgiveness for the crime of regicide.[45] Of all the members of the family of Louis XVIII, it was Marie-Thérèse whose sadness elicited both the greatest admiration and the most disdain. The mourning of Marie-Thérèse was always stronger than that of the king, and for good reason. She mourned her mother and father, and the act of mourning may have been a means for her to deal not only with their loss but also with the trauma she experienced in prison. Following the death of her aunt Elisabeth in May 1794 conditions in prison worsened for Marie-Thérèse; she lacked adequate heat, light, and food, had little with which to distract herself, and may have been physically and/or sexually abused.[46] Without giving specific details of the trauma she experienced, sources from the Restoration often depict Marie-Thérèse as haunted by her past; along these lines, much was made of her fainting when she arrived at the Tuileries palace in May 1814. Her sorrow and filial devotion allowed for depictions of the duchess that drew upon sentimental conventions, as in an 1816 print in which Marie-Thérèse, sitting before her fire with head bowed, contemplates her mother's final wishes.

The sadness of Marie-Thérèse balanced the obligations of the past with the hopes for the future incarnated by her uncle. While Louis XVIII also publicly mourned his family, he was more commonly portrayed as a figure who could heal France and replace sadness with peace, or even enthusiasm. This was possible because his niece incarnated the memory of France's crimes and as such was a figure set apart from the men in her family. As an 1816 image illustrates, Marie-Thérèse was the counterpart of the king but also distinguished from him by her special status as the daughter of Louis XVI, her sex, and her sadness. It illustrates the almost mythic status of Marie-Thérèse, who appears less like a living figure and more like an allegory of France's crimes and expiations. Hélène Becquet has argued that Marie-Thérèse was an ultraroyalist "icon."[47] While this is undoubtedly true, she was also a mythic figure in the sense elaborated by Chantal Thomas in her discussion of Marie-Antoinette; Marie-Thérèse served as a repository for a set of political values that were particularly important during the early years of the Restoration: filial devotion, faith, forgiveness, and remembrance. And although she did not have children, Marie-Thérèse acted as a mother to the children of the duchesse de Berry, keeping them with her at her court and taking charge of their education. She was also heavily involved in charitable work and was famous for her piety at a time when Catholicism was becoming increasingly feminized. As an allegory for the past, as well as in her actions, Marie-Thérèse seemed to incarnate a model of feminine virtue that aligned with the ideals of domesticity.

In the early years of the Restoration, however, female allegories did not replace all real opportunities for women to exercise power.[48] As the counterpart to a king without a living spouse, and because of her dynastic and symbolic importance as the daughter of Louis XVI, Marie-Thérèse assumed the role of queen. She appeared beside the king at ceremonial events and oversaw court etiquette and functions. She had influence with the king and other officials and wielded power through her ability to appoint the members of her household. For those not well-versed in Bourbon family relations, royal iconography gave the impression that she was in fact the queen.[49] In uniting past and present/future, Maire-Thérèse and Louis XVIII were the symbolic parents of Restoration France.

Daughter, "mother" and "queen," Marie-Thérèse also took on more controversial roles. She was in Bordeaux when Napoleon returned to France in March 1815. As the emperor's general Clauzel advanced on the city, she tried to rally the Bourbon troops, to no avail. Realizing that if she did not urge the city to surrender, its inhabitants would face serious reprisals, she told the loyal soldiers of the city's National Guard to stand down, and left to join her family in exile. The bravery of Marie-Thérèse was celebrated in a painting by Antoine-Jean Gros destined for the Tuileries palace, in which the duchess, in white and with arms outstretched toward the desolate Bordelais, embarked on the ship that would take her to safety.[50] As with the painting, accounts of the event depict the strong bond between the duchess and the inhabitants of Bordeaux as one of shared sorrow. According to the writer Alphonse de Beauchamp, "The Princess . . . responded to so many tears with her tears, to oaths of fidelity with her promises to remember." In a later account of the same scene, Beauchamp wrote, "At the sight of the profound sorrow spreading over the features of the august princess, [the National Guard] voiced unanimous cries of respect and love."[51] The painting of the duchess's departure contrasts greatly with another work by Gros meant to be its pendant, depicting a much less heroic moment: the king's abandonment of his assembled courtiers at the Tuileries palace.[52] While the king also reaches out to his soldiers, his face and gestures are less expressive than those of Marie-Thérèse, creating an emotional distance from those around him. The symbolic position of the duchess in the royal family encouraged others to see her as suffering with and for the French, whereas depictions of the king that associated him with positive emotions made it harder to see Louis XVIII as sharing the sorrows of his subjects.

That Louis XVIII and Marie-Thérèse served different symbolic and emotional functions in royalist images and published works during the early years of the Restoration could thus both hurt and harm the monarchy. In addition repeated recourse to family imagery could foster confusion. On the most crass level, the confusion between Marie-Thérèse as "daughter" of Louis XVIII and as "queen" raised the specter of incest. Incest and sexual misconduct in general was a theme that ran through condemnations of Marie-Antoinette and other members of the royal family before and during the Revolution, and one that was not easily forgotten. Before the Revolution, pornographic pamphlets targeting Marie-Antoinette attributed the paternity of Marie-Thérèse to the comte d'Artois (the brother of Louis XVI and Louis XVIII).[53] While this charge may have gone underground during the Restoration, it immediately reappeared with the July Revolution. In 1830 the writer Horace Raisson published the two-volume *Amours secrètes des Bourbons, depuis le mariage de Marie-Antoinette jusqu'à la chute de Charles X, par la Comtesse de C****, in which he brought back to life the old charges of sexual promiscuity against Marie-Antoinette, including the rumor that the comte d'Artois was the father of Marie-Thérèse. He described the duke and duchess d'Angoulême as "at once brothers [*sic*] and spouses."[54] Raisson also portrayed the young Louis XVIII and the duc de Berry as libertines, in this half-"history", half-fiction.

Also in 1830 two pamphlets accused the duchesse d'Angoulême of multiple sexual affairs, especially with members of the clergy. In one the bustle of the duchesse de Berry accuses Marie-Thérèse's petticoat of having "relations with priests, generals, bourgeois, the French, the English even more, the Russians, the Prussians."[55] Similarly, in an image from 1815, the duchesse pushes her uncle the king, who is trying to hold up an inverted candle snuffer into which members of the government are throwing the Charter, medals of the Legion of Honor, and a list of soldiers who had died for their country. Behind an elderly Marie-Thérèse stands a priest who lasciviously places his hands on her behind.[56] Marie-Thérèse was also portrayed much as Marie-Antoinette had been during the Revolution, as wanting to shed the blood of the people of France. One of the pamphlets proclaimed that if the duchess became queen, the day after "she would make the blood of the French flow"; according to the author, "*vengeance . . .* was the word that was constantly on the lips of this woman!"[57] The theme of Marie-Thérèse seeking to inflame passions and start a civil war first appeared during the Hundred Days in antiroyalist propaganda, as a response to her actions in Bordeaux.[58] It was renewed at the end of the Restoration, as in a print wherein an aged Marie-Thérèse has unsheathed her sword, in contrast to the weeping Charles X and an insouciant duc d'Angoulême.[59] These images transformed the positive association between Marie-Thérèse and Joan of Arc that circulated shortly after the Hundred Days into a critique of the monarchy based on a reversal of gender roles.[60]

Despite her supposed sexual promiscuity, detractors frequently portrayed Marie-Thérèse as aged and possessing either a masculine body or face or male attributes, such as a sword. A good example is the print *L'Antigone moderne*, which played on the comparison between Marie-Thérèse and the devoted daughter of *Oedipus at Colonus*, a popular play during the Restoration.[61] In this satirical print an unattractive Marie-Thérèse embraces a fat Louis XVIII. Depictions of Marie-Thérèse as an old woman emphasized her childlessness. Although royalists, and by all accounts the duchess herself, had hoped that she would become pregnant after returning to France, she never bore children.

This raised concerns for the future of the dynasty, until the duchesse de Berry gave birth to a son several months after her husband's assassination in 1820. Rumors that it was not really his child or that the baby was a girl that had been secretly switched to ensure the continuation of the royal dynasty circulated almost immediately and were repeated in the attacks on the royal family that appeared in 1830. Although the duchesse de Berry was a mother, she was not a solid maternal figure that could ground the family in the domestic mores of the day, and thus also came under attack.[62]

Images and displays of family unity and portrayals of Marie-Thérèse as a devoted daughter and pious "queen" did not protect her from criticism and may even have encouraged attacks against her due to her involvement in politics. After the Hundred Days, Marie-Thérèse and the comte d'Artois felt that Louis XVIII had been too indulgent toward Napoleon's supporters. They advocated a hard line against regicides and were at the center of the ultraroyalist faction. Louis XVIII seems to have been inclined to follow a more moderate course, hoping to find in forgiveness a path to political stability. However, the family politics of Louis XVIII worked against compromise. A good father, according to the authors of the Civil Code, was one who used his power within the family to protect its honor and to maintain order and stability. This meant, as Desan has argued, that a father could not follow his personal inclinations if the result would bring dishonor or disunity to the family.[63] As father, a man used his authority within the family to banish discord, knowing he was acting for the good of the whole. As king, Louis XVIII appeared to wish to do the same. Yet when these two families—his blood relations and his "great family" of the French people—disagreed, where did his loyalties lie?

In 1819 the family politics of Louis XVIII were tested when liberals introduced a project to allow regicides who had supported Napoleon to return to France. The duchesse d'Angoulême opposed it.[64] The family politics of Louis XVIII made it impossible for the king to oppose his niece, as a rift in the family would have destroyed the central legitimating image of the restored monarchy. Furthermore, as a member of Decazes's cabinet stated, to ask the king to allow the return of the regicides would be to ask him to forgive those who murdered his brother and would thereby "violate the most powerful moral sentiment," the love of one family member for another.[65] To this appeal to family loyalties liberals responded by arguing that the king was abandoning his promise to forget the divisions of the Revolution. This opened the royal family to charges of hypocrisy, both in their public, political lives and in their private, familial lives. The crisis of 1819 shows that by making the family the centerpiece of his efforts at shoring up his legitimacy, Louis XVIII could not turn against it by going against the wishes of his niece or by seeming to put aside the memory of his dead brother. By remaining loyal to his family, Louis XVIII followed the logic of his family politics, but it cost him. Not only did the liberals withdraw their support, but the ultras never rallied to him completely. And the memory of the family of Louis XVI became a weight on the regime as years passed. Already by 1822 funeral services for Marie-Antoinette were poorly attended, and by 1823 numbers were falling at services for Louis XVI as well.[66]

In post-Rousseauian, postrevolutionary, and post–Civil Code France, employing family imagery to legitimate the reign of Louis XVIII made a lot of sense. In images and texts produced for the monarchy and by its supporters, the royal family was depicted as united by strong, authentic bonds of affection. It was a family whose members had suffered during the Revolution but that was also meant to be the source of renewed happiness. In this family the father was meant to be a gentle leader and a symbol of regeneration. The daughter was meant to be a devoted incarnation of filial love, as well as a reminder of the excesses of the Revolution. In its ideal incarnation the royal family corresponded to the model of a family guided by a loving father and characterized by a division of gendered roles whose legal manifestation was found in the Civil Code. It also exceeded these norms. Marie-Thérèse—as "queen" and as the "heroine" of 1815—also incarnated older and more troubling visions of feminine power. Finally, the royal family was a family like any other of the time, including the great family of France. Its members had experienced the Revolution in different ways, reacted to the traumas of the Revolution in the manner that best fit their personalities, and did not always agree on what was best for the country. Family divisions undermined the image of family unity and balance.

We see in the royal family of Louis XVIII how the model of an ideal family could serve as an important legitimating tool, while also undermining those in power. Much research remains to be done on the topic of family politics in the nineteenth century, but we can hypothesize that the failure of the family politics of Louis XVIII may have contributed to a decline of family imagery and family visibility among political leaders, as well as a devaluation of sentiment in politics.[67] This is not to say that the family became irrelevant to politics. Both Louis Philippe and Louis Napoleon sanctioned images of their families and appeared in public with their wives and children. But their wives played roles that were strongly shaped by actual and social motherhood.[68] By contrast, Marie-Thérèse participated in the polity in a variety of ways, and depictions of her drew upon diverse conceptualizations of women's civic roles and responsibilities. The tremendous importance of the family in Restoration politics conferred upon Marie-Thérèse great influence and agency, while also providing the means with which to attack her authority and that of her family. Rather than seeing the family as a unit that constrained women to domestic roles, the example of Marie-Thérèse demonstrates how family belonging could also provide women with novel ways of exercising civic participation.

Notes

1. Charles-Paul Landon et al., *Annales du Musée et de l'école moderne des beaux-arts: Salon de 1814. Recueil de morceaux choisis parmi les ouvrages de peinture et de sculpture exposés au Musée du Louvre* (Paris: Chaignieau aîné, 1814), 15, 11, 13, 23, 9.

2. Landon et al., *Annales du Musée*, 110. The painting by Raphael is *La Sainte Famille, dite La Grande Sainte Famille de François Ier* (1518).

3. Christine Le Bozec, *Lemonnier, un peintre en révolution* (Rouen: Publications de l'Université de Rouen, 2000), 124.

4. The caption to an 1813 engraving of the painting made clear that it was intended to celebrate Josephine as a patron of the arts. Jean-Pierre-Marie Jazet, *Le siècle de François Ier (Epoque de 1518)*, (1813). On Josephine as art patron and collector see Alain Pougetoux and Celine Meunier, "Joséphine,

la passion des collections," in *Joséphine*, ed. Etablissement public de la Réunion des musées nationaux et du Grand Palais des Champs-Elysées (Paris: Réunion des musées nationaux-Grand Palais, 2014), 28–35.

5. On the political uses of Louis XVI see Emmanuel Fureix, *La France des Larmes: Deuils Politiques à l'Âge Romantique (1814–1840)* (Paris: Champ Vallon, 2009), especially 151–67. On Henri IV, see Victoria E. Thompson, "The Creation, Destruction and Re-creation of Henri IV: Seeing Popular Sovereignty in the Statue of a King," *History and Memory* 24, no. 2 (2012): 5–40; Kimberly Jones, "Henri IV and the Decorative Arts of the Bourbon Restoration, 1814–1830: A Study in Politics and Popular Taste," *Studies in the Decorative Arts* 1, no. 1 (1993): 2–21.

6. The political motivations behind representing Louis XVIII as a good father are most fully explored in Natalie Scholz, "La monarchie sentimentale: Un remède aux crises politiques de la Restauration?," in *Représentation et pouvoir: La politique symbolique en France (1789–1830)*, ed. Natalie Scholz and Christina Schroër (Rennes: Presses Universitaires de Rennes, 2007), 185–98.

7. Martin Wrede and Christine Weil, "Le portrait du roi restauré, ou la fabrication de Louis XVIII," *Revue d'histoire moderne et contemporaine* 53, no. 2 (2006): 133.

8. The images discussed in this chapter come from two collections from the Bibliothèque nationale de France, both of which have been digitized in their entirety and are available at gallica.bnf.fr. See *Collection Michel Hennin: Estampes relatives à l'Histoire de France*, 169 volumes (hereafter referred to as "Hennin"), and *Collection de Vinck: Un siècle d'histoire de France par l'estampe, 1770–1870*, 248 volumes (hereafter referred to as "De Vinck").

9. Sarah Maza, "Commerce, Luxury and Family Love," in *The Myth of the French Bourgeoisie: An Essay on the Social Imaginary, 1750–1850* (Cambridge MA: Harvard University Press, 2003), 41–68.

10. Meredith Martin, *Dairy Queens: The Politics of Pastoral Architecture from Catherine de' Medici to Marie-Antoinette* (Cambridge MA: Harvard University Press, 2011), 248.

11. Jean-Claude Bonnet, "De la famille à la patrie," in *Histoire des pères et de la paternité*, ed. Jean Delumeau and Daniel Roche (Paris: Larousse, 1990), 252. On the rise of the good father as a model for the king see also Jeffrey Merrick, "Fathers and Kings: Patriarchalism and Absolutism in Eighteenth-Century French Politics," *Studies on Voltaire & the Eighteenth Century* 308 (1993): 281–303.

12. Central to this attack on the royal couple was a flood of political pornography. See Lynn Hunt, "The Many Bodies of Marie Antoinette: Political Pornography

and the Problem of the Feminine in the French Revolution," in *Eroticism and the Body Politic*, ed. Lynn Hunt (Baltimore: Johns Hopkins University Press, 1991); Jacques Revel, "Marie-Antoinette in Her Fictions: The Staging of Hatred," in *Fictions of the French Revolution*, ed. Bernadette Fort (Evanston IL: Northwestern University Press, 1991), 111–29; Elizabeth Colwill, "Pass as a Woman, Act Like a Man: Marie-Antoinette as Tribade in the Pornography of the French Revolution," in *Homosexuality in Modern France*, ed. Jeffrey Merrick and Bryant Ragan (New York: Oxford University Press, 1996), 54–79; Chantal Thomas, *The Wicked Queen: The Origins of the Myth of Marie-Antoinette* (New York: Zone Books, 1999), published in French in 1989. On depictions of the king and queen as animals see Annie Duprat, "La dégradation de l'image royale dans la caricature révolutionnaire," in *Les images de la Révolution française*, ed. Michel Vovelle (Paris: Publications de la Sorbonne, 1988), 167–76.

13. Lynn Hunt, *The Family Romance of the French Revolution* (Berkeley: University of California Press, 1992), 8.

14. Suzanne Desan, *The Family on Trial in Revolutionary France* (Berkeley: University of California Press, 2004).

15. Two recent studies in English that demonstrate the impact of the Revolution on families are Siân Reynolds, *Marriage and Revolution: Monsieur et Madame Roland* (Oxford: Oxford University Press, 2012) and Lindsay A. H. Parker, *Writing the Revolution: A French Woman's History in Letters* (Oxford: Oxford University Press, 2013). On the impact of legal reform see Desan, *The Family on Trial*.

16. Rachel G. Fuchs, *Contested Paternity: Constructing Families in Modern France* (Baltimore: Johns Hopkins University Press, 2008), 52.

17. Desan, *The Family on Trial*, 315, 316.

18. Fuchs, *Contested Paternity*, chap. 2.

19. Sarah Horowitz, *Friendship and Politics in Post-Revolutionary France* (University Park: Pennsylvania State University Press, 2013); Denise Davidson, *France after Revolution: Urban Life, Gender, and the New Social Order* (Cambridge MA: Harvard University Press, 2007); Steven Kale, *French Salons: High Society and Political Sociability from the Old Regime to the Revolution of 1848* (Baltimore: Johns Hopkins University Press, 2004); Anne Martin-Fugier, *La vie élégante, ou la formation du Tout-Paris (1815–1848)* (Paris: Fayard, 1990); Philip Mansel, *The Court of France 1789–1830* (Cambridge, UK: Cambridge University Press, 1988).

20. This argument was made most forcefully by Joan B. Landes in *Women and the Public Sphere in the Age of the French Revolution* (Ithaca NY: Cornell University Press, 1988).

21. Mira Morgenstern, *Rousseau and the Politics of Ambiguity: Self, Culture, and Society* (University Park: Pennsylvania State University Press, 1996). Morgenstern also notes how Rousseau undermines his vision of the ideal family.

22. Jennifer Popiel, *Rousseau's Daughters: Domesticity, Education, and Autonomy in Modern France* (Durham: University of New Hampshire Press, 2008), 47.

23. Annie K. Smart, *Citoyennes: Women and the Ideal of Citizenship in Eighteenth-Century France* (Newark: University of Delaware Press, 2011), 14.

24. Margaret H. Darrow, "French Noblewomen and the New Domesticity, 1750–1850," *Feminist Studies* 5, no. 1 (1979): 41–65.

25. Jennifer Heuer and Anne Verjus, "L'invention de la sphère domestique au sortir de la Révolution," *Annales historiques de la Révolution française* no. 327 (January–March 2002): 9. See also Raymonde Monnier, ed., *Citoyens et citoyenneté sous la Révolution française: Actes du colloque de Vizille 24 et 25 septembre 2004* (Paris: Société des Etudes Robespierristes, 2012); Jennifer Ngaire Heuer, *The Family and the Nation: Gender and Citizenship in Revolutionary France, 1789–1830* (Ithaca NY: Cornell University Press, 2005); Anne Verjus, *Le cens de la famille: Les femmes et le vote, 1789–1848* (Paris: Belin, 2002).

26. "Entrée du Roi à Paris," *L'ami de la religion et du roi: Journal ecclésiastique, politique et littéraire* 1, no. 5 (1814): 74.

27. M. Patricia Dougherty, "The Rise and Fall of *L'ami de la religion*: History, Purpose, and Readership of a French Catholic Newspaper," *Catholic Historical Review* 77, no. 1 (1991): 21.

28. On Picot see [Hippolyte Barbier], *Biographie du clergé contemporain, par un solitaire*, 10 volumes (Paris: A. Appert, 1848), 6:109–44.

29. "Entrée du Roi à Paris," 72, 65.

30. Eric Pierre, "Père affaibli, société en danger: La diffusion d'un discours sous les monarchies," *Le movement social* no. 224 (July–September 2008): 12, 14; Claudia Bernard, *Penser la famille au dix-neuvième siècle, 1789–1870* (Saint-Etienne: Publications de l'Université de Saint-Etienne, 2007), 210.

31. Marie-Thérèse was the one exception, due to her importance in royalist propaganda. See Hélène Becquet, *Marie-Thérèse de France: L'orpheline du temple* (Paris: Perrin, 2012); Hélène Becquet, "La fille de Louis XVI et l'opinion en 1795: Sensibilité et politique," *Annales historiques de la Révolution française* 341 (July–September 2005): 69–83.

32. Wrede and Weil, "Le portrait du roi restauré," 133.

33. The duc d'Angoulême was the oldest son of the comte d'Artois, the younger brother of Louis XVIII. The comte d'Artois's second son was the duc de

Berry. In marrying the duc d'Angoulême, who was next in the line of succession following the comte d'Artois, Marie-Thérèse would be in position to give birth to a boy and thus strengthen the line of succession. She did not have children, however, and although the wife of the duc de Berry did give birth to a son, no one in 1830 supported her as regent. During the Restoration Louis XVIII and his family members, as well as the *royalistes purs*, those most devoted to the Restoration of the Bourbons on the lines of the Old Regime monarchy, did not wish to see the crown go to the younger branch of the family, the Orléans, since Philippe d'Orléans had voted for the death of Louis XVI, and his son, Louis-Philippe, had liberal sympathies.

34. Many works have been written about Louis XVIII and Marie-Thérèse. Two of the best are Mansel, *Louis XVIII* (Stroud, UK: Sutton, 1999); Becquet, *Marie-Thérèse.*

35. Scholz, "La monarchie sentimentale," 196.

36. L Colomb-Menard, *Louis XVI, prisonnier dans la tour du Temple, à Marie-Antoinette Joséphe-Jeanne de Lorraine, archiduchesse d'Autriche et reine de France, détenue dans une autre prison de la même tour: héroïde avec des notes historiques* (Naisses: Chez l'auteur et chez Gaude fils, 1816), 9.

37. Philip Mansel, *Monarchy and Exile: The Politics of Legitimacy from Marie de Medicis to Wilhelm II* (London: Palgrave Macmillan, 2011), 199.

38. François-René de Chateaubriand, *De Bonaparte, des Bourbons, et de la nécessité de se rallier à nos Princes légitimes, pour le bonheur de la France et celui de l'Europe*, March 31, 1814, 45.

39. Sheryl Kroen, *Politics and Theater: The Crisis of Legitimacy in Restoration France, 1815-1830* (Berkeley: University of California Press, 2000).

40. Emmanuel Fureix, *La France des larmes: Deuils politiques à l'âge romantique (1814-1840)* (Paris: Champ Vallon, 2009), 139.

41. "Entrée du Roi à Paris," 67.

42. Normand, *Oraison funèbre de Sa Majesté Louis XVI, Roi de France et de Navarre, prononcée dans la cérémonie du Service expiatoire, célébré à Tours, dans l'église de St.-François-de-Paule, le 28 juillet 1814. En mémoire de Leurs Majestés Louis XVI, Roi de France et de Navarre; Marie-Antoinette-Joséphine-Jeanne de Lorraine, Archiduchesse d'Autriche, Reine de France et de Navarre; Louis XVII, Roi de France et de Navarre; et de Son Altesse Royale Madame Elisabeth de France.* (Tours: Chez Letourmy, 1814), 17-18.

43. Jean-Bernard Roger, *Ode à la France dédiée à sa fille, Madame, Duchesse d'Angoulême* (Paris: Lebègue, n.d.), 5.

44. *L'ami de la religion et du Roi: Journal ecclésiastique, politique et littéraire* 2, no. 59 (1814): 223.

45. *Journal des débats*, May 15, 1814, quoted in Becquet, *Marie-Thérèse*, 240; see also 240–41.

46. Becquet, *Marie-Thérèse*, 82–83.

47. Becquet, *Marie-Thérèse*, 210.

48. This argument has been made by Madelyn Gutwirth in *Twilight of the Goddesses* (New Brunswick NJ: Rutgers University Press, 1992) and by Joan B. Landes, *Visualizing the Nation: Gender, Representation, and Revolution in Eighteenth-Century France* (Ithaca NY: Cornell University Press, 2001).

49. In the Chamber of Deputies a portrait of the duchesse d'Angoulême served as a pendant to that of Louis XVIII (Becquet, *Marie-Thérèse*, 209).

50. Antoine-Jean Gros, *Embarquement de la Duchesse d'Angoulême à Pauillac*, 1818.

51. M.A.D.B.P. [Alphonse de Beauchamp], *La duchesse d'Angoulême à Bordeaux, ou Relation circonstanciée des Evènemens politiques dont cette ville a été le théâtre en mars 1815* (Versailles: J.-A. Lebel, 1815), 74–75; Alphonse de Beauchamp, *Histoire des campagnes de 1814 et de 1815 . . . Seconde partie, Comprenant le récit de tous les événemens survenus en France en 1815* (Paris: Le Normant, 1817), 491.

52. Antoine-Jean Gros, *Adieux de Louis XVIII quittant le palais des Tuileries, dans la nuit du 20 mars 1815*, 1817.

53. Hunt, *The Family Romance*, 113.

54. [Horace-Napoléon Raisson], *Amours secrètes des Bourbons, depuis le mariage de Marie-Antoinette jusque'à la chute de Charles X, Pars la Comtesse du C****, 2 volumes (Paris: Imprimerie de Chaignieau fils aîné, Jules Lefebvre, 1830), 2:190–91.

55. *Histoire d'un jupon de la duchesse d'Angoulême et d'un polisson de la duchesse de Berry, trouvés aux Tuileries: Suivie d'une Correspondance secrète découverte dans un ridicule appartenant à une dame de la Cour, et précédé d'une romance sur les polissons* (Paris: Au Bureau, rue Montmartre n. 54, n.d. [1830]), 4.

56. *Exercise du Royal éteignoir*, n.p, n.d., De Vinck 80:10295.

57. *Aventures secrètes de la duchesse d'Angoulême et d'un prélat fort connu dans Paris* (Paris: Au Bureau, rue Montmartre, n. 54, n.d. [1830]), 3, 4.

58. Susan Nagel, *Marie-Thérèse: The Fate of Marie Antoinette's Daughter* (London: Bloomsbury, 2018), 263–67.

59. Victor Ratier, *Pleure donc feignant*, n.d., Hennin, 14472.

60. On Marie-Thérèse as Joan of Arc, see the print *L'Héroïne de Bordeaux*, n.p, n.d., De Vinck 72: 9490. According to Susan Dunn, royalists during the Restoration argued that Joan was of royal blood; this image along with its companion print of Joan of Arc thus situated Marie-Thérèse within an alternate royal genealogy. Dunn, *The Deaths of Louis XVI: Regicide and*

the French Political Imagination (Princeton NJ: Princeton University Press, 1994), 40n8.

61. On Marie-Thérèse as Antigone see Becquet, *Marie-Thérèse*, 159–60.

62. See, for instance, *Histoire d'un jupon de la duchesse d'Angoulême*. On the image of the duchess de Berry and her relations with the royal family see Jo Burr Margadant, "The Duchesse de Berry and Royalist Political Culture in Postrevolutionary France," in *The New Biography: Performing Femininity in Nineteenth-Century France*, ed. Jo Burr Margadant (Berkeley: University of California Press, 2000), 33–71.

63. Desan, *The Family on Trial*, 296.

64. Emmanuel de Waresquiel and Benoît Yvert, *Histoire de la Restauration, 1814–1830: Naissance de la France moderne,* 2nd edition (Paris: Perrin, 2002), 269.

65. Pierre-François-Hercule, comte de Serre, speech of May 17, 1819, quoted in Waresquiel and Yvert, *Histoire de la Restauration*, 269.

66. "Police surveillance, service pour Marie-Antoinette," 1822, and "Rapport du 21 janvier 1823," AA 363, Archives de la Préfecture de Police de Paris.

67. On the demise of family imagery in the political struggles of the 1840s see Jo Burr Margadant, "Gender, Vice and the Political Imaginary in Postrevolutionary France: Reinterpreting the Failure of the July Monarchy, 1830–1848," *American Historical Review* 10, no. 4 (1999): 1460–96. On the shift away from sentimentalism in politics see William M. Reddy, *The Invisible Code: Honor and Sentiment in Postrevolutionary France, 1814-1848* (Berkeley: University of California Press, 1997).

68. Jo Burr Margadant, "Representing Queen Marie-Amélie in a 'Bourgeois' Monarchy," *Historical Reflections/Réflexions Historiques* 32, no. 2 (2006): 421–51; Alison McQueen, "Women and Social Innovation during the Second Empire: Empress Eugénie's Patronage of the Fondation Eugène Napoléon," *Journal of the Society of Architectural Historians* 66, no. 2 (2007): 176–93.

3

Gender, Immigration, and the Everyday Practice of Social Citizenship

NIMISHA BARTON

Studies of citizenship in modern France have revolved around threshold questions—that is, who receives formal citizenship status and who does not. Drawing on Marxist, feminist, queer, and postcolonial theory, French historians have demonstrated how the state prevented the full incorporation of workers, women, immigrants, colonial, and postcolonial subjects into the national polity through restrictive laws and policies.[1] Through the lens of social reform, in particular, historians have demonstrated how members of these groups nevertheless acquired political, economic, and social rights in a piecemeal fashion.[2] Over time, they show, certain members (particularly white working-class Frenchmen) would move closer to full citizenship status than others (primarily women, immigrants, and colonial subjects) when ranged along a spectrum. Yet these interpretations tend to privilege the attainment of formal citizenship status as the ultimate litmus test for belonging in the national community, despite themselves demonstrating the gradual though disjointed acquisition of rights, benefits, and privileges that members of different groups successfully claimed. Moreover because of the emphasis on citizenship as status, they do not consider the importance of citizenship as daily practice and lived experience nor how subjects themselves could successfully craft and deploy the rights of citizenship on the ground.[3]

Drawing on new methodological approaches in the field that examine citizenship as practice and thereby restore the agency of subjects to the analysis, this chapter examines how working-class French and immigrant women navigated the choppy waters of social citizenship in early twentieth-century France.[4] Though shorn of formal citizenship status as a result of their gender and/or nationality, working-class French and immigrant women nevertheless deployed state and legal resources effectively and imaginatively to get what they needed in order to ensure their survival. In the process they successfully laid claim to social citizenship and the various, rapidly multiplying rights that flowed therefrom in fin-de-siècle and twentieth-century France. As scholars of women in France have demonstrated, the so-called crisis of depopulation that appeared full force in the late nineteenth century made women, children, and families central to the project of national regeneration.[5] Consequently, from the end of the nineteenth century onward, the French state deliberately leaned toward women in the paternalist spirit of protecting them and the populationist spirit of providing for them and their children, a development inseparable from the state's tighter regulation of bachelors through the institution of marriage.[6]

Firmly in line with feminist analyses that acknowledge both the peril and the promise of an embodied self at the center of modern incarnations of citizenship, this chapter argues that French and foreign women co-opted a wide network of overlapping regulatory systems trained on the surveillance of both single immigrant men and negligent breadwinners and used it to their own ends. In women's daily interactions with paternalist French state officials, this chapter argues, French and immigrant women practiced social citizenship. The practice was of an everyday variety as exercised by ordinary people focused on the well-being of themselves and their families.[7] Importantly, it was also an interaction mediated through the gendered identities of middle-class, educated male state officials, on the one hand, and their working-class female clients, on the other. That French and immigrant wives, widows, and mothers possessed and performed social identities that the state valued, incentivized, and amply rewarded during this period was key to their success but does not undermine their successes nor the savviness of their strategies.[8]

This chapter consists of two parts. First, I depict mixed and immigrant working-class conjugal households in Paris between the wars, when immigration to modern France first soared to new heights. In these households, buffeted by the rise and fall of political, economic, and familial fortunes during the turbulent interwar decades, the male wage was of paramount importance; without it households were condemned to struggle. Yet myriad factors whisked away foreign male breadwinners; whether due to death, disease, war, or (mis)adventure, the absence of men and their wages left women—especially immigrant women—the sole providers of large households. Thus French and foreign wives, widows, and mothers left behind used available state, municipal, and local resources to locate errant breadwinners and demand compensation.

Next I demonstrate how both French and foreign women turned the pro-marital, pro-natal, and pro-familial orientation of policing bodies within and between states to their own advantage. Of their own volition and on the advice of others, French and foreign women used both state and police powers to surveil potential foreign spouses, as indeed the entire state and police apparatus had been developing toward the surveillance of mobility—especially foreigners' mobility—from the nineteenth century onward.[9] In so doing women adapted preexisting traditions of familial intervention and monitoring of potential suitors to the perils and pitfalls of sexual intimacy in an era of mass mobility, primarily by seeking official intervention.[10] Throughout I illustrate how French and foreign women formulated their claims to bureaucrats and local police officials, above all by underscoring their status as women in need of the state's muscular protection from ill-intentioned men. Together these arguments reinforce the central theme of this volume: that the institutional structure, ideology, and bureaucracy of the French state provided women—both French and foreign—with a margin of maneuverability that many used to their own advantage. In practice women's citizenship proved more fluid in twentieth-century France than current scholarly opinion allows.

The Wages of Marriage

Beginning in the 1880s the rise and fall of political regimes, the violence and turbulence of war and poverty, and the rapid disintegration of empires across the continent left Europe and its people in turmoil. As a result of depopulation and concomitant labor shortages heightened after the bloodbath of World War I, France emerged as an ideal destination for migrant workers, political exiles, refugees, and asylum seekers as well as their families. France drew not only Europeans but also colonial soldiers and workingmen from French North Africa and Indochina. In 1911 foreigners represented just 3 percent of the population in France; by 1931 they represented over 7 percent, accounting for nearly three million inhabitants.[11] Though labor shortages throughout the country brought immigrants to every corner of France, Paris emerged as the immigrant destination par excellence in the early twentieth century, growing from a foreign population of just 6 percent in 1911 to over 10 percent by 1926.[12] Within the lively urban spaces that Paris furnished, French and foreign men and women met and mingled. As a result rates of intermarriage soared between the wars and mixed and foreign households became increasingly common in Paris.[13] As French people and foreigners established intimacies in the early decades of the twentieth century, they entered fraught terrain where women, work, and marriage were concerned.

Although Frenchwomen, both married and single, worked at higher rates in France than elsewhere in modern Europe, the era of industrial transition overall witnessed their relegation to the lower rungs of the occupational ladder.[14] This trend accentuated during and after World War I, when women were first called to munitions and wartime factories, then pushed out of the workforce after the war to make room for returning veterans. Those women who remained active in the labor force endured the contraction of employment opportunities, the deskilling of their occupational sectors, and concomitant pay cuts and job insecurity.[15] The Great Depression drove home the gendered economic lesson of the era—namely, that work was a male prerogative. Employers, state officials, politicians, and even a handful of benevolent *bourgeoises* from across the political spectrum appealed to workingwomen to yield their jobs to men, and above all for married women to return to the *foyer* where they supposedly belonged. Populationism played its part also, as these same critics of workingwomen placed renewed emphasis on the female obligations of childbearing and childrearing—not breadwinning.[16]

Throughout the 1930s the French state also enacted a variety of social policies that contributed to the propagation of the male breadwinner ideal, though perhaps less blatantly than in the British context.[17] Above all, the state linked entitlements to the employment status of male heads of household, incorporating assumptions about women's presumed dependence on men in the process. These were the same groups that supported unwaged mothers' allowances and argued for the primacy of women's maternal roles throughout the 1920s.[18] Thus during the interwar decades women found recourse to marriage and marriage-like household formations increasingly necessary to support themselves financially. While of course many wives had little choice but to work, considering the economic realities of their working-class lives, their wages were typically low, unstable, and largely supplemental to the household income. By contrast, the male wage—larger and more stable—was central to the survival of working-class households.

Mixed and immigrant households in Paris were no exception to this general trend in the history of marriage, work, and women in France and beyond.[19] Of course there were specificities to their situation. French wives of foreign men were more likely than immigrant wives to work, and they were more likely to work outside the home. There is also evidence that immigrant wives may have opted not to work in accordance with husbands' preferences. In such cases the element of choice was highly circumscribed. Although Manuela Martinez worked in Spain before her migration to Paris in 1928, her husband, Vicente, grew tired of her occupational distractions, claiming that she did not spend enough time keeping house and caring for their five-year-old son. Though she worked for a time selling oranges and bananas at a stall in the center of Paris, Vicente eventually forbade her to work, citing "the negligence and disorder" of their household as the primary cause. Instead he demanded that Manuela "devote herself uniquely to her [household] interior and to her child."[20]

In this particular instance expectations about wives' proper place and duties even took priority over the economic realities of the household. When confronted about her supposed negligence and the household's reputed disorder, Manuela justified herself thus: "I was always worried about keeping my house in order. But at one time, we needed money, and I went to sell oranges at the door of a café. That is what explains why, sometimes, everything was not perfectly in order in my home."[21] In fact the economic pressures on the household were so great in 1931 that, unbeknownst to her husband, she started taking in laundry from the neighborhood to supplement the household's income.[22] But the fact that she hid this economic activity from her husband underscores that some husbands saw the realm of work as their unique prerogative in the household, as indeed the wider economic, social, and political climate encouraged.

If husbands declared waged work their province, then some French and foreign wives nursed financial expectations of what husbands ought to provide. Naturally these expectations were most visible when they were not met. One Polish immigrant, Rachel Lewinsky, refused a marriage proposition by her compatriot Jean Swiderski, whose breadwinner potential she seriously doubted. Lewinsky explained, "Since he did not want to give me money and since I am not the kind of woman who provides for a man [*entretenir un homme*], I threw him out."[23] When marital discord reached a fevered—not to say murderous—pitch, friends, neighbors, and community members often cited husbands' failures to financially provide for their wives and children as a primary irritant in the relationship. Alice Plourde, for instance, testified that her friend Suzanne Genevrier complained often of her Algerian husband's miserliness; for his own part, Arezki Slimani found fault with a wife who "spent all [his] savings and then wanted to leave [him]."[24]

It was well-known by her intimate acquaintances on Cité Industrielle in Sainte Marguerite that Emilia Leon's Italian husband beat her for failing to use precious household resources such as coal sparingly. Neighbor women considered Jacques Violina stingy, not "frugal," as he was described in official reports. He told a different story, however, claiming that his Luxemburg-born wife beat him: "She reproached me for not giving her enough money."[25] Thus, while political and economic pressures worked to increase wives' dependencies on husbands, wives too came to have certain financial expectations of husbands upon whom they relied to maintain and replenish household coffers.

Adultery provides another illustrative example of the material importance of the male income to mixed and immigrant working-class households. In cases of adultery, the primary concern working-class wives expressed was not a sense of sexual or even emotional betrayal but immense frustration and resentment at the loss of male wages. This was as true for French as for immigrant wives. When the confectioner David Botton, a Greek immigrant, left his French wife and their four children to take up with his mistress, Yvonne Botton worked hard to remain in close contact with him in order to access his wages. Her estimate of the financial loss his absence inflicted on the household was quite specific: "At the start of our marriage, he gave me seventy francs a day to buy clothes for the children or fix their shoes. . . . Since meeting Mademoiselle Malfatti, he will not give me more than thirty francs a day and he has innumerable difficulties participating in the maintenance of the children." Rather than spend his wages providing for his legitimate family, Yvonne claimed, her adulterous husband spent his money on his new mistress.[26] A friend of a brother-in-law drily summarized David's financial situation: "It is certain that with a wife, four children, and a mistress, Botton has monetary needs."[27] When the Italian immigrant Henri Ferrari left his family for a French mistress, his wife, Emilie, needled him incessantly for financial help, even enlisting the aid of his employer in her campaign to extract money from the wayward spouse.[28] His failure to send a portion of his wages back to the wife and children he left behind was the substance of the complaint Emilie's mother, the widow Dimascio, sent to police officials. Specifically she reproached Henri, "who had never sent a *centime* to support his four small innocent children."[29]

In fact wives considered the evaporation of male wages a sure sign that funny business was afoot. Although the Russian immigrant Antonine Smaguine did not know for sure that her husband was cheating on her, she had begun to have her suspicions "since for three months he did not give [her] money for the household." He left her for his French mistress a few months later, in December 1930.[30] Thus wives experienced extramarital affairs not just as emotional strains on the family but primarily as financial burdens on the household.

Illness and death were factors that impinged on mixed and immigrant working-class households to a perhaps greater degree than French households. In households organized around an immigrant male breadwinner, the fragile health of these men posed an ever-present threat to the financial security of the entire family. After all, throughout the interwar decades immigrant men tended increasingly to work in the most unhealthful industries (such as chemical and metallurgical plants and refineries) and the most arduous trades (construction, agriculture), which French workingmen had deserted.[31] Moreover they lived in spaces more cramped and crowded than did their French counterparts, spaces in which diseases bred and claimed victims with relative ease.

Although statistics from the period show that there were significantly more female widows than male widowers in France generally, there is reason to believe that immigrant wives were more impacted by the premature death of spouses than other segments of the population. In 1926 French statisticians noted that immigrant widows were the heads of household for the largest families in France, proportionately speaking. This could only be the result of the premature death or unexplained disappearance of a breadwinner.[32] Of course husbands suffered from the illness and death of wives, as well. Considering the gendered division of household labor, however, a wife's illness or death deprived him of child care provider, cook, seamstress, maid, and laundress. For example, when Michel Polycar's wife died of pneumonia three years after the Turkish family's arrival in Paris, he moved quickly to fill her position. After trying and failing to woo his niece, he set his sights on a Turkish neighbor and wed her six months later. According to social workers investigating familial discord between the new stepmother and her three stepsons, "Monsieur Polycar only considers his second wife as a domestic servant charged with household responsibilities."[33] The judgment might seem unduly harsh were it not for the fact that the new Madame Polycar concurred with their assessment.[34] Thus while the death of a wife incurred certain inconveniences, it did not, as other historians of workingwomen have noted, imperil the husband's livelihood in quite the same way as the death of a husband imperiled the wife he left behind.[35] The death, illness, or absence of wives and husbands impacted households in very different ways.

The onset of the Great Depression only exacerbated the fragility of working-class households, especially those dependent on immigrant male breadwinners. As the Depression deepened, the French state enacted restrictive measures to protect native labor against the immigrant workforce. Consequently employers began to dismiss their immigrant employees at a rapid pace.[36] Foreign workingmen, especially bachelors, were repatriated.[37] Women's work was not as severely impacted, in part because women's jobs were already so deskilled and low-paying.[38] In mixed and immigrant households of Paris, wives increasingly went to work to support children who depended on them and husbands who would now have to as well. For instance, when the Polish immigrant Dimitri Wandiak lost his job as an electrician in 1932, his wife, Anne Bugajsi, was forced to find regular employment in France for the first time. But mind-sets do not change overnight, even if markets do. From the start, Bugajsi made it very well-known to both her spouse and all her intimate acquaintances at the clothing workshop where she found employment that she resented supporting him. According to the concierge of her building, "In the month of June 1932, the wife left him because he no longer worked and she did not want to continue feeding him."[39]

With foreign husbands down on their luck, French and foreign wives emerged as the fragile breadwinners of Depression-era mixed and immigrant working-class households. But just as some wives struggled to adjust to their new role, so too did husbands experience difficulty coming to terms with the sudden role reversal. In certain instances the inversion of gender roles at home could prove a considerable source of shame for them. Amerigo Brunetti, a sculptor from Italy, allowed himself to be baited by a compatriot named Bertolucci, "who said he [Brunetti] had not been happy since he lost his job and since his wife had to provide for him." Deeply offended, Brunetti responded, "You know nothing, young man, of how I have worked in my life and you do not have the right to speak about my wife like that." A scuffle between the men ensued shortly thereafter at the *débit* on rue Hallé in the 14th arrondissement.[40] In February 1939 an Algerian immigrant named Mohamed Salah beat and killed his prosperous cousin, who dared to mock his unemployment in front of a room full of acquaintances at a restaurant in the 18th arrondissement.[41]

Of course in the midst of the Depression, neither French nor immigrant wives found easy, stable employment. By and large they simply increased the frequency of their participation in unstable, sporadic economic pursuits to make ends meet. Above all, immigrant women found themselves cleaning houses in their neighborhoods. For instance, when the Italian immigrant Jean Cauda lost his job as a mechanic, his wife was suddenly thrust into the job market. Tellingly officials registered surprise at the lack of marital discord given the absence of a male wage, indicating how tethered the two factors were even in the official mind. According to a stunned Police Inspector Lasigne, "Despite his unemployment, the household seems to get by without apparent difficulty, probably thanks to the aid furnished by unemployment funds and the salary of Madame Cauda, employed in cleaning houses in the neighborhood."[42] In worst-case scenarios, married immigrant women might engage in prostitution to support husbands and families in the 1930s. For instance, when Jean Schwiderski, an out-of-work baker originally from Poland, fell on hard times, he pimped out his wife, Fajga, to support the household. For a brief time he even sent her to work at a *maison de tolérance* in Tunis, collecting her wages from Paris.[43] But this is an admittedly extreme example. What is important is the way in which macro-level shifts in the economy initiated subtle and not so subtle shifts in gender relations between spouses. While women may have found themselves increasingly responsible for providing for the households, the larger political and economic climate made it impossible for them to match the earning potential of men. Working wives and mothers were poor substitutes for male breadwinners.

Finally, the larger-than-life events of the period could separate husbands and wives just as easily and, in some cases, far more effectively. In 1914 Catherine Girardo's husband, Lorenzo, was called away to serve in the Italian Army. During the war years she remained in Paris working as a domestic servant with her two young daughters, Anna and Madeleine, until Lorenzo returned in 1919.[44] Not all foreign women in a similar predicament could expect a similar outcome. Jeanne Alcail was a Spanish woman who had lived and worked in Paris since 1913 with her husband and son, Charles. In 1915 her husband left to fight in the war and never came back.[45] This is to say nothing of the countless immigrant women, such as Rachel Goichmann from Russia, who, like French wives, were widowed by the war their husbands fought on behalf of France.[46] Indeed war swept husbands away, sometimes temporarily, as in Catherine Girardo's case, but other times permanently, as the stories of Jeanne Alcail and Rachel Goichmann indicate.

Still others found themselves "abandoned" by husbands called away by business or pleasure—or both. This was the case for Sophie Malkine, a native of Odessa, Russia, whose husband, an employee at Standard Oil in Bakore, India, had some years earlier left for the United States on business. She was not to hear from him again; thus it fell to her to support her mother, her brother, and her two Paris-born sons.[47] Others may have been called away by the siren song of adventure, which had the same effect of removing the all-important breadwinner from mixed and immigrant households altogether. Although the dissolution of households removed the male wage, as long as legitimate husbands and fathers could be located, a breadwinner could in fact be won.

In the first few decades of the twentieth century, men were taken away by death and disease, war and revolution, economic ventures and extramarital adventures. Regardless of the reason, the absence of a male wage was debilitating for households, especially immigrant households situated on the outer edges of working-class poverty. These debilitating effects worsened considerably with the onset of the Great Depression. Although female unemployment was often lower than male unemployment during this period, wives and mothers rarely found stable work that would provide sufficiently for their dependents. Rather women's work during these years was often low-skill, low-paying, and sporadic, an unpredictable kind of labor yielding an unsteady and unreliable kind of income. Women simply would not do as breadwinners—the logical material outcome of gendered inequalities built into the French economic system and nourished by the wider political and social climate of the 1920s and 1930s, especially. Households thus depended on male wages for survival, which is why so many French and foreign women would go to great lengths to track down their men.

Locating Men: Women Using Consular and Colonial Authorities

Between the wars French and immigrant women brought the policing power of French and foreign states to bear on breadwinning immigrant men with whom they had formed relationships. In so doing they took advantage of the state's increasing propensity to police foreign male mobility as well as foreign male sexual morality and marital probity.[48] Importantly, women availed themselves of the state's paternalist inclination to protect "vulnerable women." While there was a kernel of truth in this description (after all, as the preceding section has shown, women simply *were* more economically, socially, and politically vulnerable than men in important ways), French and foreign women nevertheless were quite adept at presenting themselves as in need of paternalist intervention all the while using state means to engage in the spousal regulation of husbands and would-be husbands.

Social historians have long documented the fluid sexual atmosphere that reigned in popular neighborhoods of Paris. For women, these liaisons always carried with them the possibility of pregnancy, a risk that was especially great for single women to whom men owed nothing. Sexual dalliances with foreign men heightened the danger of "abandonment," for many immigrant men were indeed here today, gone tomorrow. Moreover, as an immigrant he was an unknown quantity to friends, family, and the wider community, who traditionally brought community standards to bear on "seducing" parties by forcing marriage in the case of pregnancy.[49] The image of the foreign man who seduced women, then left them high and dry once pregnant, became something of a trope for maternalist social service organizations in the capital during the interwar period. Germaine Besnard de Quelen, founder and director of the League for the Protection of Abandoned Mothers, a maternalist welfare organization for working-class mothers, spun one such tale to her audience of social workers and supporters in 1937: a young girl from the provinces met "a handsome foreigner" who "seduced her with his promises." Finding herself pregnant and abandoned, she suffered further disgrace when her parents disowned her. Like other single mothers whom Besnard imagined, "she wandered, aimlessly, this immense and devouring Paris that she knew not, [when,] directly in front of her: she arrives at the Seine." There, in her bleakest moment, she contemplated suicide.[50]

The trope of the seduced single woman throwing herself into the Seine to end her misery was well-known to Parisians from the nineteenth century onward.[51] But despite such harrowing tales, certain women proved themselves less despairing and more resourceful when they found themselves in similar situations. And there were many such women. Of the thousands of unmarried and pregnant French and foreign women who found solace at LPAM, several singled out a foreign man as the offending party.[52] For instance, Suzanne Balivet, a seventeen-year-old housemaid, was abandoned by her Serbian fiancé. Although he "led her to believe that he was happy with his impending paternity," he left without a word after she presented him to her mother, who lived just outside of Paris, in the *banlieue* of Seine-et-Oise.[53] Isaline Bron, a thirty-four-year-old housemaid also living in the 16th arrondissement, admitted with "much chagrin" that she had loaned her Armenian lover over 5,000 francs for his naturalization, with the expectation that he would marry her. She was sorely disappointed when he disappeared from their home only a few weeks later.[54] In the neighborhood of Sainte Marguerite, the Frenchwoman Marie Anne Léontine Goasdaiff had a similar experience with an Italian man who returned to his country after their tryst, leaving her five months pregnant.[55] Such stories abound in the archives.[56] Of course fingering a mysterious foreigner, vanished without a trace, may have been a convenient and far less shameful narrative choice for unmarried pregnant women who were left alone to bear the stigma of unwed pregnancy. When a young Frenchwoman, Simone Gaudinot, claimed to have been "raped by an Italian," the social worker handling her case at the Social Service for Children in Moral Danger dismissed it as "a fairly improbable story" fabricated in light of her imminent medical examination and what it would likely turn up about her sexual experience.[57] Yet the fact that many women took additional steps to locate foreign men suggests that, for a number of them, these claims were more than mere fabrications.

In fact certain French and foreign women found ways to bring state powers to bear on recalcitrant foreign lovers, fiancés, and spouses. In this social workers sought to connect foreign women to resources in the capital that would permit them to bring state power—any state's power—to bear on wayward partners. For instance, LPAM workers frequently sent married foreign women and immigrant mothers to the appropriate consular authorities when their husbands left them. When a twenty-three-year-old Czech immigrant, Roza Albertilikova, a factory worker in Argenteuil, was abandoned by a compatriot and the father of her child, social workers recommended that she pay a visit to the Czech consulate.[58] Madame Michel counseled Vicenta Dasi, a thirty-eight-year-old domestic servant in the 16th arrondissement whose Spanish husband left her in 1930, to drop in at the Spanish consulate.[59] It remains unclear whether foreign women and French social workers believed foreign consulates would simply aid in locating foreign husbands or go one step further, perhaps by providing assistance—material or otherwise—to the jilted foreign wife in question. But the expectation of some aid is quite clear.

Social workers, lawyers, and legal consultants at social service organizations recommended this line of action, but it would appear that women arrived at this conclusion on their own as well. For instance, a handful of resourceful Frenchwomen turned to foreign consulates on their own initiative for help locating a man who had left them in the lurch. Take, for instance, Yvonne Lecoz, a twenty-one-year-old factory worker. In 1931 Lecoz's partner, "an Italian lift-boy," abandoned her when she was eight months pregnant. Even before she sought help from LPAM social workers, she had already gone to the Italian consulate "to obtain some information about him."[60] Lecoz's behavior suggests a certain economy of information shared among working women who knew where to go and whom to talk to when a romance with a foreign partner went awry.

Frenchwomen might also approach consular authorities if they even nursed suspicions about the moral (and marital) probity of their beloved. The marital status of Italians in France was a particularly problematic one after Mussolini outlawed divorce in 1928. In France the Italian law cast suspicion on Italian men who did not act quickly—or quickly enough—in the eyes of their partners. This was the case for Pascal Fenile, a thirty-four-year-old entrepreneur who did indeed leave his wife behind in Italy when he came to France. Soon after his arrival he began courting a young Frenchwoman, Suzanne Lurin, all the while "carefully dissimulating his familial situation," as prosecutors would later put it. Court officials noted that he promised Lurin marriage in order to "win over her resistance," a euphemism indicating that he lied to her in order to lay with her. They moved to Paris together, but months and years passed and still the young Lurin remained unmarried. In July 1931 she and her mother, "wearied by the inexplicable eternalization of an irregular and humiliating situation," appeared on the doorstep of the Italian consulate in Paris to look into the background of this mysterious foreign beau. There it was at last revealed to mother and daughter that Fenile did indeed already have a wife in his home country. Thus Frenchwomen learned to maneuver the international system to their own advantage, gaining information about former and would-be spouses from consular authorities.[61] In this sense Frenchwomen accommodated themselves to a new age in which family, friends, and neighbors could no longer be relied upon either to vet a potential spouse or to ensure that potential spouses remained in the event of an unplanned pregnancy. In an era of mass mobility, then,

Frenchwomen found recourse in international and state power that, for their own part, leaned toward these women in return.

Married and unmarried foreign women employed similar methods when dealing with their foreign spouses and partners in France. For instance, Emilia Leon, a native of Luxemburg mentioned previously, developed a very close friendship with her French concierge, a relationship mostly cemented over her ongoing domestic troubles. Leon regarded her husband, an Italian immigrant locksmith named Jacques Violina, as an endless source of trouble, and her concierge concurred. The official inquest, however, yielded a different story. Despite her complaints, officials determined instead that the household was marred by Leon's violence against her husband. The abuse her husband was subjected to, so the story went, prompted him to quit the marriage in 1935, after seven years. When he departed he took with him their six-year-old son. In the hopes of learning their whereabouts, Leon immediately sought out the Italian consulate. In this particular instance foreign consular authorities even acted as informal marriage counselors. According to official reports, "the Vice-Consul [of the Italian consulate] attempted a reconciliation, but in vain."[62] Although Leon's search for husband and child was not fruitful in the end, her actions suggest that, at the very least, some foreign women, like many Frenchwomen, believed they would find a sympathetic ear in official circles.

French and foreign women who suffered from domestic abuse regularly filed their complaints with neighborhood authorities, recording their suffering at the local police station. Considering the networks of information among workingwomen in the capital, it is rather unsurprising that immigrant women would have taken advantage of the local police as a regulatory apparatus. Additionally, both French and foreign women involved with North African men used a special regulatory apparatus in the capital aimed at policing the mores and behaviors of colonial subjects: the North African Brigade, the police arm of the Service des Affaires Indigènes Nord-Africaines (SAINA), established in the summer of 1925. The North African Brigade was a special division of the Paris Prefecture of Police vested with the authority to monitor, surveil, and otherwise harass North African migrants in Paris. The creation of the office in the 7th arrondissement was the outcome of political consensus across the board on the issue of North African "criminality."[63] Although the service was intended to investigate major crimes involving North African colonial subjects, such as murder, Parisian women, both French and foreign, used these policing institutions for their own personal ends. That is, immigrant and French women at times sought recourse in the North African Brigade to protect them against men whom they considered—or at least portrayed as—violent North African lovers and spouses.

Blanche Sadoun, for instance, was a Tunisian Jew who migrated to Paris in the 1920s and worked as a dancer in a *café maure* called El Maghreb in the 5th arrondissement. In 1929 she married a Moroccan, Mohamed ben M'Barek Cheradi, *selon le rite musulman* in Marrakesh. Their union later disintegrated due to *mésintelligence*, or discord, between the two partners. When she became the object of domestic abuse, Sadoun chose to seek help from SAINA authorities. There she claimed that her husband treated her savagely, no better than "a slave that one beats, at his pleasure, without end." "My life as you have recorded is in perpetual danger," she told them. Later reports mixed pronouns, making it difficult to separate Sadoun's own voice from that of officials. Nevertheless documents recorded, "She knew that she would be spared any danger only if the Service des Affaires Indigènes from whom I solicit protection, agrees to look after me."[64] Sadoun thus invited police intervention into her relationship, a relationship she characterized as violent. In so doing she portrayed herself as a (female) victim in need of (male) protection from an abusive husband. That Cheradi later murdered her would seem to indicate that she was not exaggerating the danger. Most important, the authorities to whom she addressed herself and the manner in which she formulated those claims indicate that foreign wives sought to harness and direct the surveilling and policing bodies of the state for their own ends.

While women like Blanche Sadoun used police power to try to protect themselves from violent men, other women turned state and local power to their own advantage, misrepresenting details of their acquaintanceship with North African men in the hopes that officials would intervene on their behalf. In so doing they highlighted both gendered and racial dimensions of their relationships with colonial men, perhaps knowing that state and municipal officials would be that much more sympathetic to their side of the story. For instance, Victorine Louise Morot was the French hotel operator of a small pension in Villecomble during the 1920s, where she had occasion to meet one of her lodgers, a young Algerian man by the name of Touhami Boubeker. Boubeker entrusted her with his money because, by his own admission and that of others, "not knowing French and unable to get by [*se débrouiller*] in Paris, he found recourse in her."[65] According to another testimonial drawn from Boubeker, this was something of a pattern for him, for, "knowing neither how to read or write, saving his money in case of unemployment or sudden illness, he entrusted his money voluntarily to this or that one of his employers or *hôteliers*." Boubeker and Morot agreed that once he had accumulated 10,000 francs, she would help him open a savings account.

By all accounts Morot hoodwinked Boubeker. After several months of collecting his money, she suddenly became difficult to locate. According to Boubeker, whenever he did manage to find her and question her about his savings, she would "always threaten to have him arrested if he did not let her be." Some time later Morot made good on her threats, filing a complaint against him on March 12, 1934, with the North African Brigade. She claimed "that she was the object of death threats on the part of Boubeker and demanded to be protected."[66] She even told her employer, Jean Gervet on rue Amelot, that an Algerian whom she used to do laundry for was coming around threatening her "for incomprehensible and futile motives" and that she had gone to the North African Brigade out of fear.[67] While there were rumors of a love affair between them, Boubeker adamantly denied them and insisted that he sought her out solely in the interest of seeing his small fortune returned to him.[68] Morot, on the other hand, let friends, neighbors, and employers intuit a vague romantic connection between the two. By insinuating the existence of a sexual relationship, Morot invited a particularly interested form of police intervention, taking advantage of the state's disciplinary predisposition to surveil colonial subjects in the metropole, above all when a sexual relationship with a white woman was concerned. Morot used the state's gendered and racist policing predisposition in her private dealings with Boubeker, indicating that at least some Frenchwomen learned to use state and police powers against foreign bachelors and colonial subjects. Moreover they knew to insinuate something torrid even when sex, marriage, and pregnancy were not at issue. In both instances French and foreign women relied on colonial police units of the Paris Prefecture—the North African Brigade—to find what they themselves termed "protection."

Conclusion

Both of their own volition and on the advice of friends, neighbors, and concerned social workers, French and foreign women adeptly used state and police power to regulate foreign-born lovers and partners, former husbands and would-be spouses. Using the legal apparatus of French and foreign states, women thus adapted to an era of mass mobility in which the stakes of romantic and sexual liaisons were higher and the sexual risks greater because men were increasingly mobile, unknown quantities. More significantly, their dealings with international, state, and municipal officials suggest the crystallization of a certain sociopolitical configuration that, while certainly premised on women's formal disenfranchisement, nevertheless provided them with power from the margins, as mediated through their identities as wives, widows, and mothers. Though lacking formal citizenship status, both French and immigrant women mobilized identities that disposed the state and its officials to help them, indeed to protect them. Though it was a different model of citizenship than that accorded to men, this version of citizenship as practiced by women nevertheless entailed a variety of social and economic benefits that allowed them to regulate their daily lives and ensure the livelihood of themselves and their families.

Notes

1. On workers and citizenship in France, see Judith Stone, *The Search for Social Peace: Reform Legislation in France, 1890-1914* (Albany: State University of New York Press, 1985). On women, gender, and citizenship,

see Jennifer N. Heuer, *The Family and the Nation: Gender and Citizenship in Revolutionary France, 1789–1830* (Ithaca NY: Cornell University Press, 2005); Laura L. Frader, *Breadwinners and Citizens: Gender in the Making of the French Social Model* (Durham NC: Duke University Press, 2008); Judith Surkis, *Sexing the Citizen: Morality and Masculinity in France, 1870–1920* (Ithaca NY: Cornell University Press, 2006); Andrea Mansker, *Sex, Honor and Citizenship in Early Third Republic France* (Basingstoke, UK: Palgrave Macmillan, 2011); Geoff Read, *The Republic of Men: Gender and the Political Parties in Interwar France* (Baton Rouge: Louisiana State University Press, 2014). On race, empire, and citizenship, see Laura Levine Frader, *Breadwinners and Citizens: Gender in the Making of the French Social Model* (Durham NC: Duke University Press, 2008); Elisa Camiscioli, *Reproducing the French Race: Immigration, Intimacy, and Embodiment in the Early Twentieth Century* (Durham NC: Duke University Press, 2009); Emmanuelle Saada, *Empire's Children: Race, Filiation, and Citizenship in the French Colonies* (Chicago: University of Chicago Press, 2012). On immigration, *sans-papiers*, and citizenship, see Gérard Noiriel, *Le Creuset français: Histoire de L'immigration, XIXe–XXe Siècles* (Paris: Seuil, 1988); Rogers Brubaker, *Citizenship and Nationhood in France and Germany* (Cambridge MA: Harvard University Press, 1992); Patrick Weil, *Qu'est-Ce Qu'un Français: Histoire de la nationalité français depuis la Révolution* (Paris: Grasset, 2002); Peter Sahlins, *Unnaturally French: Foreign Citizens in the Old Regime and After* (Ithaca NY: Cornell University Press, 2004); Mary Dewhurst Lewis, *The Boundaries of the Republic: Migrant Rights and the Limits of Universalism in France, 1918–1940* (Stanford CA: Stanford University Press, 2007); Catherine Raissiguier, *Reinventing the Republic: Gender, Migration, and Citizenship in France* (Stanford CA: Stanford University Press, 2010).

2. Henri Hatzfeld, *Du paupérisme à la sécurité sociale: Essai sur les origines de la sécurité sociale en France, 1850–1940* (Paris: A. Colin, 1971); François Ewald, *L'Etat providence* (Paris: B. Grasset, 1986); Susan Pedersen, *Family, Dependence, and the Origins of the Welfare State: Britain and France, 1914–1945* (Cambridge, UK: Cambridge University Press, 1993); Elinor A. Accampo, Rachel G. Fuchs, and Mary Lynn Stewart, eds., *Gender and the Politics of Social Reforms in France, 1870–1914* (Baltimore: Johns Hopkins University Press, 1995); Paul V. Dutton, *Origins of the French Welfare State: The Struggle for Social Reform in France, 1914–1947* (New York: Cambridge University Press, 2002).

3. For overviews of these debates, see Ronald Beiner, ed., *Theorizing Citizenship* (Albany: State University of New York Press, 1995); Gershon Shafir, ed.,

The *Citizenship Debates: A Reader* (Minneapolis: University of Minnesota Press, 1998); Linda Bosniak, *The Citizen and the Alien: Dilemmas of Contemporary Membership* (Princeton NJ: Princeton University Press, 2006).

4. See especially Raissiguier, *Reinventing the Republic*; Elizabeth Heath, *Wine, Sugar, and the Making of Modern France: Global Economic Crisis and the Racialization of French Citizenship, 1870-1910*, New Studies in European History (Cambridge, UK: Cambridge University Press, 2014); Minayo Nasiali, *Native to the Republic: Empire, Social Citizenship, and Everyday Life in Marseille Since 1945* (Ithaca NY: Cornell University Press, 2016).

5. Accampo et al., *Gender and the Politics of Social Reform in France*; Rachel G. Fuchs, *Contested Paternity: Constructing Families in Modern France* (Baltimore: Johns Hopkins University Press, 2008).

6. Surkis, *Sexing the Citizen*; Read, *The Republic of Men*; Nimisha Barton, "Marrying into the Nation: Immigrant Bachelors, French Bureaucrats, and the Conjugal Politics of Naturalization in the Third Republic," *French Politics, Culture & Society* 34, no. 3 (2016): 23. For revolutionary antecedents, see E. Claire Cage, *Unnatural Frenchmen: The Politics of Priestly Celibacy and Marriage, 1720-1815* (Charlottesville: University of Virginia Press, 2015).

7. This methodological approach has been most clearly articulated by Nasiali, *Native to the Republic*. For historiographical antecedents, see Rachel G. Fuchs, *Poor and Pregnant in Paris: Strategies for Survival in the Nineteenth Century* (New Brunswick NJ: Rutgers University Press, 1992); Fuchs, *Contested Paternity*.

8. Here I am influenced by Karen Offen's analysis of middle-class French-women's familial feminism that made republican motherhood central to the struggle. As Offen argues, it was a successful vehicle to transform the status of women and to subvert the sexual system from within—strategies that made them "politically astute." See Karen Offen, "Depopulation, Nationalism, and Feminism in Fin-de-Siècle France," *American Historical Review* 89, no. 3 (1984): 648-76.

9. Noiriel, *Le Creuset français*, chap. 2, "The Card and the Code," especially; John C. Torpey, *The Invention of the Passport: Surveillance, Citizenship, and the State* (Cambridge, UK: Cambridge University Press, 2000); Clifford D. Rosenberg, *Policing Paris: The Origins of Modern Immigration Control Between the Wars* (Ithaca NY: Cornell University Press, 2006).

10. Rachel G. Fuchs and Leslie Page Moch, "Pregnant, Single, and Far from Home: Migrant Women in Nineteenth-Century Paris," *American Historical Review* 95, no. 4 (1990): 1007-31; Leslie Page Moch and Rachel G. Fuchs, "Getting Along: Poor Women's Networks in Nineteenth-Century Paris,"

French Historical Studies 18, no. 1 (1993): 34–49; Leslie Page Moch, *The Pariahs of Yesterday: Breton Migrants in Paris* (Durham NC: Duke University Press, 2012), chap. 2.

11. Michel Huber, *La Population de la France pendant la guerre, avec un appendice sur les revenus avant et après la guerre* (Paris: Les Presses universitaires de France, 1931), 6–7, 453, 526.

12. These statistics are based on data from M. Galmiche, "Extrait: Les Etrangers dans l'agglomération parisienne d'après le recensement de 1921," *Bulletin de la Statistique générale de la France et du Service d'observation des Prix* 11, no. 3, April 1922, in Archives nationales (hereafter AN) 50 AP 62; "Dénombrement effectué en septembre 1914, à la demande de l'autorité militaire. Ville de Paris.—Population présente," *Annuaire Statistique de la Ville de Paris* (hereafter ASVP) (1915–18), 929; "Ville de Paris.—Population domiciliée.—Population française et population étrangère," ASVP (1921–22), 284–85; "Ville de Paris.—Recensement de 1926," ASVP (1923–24), 295–96; "Ville de Paris.—Recensement de 1931," ASVP (1927–28), 140–41.

13. From the declaration of war in August 1914 through 1932, nearly 285,000 mixed marriages were concluded in France; from 1915 until 1940, over 64,000 alone took place in Paris. Over the course of both decades the rate of intermarriage in Paris hovered between 7 and 10 percent, twice that of France overall. (Data based on marital statistics recorded every year since 1915 in the ASVP).

14. Louise Tilly and Joan Wallach Scott, *Women, Work, and Family* (New York: Holt, Rinehart and Winston, 1978), 150–51.

15. Laura Lee Downs, *Manufacturing Inequality: Gender Division in the French and British Metalworking Industries, 1914–1939* (Ithaca NY: Cornell University Press, 1995).

16. Françoise Thébaud, *Quand nos grand-mères donnaient la vie: La maternité en France dans l'entre-deux-guerres* (Lyon: Presses universitaires de Lyon, 1986), 23–25; Frader, *Breadwinners and Citizens*, chap. 6.

17. In *Family, Dependence, and the Origins of the Welfare State*, Pedersen draws a stark contrast between welfare schemes centered on the male breadwinner ideal that predominated in Great Britain between the wars and the familialist welfare schemes in interwar France that redistributed income from the childless to mothers and families.

18. Frader, *Breadwinners and Citizens*, chap. 6.

19. On gendered expectations of household management among fin-de-siècle working-class Parisians, see Eliza Earle Ferguson, *Gender and Justice: Violence, Intimacy and Community in Fin-de Siècle Paris* (Baltimore: Johns

Hopkins University Press, 2010), chap. 2. On the problem of women's economic dependencies among the popular classes of nineteenth-century New York and London, respectively, see Christine Stansell, *City of Women: Sex and Class in New York, 1789–1860* (New York: Knopf, 1986), chap. 2 especially; Ellen Ross, *Love and Toil: Motherhood in Outcast London, 1870–1918* (New York: Oxford University Press, 1993), chap. 3 especially.

20. Ordonnance de Transmission de la Procédure, Tribunal de première instance (hereafter TPI), March 4, 1931, Archives de Paris (hereafter AdP), D2U8 320.

21. Procès-verbal d'interrogatoire et de confrontation, January 22, 1932, AdP, D2U8 320.

22. Renseignements demandés, TPI, Petit Parquet, October 25, 1931, AdP, D2U8 320.

23. Déposition de Rachel née Lewinski femme Gerber, TPI, September 10, 1934, AdP, D2U8 390.

24. Audition d'Alice Plourde, Commissariat de Police de la Goutte d'Or, October 20, 1933; Ordonnance de Transmission de la Procédure à M. le Procureur Général, TPI, January 30, 1934, AdP, D2U8 369.

25. Déposition de Léontine Aline Armand Marinier née Tissard, TPI, February 19, 1936; Déposition de Jacques Violina, TPI, December 9, 1935; Réquisitoire définitif, April 6, 1936, AdP, D2U8 496.

26. Déposition de Yvonne femme Botton née Divrechy, TPI, February 16, 1937, AdP, D2U8 540.

27. Déposition de Flore Saltiel Amar, TPI, February 2, 1937, AdP, D2U8 540.

28. Déposition d'Edouard Boutier, TPI, October 19, 1932, AdP, D2U8 345.

29. Letter, Widow Dimascio to the Procurer General, October 25, 1932, AdP, D2U8 345.

30. Déposition d'Antonine née Jankowska femme Smaguine, TPI, May 6, 1936, AdP, D2U8 499.

31. Gary S. Cross, *Immigrant Workers in Industrial France: The Making of a New Laboring Class* (Philadelphia: Temple University Press, 1983), 9–10.

32. Statistique Générale de France, *Statistique Des Familles en 1926* (Paris: Imprimerie nationale, 1932), 28.

33. Polycar, dossier familial, p. 6, AdP, 1368W/31, no. 2356.

34. In fact Madame Polycar declared to social workers after a particularly "violent" scene between herself and her husband, "She is not surprised that [her stepsons] Maurice and Marcel neither respect nor love her since the father denigrates her constantly in their presence" (Polycar, dossier familial, p. 4, AdP, 1368W/31, no. 2356).

35. Stansell, *City of Women*, 45.

36. Cross, *Immigrant Workers in Industrial France*, chap. 9.
37. Lewis, *Boundaries of the Republic*, chap. 4.
38. Frader, *Breadwinners and Citizens*, 195–208.
39. Déposition d'Antonine Drouart née Beaujean, TPI, December 3, 1932. This fact appears in other testimonies: Déposition de Louis Koppus, TPI, December 3, 1932. By Wandiak's own admission, "She left me because, being without work, I no longer had money" (Procès-verbal d'interrogatoire et de confrontation, TPI, October 26, 1932, AdP, D2U8 351).
40. Déposition d'André Giromini, TPI, November 24, 1933, AdP, D2U8 375.
41. Acte d'Accusation, July 29, 1939, AdP, D2U8 605.
42. Rapport de la Police Judiciaire fourni par l'Inspecteur Lasigne au sujet du nommé Cauda, August 27, 1934, AdP, D2U8 391.
43. Déposition de Joseph Dyzenchanz, TPI, May, 11 1934; Déposition de Chana Lewinska, TPI, June 4, 1934; Réquisitoire définitif, November 2, 1934, 5; Acte d'Accusation, December 4,1934, AdP, D2U8 390.
44. Procès-verbal d'intérogatoire et de confrontation, TPI, July 26, 1930, AdP, D2U8 300.
45. Procès verbal d'interrogatoire et de confrontation, TPI, October 10, 1932, AdP, D2U8 339.
46. Letter from Widow Goichmann to Minister of Justice, May 20, 1926; Demande de Naturalisation for Widow Goichmann, June 24, 1926, in Rachel Goichmann née Schwartz, AN, 16875x14.
47. Sophie Malkine, folio no. 1796, AdP, D84Z 146.
48. Noiriel, *Le Creuset français*, chap. 2 especially; Torpey, *The Invention of the Passport*; Rosenberg, *Policing Paris*.
49. Fuchs and Moch, "Pregnant, Single, and Far from Home"; Moch and Fuchs, "Getting Along"; Moch, *The Pariahs of Yesterday*, chap. 2.
50. Germaine Besnard de Quelen, "Rapport moral de l'exercice 1937," *Compte rendu*, 20, AdP, D84Z 228.
51. Fuchs, *Poor and Pregnant*, 1.
52. On the League for the Protection of Abandoned Mothers, see Nimisha Barton, "'French or Foreign, So Long as They Be Mothers': Immigrant Women, Welfare, and the Politics of Pronatalism in Interwar Paris," *Journal of Women's History* 28, no. 4 (2016): 65–88.
53. Suzanne Balivet, folio no. 453, AdP, D84Z 145.
54. Isaline Bron, folio no. 11001, AdP, D84Z 155.
55. Marie Anne Léontine Goasdaiff, folio no. 7575 bis, AdP, D84Z 15.
56. For instance, Jeanne Sergent abandoned by "a foreigner" (folio no. 611, AdP, D84Z 145); Michaelle Valot abandoned by "an Italian whom she

learned later was married" (folio no. 985, AdP, D84Z 145); Georgette Taine abandoned by "a Spaniard" (folio no. 1285, AdP, D84Z 146).

57. Paul Gaudinot, dossier familial, p. 5, AdP, 1368w/287, no. 5514.

58. Roza Albertilikova, folio no. 1085, AdP, D84Z /145.

59. Vicenta Dasi, folio no. 3948, AdP, D84Z /148.

60. Yvonne Lecoz, folio no. 5313, AdP, D84Z /149.

61. Acte d'accusation, November 25, 1932, AdP, D2U8 350.

62. Acte d'accusation, July 16, 1936, AdP, D2U8 496.

63. Rosenberg, *Policing Paris*, 159–66.

64. Déclaration de Madame Blanche Sadoun, May 25, 1936; Acte d'accusation, January 22, 1937, AdP, D2U8 512.

65. Audition de Marie Anna Isoline née Cailleux femme Gody, May 4, 1934, AdP, D2U8 384.

66. Réquisitoire définitif, August 21, 1934, AdP, D2U8 384.

67. Audition de Jean Gervet, Commissariat de Police du Quartier de la Folie-Méricourt, March 14, 1934, AdP, D2U8 384.

68. Docteur Truelle, "Rapport médico-légal," May 24, 1934, 5-7, AdP, D2U8 384.

4

Hospital Policies, Family Agency, and Mothers at l'Hôpital Sainte-Eugénie, 1855–1875

STEPHANIE MCBRIDE-SCHREINER

In 1855 l'hôpital Sainte-Eugénie, the third children's hospital in Paris, opened its doors. Named after Empress Eugénie, the consort of Napoleon III, the hospital's establishment was part of larger state initiatives led by doctors, legislators, public administrators, and social reformers that aimed to expand medical care for poor, sick children of Paris, and therefore enhance the future health of the nation. This exertion of governmental and medical authority over individual and collective health could be viewed as part of a wider disciplinary process to know, regulate, and optimize social health and welfare. In the setting of the children's hospital, however, this process was not a one-way street, as the dependent status of children and the challenge of parental *puissance* mediated the medical and social authority of the public children's hospital. An examination of family members' decisions regarding their children's medical care vis-à-vis l'hôpital Sainte-Eugénie's policies and practices demonstrates varying degrees of cooperation and conflict between medical and administrative elites and working-class and indigent patient families.

The record of family decision-making and intervention in patient medical care at Sainte-Eugénie complicates social control theories, particular Michel Foucault's and Jacques Donzelot's arguments that medical institutions, practitioners, and the medical-legal discourses that they generated formed part of a "tutelary complex" aimed to control social behavior, particularly of the poorer classes.[1] The social control approach especially resonates with the entity of the state-sponsored children's hospital, since children were the future of the nation, and regulating and preserving their health through public welfare institutions was an avenue to extend the medical and political surveillance and governance of individuals and populations. While administrators governed hospital admissions and doctors asserted their influence in the diagnosis, observation, and treatment of children, patients' families could appeal administrative decisions or deny a doctor his patient altogether. Challenging the idea that poor families were the passive recipients of charity at Paris hospitals, this chapter demonstrates that families had a voice in children's medical matters. Furthermore I propose that interventions at l'hôpital Sainte-Eugénie represent assertions of family members' "rights" to seek or to refuse medical assistance for their children at public institutions, and in the process, families engaged in a critical form of social citizenship. This essay provides numerous examples wherein French working-class and indigent families, especially mothers, played a crucial role in securing medical attention for their children, in advocating for children's needs, and in establishing limits to health care.

Nineteenth-Century Children's Hospitals, Social Medicine, and Families

The nineteenth-century Parisian hospital has a rich history, with scholarly works documenting its rise as the premier destination for physician training, the learning of medical specialties, and the most advanced medical techniques in the first half of the century.[2] Furthermore the early nineteenth-century public health movement in France, led by doctors and hygienists who set into motion an administrative machinery based on progress, reform, education, and scientific empiricism, aimed to not only treat medical conditions but also to reduce general mortality and improve individuals' quality of life.[3] On March 3, 1848, Jules Guerin coined the term "social medicine" to advocate the use of medicine in the service of society.[4] Following the consolidation of the city's hospitals under the direction of l'Assistance publique in 1849, the public hospitals of Paris were at the forefront of this provision of social medicine.[5] Access to medical care in the capital's hospital system was considered a right (*droit*) for the neediest residents of the department, children included, and formal Assistance publique documents used this terminology.[6] The legislation of "children's rights" to protection also coincided with these midcentury institutional developments. Numerous studies have documented the crescendo of nineteenth-century child protection laws and programs, such as child labor legislation (1841, 1870), the regulation of the wet-nursing industry to reduce infant mortality (1871), and the law on *abandon moral* and the divestiture of French paternal authority (1889), all of which had crucial implications for children and families.[7] However, the nineteenth-century Parisian children's hospital and its complicated social dimensions have not yet been examined.

Considering the primary mission of the nineteenth-century Parisian children's hospital was to improve the health of the capital's poor, ailing dependent children, this study of Sainte-Eugénie underscores the connections among French medicine, public health, and social welfare policy and practice, with particular attention to the complex social interactions between children's hospitals, public health administrations, and patients and their families.[8] As dependents, child patients first and foremost relied on their families, particularly mothers, for survival. This examination builds on other works that highlight the interplay between welfare institutions and reforms and families, motherhood, and childhood in France and elsewhere later in the nineteenth century.[9] In particular, Rachel Fuchs's studies of the Paris foundling hospital that received abandoned children and the *maternités* that delivered poor mothers underscored the French state's interventions, provisions, and policies to protect dependent children and decrease child mortality, as well as mothers', albeit limited, agency in navigating the state welfare system.[10] As this study will show, mothers figured prominently in the Paris children's hospital records, supporting other scholarly works that demonstrate female agency and strong maternal bonds extended beyond the family unit and into the domain of public welfare institutions.[11] The visibility and influence of patients' mothers at Sainte-Eugénie emphasizes how, as primary caregivers, mothers were gatekeepers to their children's health and therefore played a significant role in children's medical care.

A close examination of Sainte-Eugénie's hospital records affords a more nuanced view of its patients and their families and raises important questions about social welfare institutions and poor urban family agency during this period: How pliable were administrative welfare policies, what was the nature of parent involvement in a child's medical treatment, and how might family choices affect a child's medical outcome? Drawing on the rich archival hospital records of l'Assistance publique—Hôpitaux de Paris, including admission registers (*registres d'entrées*) and administrative reports dating from 1855 to 1876, and a folio of nearly sixty letters of "exceptional admissions" between 1855 and 1880, this essay explores the children's hospital's administrative apparatus, its policies and procedures and medical activities.[12] However, reading between the lines of these archival records also reveals that French family members, particularly mothers, had options and exercised varying degrees of autonomy and authority in the face of the administrative policies of l'Assistance publique and the children's hospitals that operated under its jurisdiction.

The Setting: The Children's Hospital of Sainte-Eugénie

Sainte-Eugénie was one of three children's hospitals that operated in Paris during the second half of the nineteenth century. Like its predecessors Enfants-Malades and Enfants-Trouvés, Sainte-Eugénie was part of a vast Paris hospital network under the umbrella of a centralized welfare administration, l'Assistance publique de Paris. Established in 1855 on the former site of Enfants-Trouvés, the Paris foundling hospital, Sainte-Eugénie was monumental: four stories high, with separate floors dedicated to specific health conditions, a substantial outpatient department, as well as facilities for acute medical care and surgery.[13] With ten wards containing between thirty and sixty beds each, the hospital could house over 300 children at one time. In its opening year the hospital serviced almost 3,000 children, and for the next fifteen years maintained an average of 2,950 patients per year.[14] As one unit of a centralized, high-capacity Paris hospital system, Sainte-Eugénie was structured to receive and treat great numbers of children with efficiency and economy.

The hospital's neighborhood in the eastern Parisian periphery was home to some of the poorest members of the city's working class.[15] Sainte-Eugénie fell within the boundaries of the faubourg Saint Antoine, a neighborhood situated in the 8th arrondissement prior to 1860 and after Baron Georges-Eugène Haussmann's urban reconstruction efforts in the northwest corner of the 12th arrondissement.[16] According to l'Assistance publique statistics gathered during the 1860s, two of the three arrondissements containing the highest numbers of indigent households (*ménages*) in Paris were adjacent to the children's hospital: the 5th (to the southwest) and the 11th (to the north).[17] Sainte-Eugénie's registers confirm the hospital's proximity to Parisian poverty, with the majority of Sainte-Eugénie's patients residing in the arrondissements adjacent to the hospital.[18] Thus situated, l'hôpital Sainte-Eugénie was accessible to the city's poorest inhabitants, and prior to the introduction of the *métro de Paris*, within easy walking distance of poor families with sick children. Geospatially the urban centrality of the children's hospital, in contrast to a location outside of the city limits or in a more affluent residential locale, undoubtedly allowed for greater ease and opportunity for local family interactions with the hospital administrators and staff as well as for direct interventions.

Hospital Policies and Patient Eligibility

The hospitals of Paris were considered "pillars of social medicine," and Parisian children's hospitals like Sainte-Eugénie were building blocks for the "improvement of society through medicine" by providing medical services to its youngest and most needy residents.[19] In the view of the state's public assistance administration, the neediest children of the department had the right (*droit*) to access medical care at Sainte-Eugénie.[20] In theory, individuals were eligible for free medical care within the Paris hospital network if two key conditions were met: first, they needed to provide proof of their indigence or inability to pay for medical services; and second, they needed to live within the boundaries the Department of the Seine (essentially the city of Paris, and after 1860 Paris and its suburbs) at the time of admission. Given a policy approach based on locality and need, a parent's or guardian's ability to secure admission for a child at Sainte-Eugénie boiled down to geographic and financial eligibility. In a sample of 770 children at this hospital, approximately 95 percent fit both eligibility requirements and received free care through public assistance due to their residential address and socioeconomic status, thus confirming an impression of the children's hospital as *l'asile de misère*, the refuge of Paris's most impoverished child population.[21]

The other 5 percent of Sainte-Eugénie's patients, however, did not fit these conditions. Since not all patients were Parisian nor were completely destitute, the administration of l'Assistance publique distinguished between two sets of "exceptional" patient categories: paying patients (*malades payants/payantes*) and nonresident patients (*malades étrangers/ étrangeres*).[22] Patients fell into the *payant* category if their families had the ability to partially or fully pay for the hospital's services, while others fell into the *étranger* category if they were not residents of the Department of the Seine.[23] These two categories always overlapped when the patient was not a resident of Paris. Lacking the "right" to free hospital care, nonresidents seeking admission at any Paris hospital needed to provide proof to l'Assistance publique of their ability to pay for medical care in order to obtain written consent for admission, and so all admitted nonresidents were paying patients.[24] The following communiqué exemplifies this administrative attitude: l'Assistance publique notified Sainte-Eugénie that if the Delambardy family, who lived in an unnamed place in the country (*campagne*), could not pay the daily rate (*prix de journée*) for the full eight days due, their daughter would be sent back, "considering that she occupied a place that should be given to the indigent children of Paris."[25]

With the intention of channeling Parisian public assistance dollars toward the care of Parisians, this guiding principle was enforced but not set in stone. In children's hospitals, humanitarianism could overrule doctrinaire regulations. In cases of extreme urgency or special cases that "absolutely require turning to the talent of the medical practitioners of the capital," nonresident children could be admitted to a Paris hospital as long as l'Assistance publique was involved and maintained a close eye on those situations.[26] Due to these policies, paying patients and their families—resident and nonresident (*étranger*) alike—constituted one of the most vociferous groups at the children's hospitals. Negotiations about monetary payment (*versement*) for nonresident admittance generated a paper trail on many of these exceptional patients that demonstrate the abilities of some families to effectively navigate the hospital system. Although hospital directors and physicians took great pains to manage Sainte-Eugénie according to their standards of hospital organization and quality medical care, the human element intrinsic to the hospital experience produced change, compromise, and sometimes conflict. Administrators and doctors determined who would be admitted for medical care and how they would be treated; however, patients' families could, and did, exercise a certain degree of power in negotiation and resistance.

Resident Paying Patients (*Malades Payants*)

Paying patients who resided in the Department of the Seine composed the majority of exceptional patient admissions. Their experiences varied due to complex factors involved in determining hospital costs and family contributions, but their common residency in Paris or some other area encompassed within the Department of the Seine bound them together as an administrative category. Of the forty-three paying patients identified in the Sainte-Eugénie register, a majority were in Parisian families headed by a male breadwinner who worked in small business or had a skilled trade.[27] Some of these families sought and paid for care at the children's hospital because they could not afford a private physician but made too much money to qualify for free care. This situation was the case for Henri Bission, son of a jeweler (*bijoutier*) admitted to Sainte-Eugénie in 1869 with a fracture, and for Josèphe Thurot, son of a *maître d'hôtel*, admitted with water on the knee (hydroartrosis) in 1876. In other cases, collective family member earnings accumulated through unskilled or temporary work or income from unpredictable artistic trades may have pushed families just over the line to qualify for indigence. For example, in the Poinsot family, the patient's father worked as a painter, his mother worked as a florist, and two other members at the residence were employed, yet the family paid a reduced rate of 20 francs per month for their son's hospital stay at Sainte-Eugénie.[28]

For some Parisian families, financial assistance was not the issue; the child's affliction demanded inpatient medical care or a surgical procedure that only a hospital surgeon could provide. This situation was especially evident in cases of the croup, one of the most common respiratory illnesses noted in hospital registers and, prior to antibiotics and vaccinations, one of the deadliest. Croup involved a severe inflammation of the larynx and the trachea, but most severe cases designated as croup were most likely associated with diphtheria. These "croup" patients often had so much difficulty breathing that doctors often performed tracheotomies to open their air passages. Seven of the forty-three paying patients underwent croup operations, which were typically last-minute desperate measures to save the child's life. The probability of a child's surviving this operation was not high, and in this sample only three of the seven pulled through the procedure. Socioeconomics had little to do with whether or not a child endured this type of invasive operation; children of wine merchants (three) fared no better or worse than those of cashiers (one), artists (two), or unskilled workers (one).[29] For the Scheppe and de Bardel families, convulsions associated with chorea—now known to be symptoms of a wide range of nervous disorders—led them to Sainte-Eugénie, but their substantial household earnings had no bearing on the success or failure of this little-understood disease.[30] In situations like these, certain medical conditions exerted an equalizing force on families, regardless of their socioeconomic status or where they resided.

Nonresident Paying Patients

Due to a small but steady stream of paying patients from Paris, ward space was left open for paying patients from outside the Department of the Seine (*étrangers*). Admissions of *étrangers* recorded in the Sainte-Eugénie registers were rare, and in the words of Parisian public assistance administrators, *authorisations exceptionnelles*.[31] Outside the register sample, a cache of *authorisations exceptionnelles* letters reveals at least another sixteen children from other regions of France, including one of the African colonies, entered Sainte-Eugénie with l'Assistance publique's special consent. The small number of *étrangers* that actually made it through the hospital's doors demonstrates the vigilance of the exclusionary policy, which extended to the convalescent hospitals that exclusively served Paris children, like Berck-sur-Mer, as well as adult hospitals and houses of refuge within the capital city.[32] Over one quarter of the surviving letters about paying patients during this period involved out-of-domicile requests; though they were considered exceptional, l'Assistance publique was no stranger to these types of requests.

Nonresident admissions typically involved special surgical procedures and inpatient medical care that only the hospital setting could provide. The types of surgeries that attracted *étranger* patients to Sainte-Eugénie included operations to correct or ameliorate congenital conditions (birth defects) such as club feet (*pieds bots*) and cleft lips and palates, the removal of tumors, and other specialty operations. Particularly for families living in communes and departments immediately surrounding the Seine, the opportunity for their children to have corrective surgeries outweighed the costs and efforts involved in seeking admission at one of the children's hospitals in Paris. Occasionally a local doctor in an outlying region petitioned l'Assistance publique for a particular patient's admission to Sainte-Eugénie.[33]

Some nonresident parents took the lead in obtaining health care for their child at Sainte-Eugénie in this type of situation. In April 1874 a nine-year-old girl named Céline Jolly, the daughter of farmers from Seine-et-Oise, entered the children's hospital for surgery on her club feet. The Jolly family had either petitioned their local bureau of public assistance or written directly to the l'Assistance publique to acquire the authorization for their daughter—who was not a resident of Paris—to gain admission to the hospital. Either way, Charles Blondel, the director of l'Assistance publique, authorized her admission in a letter to the hospital director at Sainte-Eugénie, and Céline and her mother traveled between twenty and thirty miles to Paris for the operation. Some patients traveled even farther, such as a young boy from Confolens, Charente, in the southwestern region of France, with a cleft lip (bec de lièvre) as well as a cleft palate (*division de voute palatine*). The child's local doctor sought out the administration and requested the specialty surgery in Paris, which l'Assistance publique de Paris granted.[34]

The equivalent of 5 percent (one or two per yearly sample of thirty-five), the annual number of paying patients—both Parisian and *étrangers*—was small but significant, considering that Sainte-Eugénie took in an average of almost three thousand patients per year between 1855 and 1875. Their presence raises some important points about the exceptional patients and their families at the children's hospitals. Regardless of the state's residential and financial guidelines, some French family members figured out how to maneuver past the administrative hurdles and gain entry for children who would not otherwise qualify for care at the hospital.

Patients and Families: Choice and Agency

As the vast numbers of Sainte-Eugénie admissions attest, thousands of parents, guardians, or other family members chose to place their child in the care of the children's hospital. The first such hospital in Paris and in Europe, Enfants-Malades, opened in 1802—over fifty years before Sainte-Eugénie—and generations of Parisians and inhabitants across France were aware of the city's children's medical establishments. However, the gravity of a family's decision to go through with in-patient medical treatment for a child must not be underestimated. Prior to 1880 deadly childhood diseases had no cure or vaccine (excepting smallpox), antisepsis and anesthesia methods were known but relatively novel and not widespread in children's hospitals, and the children's hospitals of Paris were teaching hospitals, a constant laboratory for the development of new methods.[35] Considering varying degrees of parental anxiety about their child's illness, uncertainty about their ability to nurse their children back to health, and the reluctance to leave their children with others, the decision to seek out admittance at a children's hospital was not casual, and for many parents it may have been a particularly intense experience.[36] An already difficult decision, a parent's or family member's task in securing medical attention for a young patient was then compounded by a rigorous admissions process and eligibility requirements.

After jumping through the admission hoops, some patients' families continued to act as agents in the health and welfare of their children while they were in hospital. While rarely in consultation with physicians about medical issues, families used their voice in other ways. At both hospitals family members and guardians might take authoritative action in ways that either expanded or curtailed the limits of health care. At Sainte-Eugénie they stepped forward to work out financial issues that threatened the continuation of patient care; sometimes they stopped hospital payments altogether. The most frequent use of parental or guardian authority was the complete removal of the child from the hospital, illustrating that the ultimate decision whether to keep a child in the hospital lay with the child's family. In a handful of rare occurrences, parents abandoned their child at Sainte-Eugénie, and the child was transferred to Enfants-Assistés (formerly Enfants-Trouvés), the hospice for abandoned children.

Family Finances and Resourcefulness

Mothers, fathers, and other family members advocated for child patients in various ways, and lack of funds frequently spurred family involvement. At Sainte-Eugénie finances were a common topic of client-hospital relations when the family or a third party, such as a local public assistance bureau, paid the necessary expenses. Some families took total responsibility for the expenses, including the cost of the stay, medications, and any special surgeries or therapies. For example, on January 26, 1864, a thirteen-year-old patient from Clichy named Desirée Labourot was admitted with scrofula, an all-purpose medical term used to describe a variety of conditions ranging from skin disorders and chronic weakness to tuberculosis. Both her parents were dead, but her brother, an established baker, was able to pay for the hospital stay, which would have been quite an expense since her treatment lasted almost ten months.[37] In other cases the local bureau of public assistance subsidized all or part of the cost of hospital care. Pauline Letteron, an *étrangère* from Seine-et-Marne, received treatment for several months each year during 1864, 1865, and 1866, thanks to such an arrangement. A local bureau paid for all three of her hospital sojourns, which varied between a rate of 1 franc 75 centimes and 1 franc 86 centimes per day, depending on the year.[38] Even if their local public assistance handled the hospital costs, the families of *étranger* patients were bound to accrue related expenditures, for example, when mothers accompanied their children to the hospital. Transportation to and from Paris, temporary lodging in the capital if they had no friends or family, and perhaps lost wages of parents who accompanied their child for a portion or the entire duration of the hospital stay—these were financial burdens that some parents were willing to shoulder in order to help their child get well.

At Sainte-Eugénie some parents or family members who initially contributed to their child's hospital expenses found themselves in precarious economic situations. Lost income due to unemployment or sickness left some families unable to continue their payments to the Paris hospital. Some in this situation took a proactive stance and wrote to l'Assistance publique, claiming hardship and seeking either a reduction in their patient's daily rate or exoneration from payment altogether. This process could be time-consuming and invasive; in cases involving stopped payments or requests for financial help, l'Assistance publique made formal inquiries into a family's or guardian's economic situation. If the request was justified, or if removing the patient from the hospital threatened his or her chance of recovery, the administration either reduced the daily rate or offered to cover the remainder of the hospital bill.

Mothers of patients at Sainte-Eugénie were particularly forthright in demanding financial assistance. Of the remaining letters concerning admissions between family members and l'Assistance publique administration between 1855 and 1875, over half involved mothers seeking additional funds to continue medical care for their child. For example, in a letter dated September 18, 1855, Elisa Robardy informed the administration that the family fell on hard times and could no longer afford her son's daily rate.[39] Upon investigation, her story was validated and her five-year-old son, Charles, was allowed to remain at Sainte-Eugénie free of charge for the rest of his hospital stay. In early 1856 Eugénie Choquet wrote on behalf of her eleven-year-old daughter, Pauline, who was admitted in November of the year before with a fever. As it turned out, the fever was actually an epileptic spell. When her daughter needed to remain in the hospital for months longer than anticipated, Madame Choquet, a dressmaker and single mother, requested public assistance. L'Assistance publique responded by covering the additional 123 days of Pauline's treatment. In these cases, if the mother's plea was justified according to administrative inquests, l'Assistance publique accommodated the request.

Family Requests, Refusals, and Patient Removals

Documentation of family advocacy concerning direct requests for specific medical care at Sainte-Eugénie is rare, likely since parents and other family members knew little of the classification, diagnosis, and treatment of childhood diseases. Most family members and friends brought children to the hospital because they had few alternatives and could not afford private physician care. In rare cases parents ventured to ask for specific doctors or surgeons to treat their children, and Sainte-Eugénie's hospital administrators mediated such requests. For example, Amélie Poutrel entered the children's hospital with a diagnosis of necrosis (*nécrose*), a debilitating condition often related to tuberculosis that resulted in cellular degeneration, usually of the bone. In a letter from Armand Husson, head of l'Assistance publique, to the hospital director, Husson indicated that the patient's father had requested Dr. Marjolin, one of the hospital's most renowned surgeons at the time, to take charge of his daughter's treatment, which probably required surgical removal of the diseased bone tissue.[40] Based on recommendations by other doctors, family members, or friends, other French parents likely made such appeals. Due to the presence of the adjoining outpatient department, other parents and guardians would have interfaced with attending medical personnel through previous visits and sought out familiar names and faces if their child had an emergency or needed inpatient care.

Although hospital doctors were the medical experts, ultimately a parent or guardian had power over their child's medical care. As their only leverage when unsatisfied, unwilling, or without hope, they wielded this authority by refusing to consent to a surgery or treatment. Understandably surgeries posed a problem for parents because of their evasive, traumatic, even brutal nature. Operations to extract tumors or diseased joints or limbs were particularly unpopular, due not only to the seriousness of the condition but to the postsurgical consequences (including death from infection) if a child lost part of an arm, a leg, or a foot, or a combination of these. At Sainte-Eugénie eleven-year-old Marguerite Lauer did not have an operation to remove a tumor on her right elbow because her father would not allow it.[41] Parents of patients were also unwilling to consent to operations because it required a longer hospital stay, and a lengthy convalescence might lead to the contraction of an infectious disease that appeared and spread on the ward. For example, while in the hospital for a club foot operation, Céline Jolly contracted measles (*rougeole*). She survived and returned home, but when Céline later developed eye problems, her mother refused to allow her daughter to stay at Sainte-Eugénie.[42]

Although not typical, one recourse was to simply curtail the hospital's access to their child and demand the young patient's early release. In the decades after Sainte-Eugénie opened, mothers, fathers, and other guardians increasingly exercised their power of parental authority and demanded that their children be returned to them. While some of this increase corresponds to greater numbers of total patients at both hospitals, if the record keeping on the topic remained relatively stable, instances of parents removing patients gradually rose over time at both institutions. For example, at Sainte-Eugénie, records show only five instances of children willfully removed from hospital care between the years 1855 and 1870.[43] In contrast, between 1871 and 1876 fifteen children were removed due to the demand of a parent, with removals peaking in 1872 and 1875 and involving 11 percent (four out of twenty-five) of all patients in that sample year.[44] Part of this increase in parent intervention may reflect a general sense of uncertainty and upheaval among Parisians in the chaotic years following the Franco-Prussian War, the Paris Commune, and the forging of the Third Republic. Parental reactions to greater state and medical intervention into working-class domestic life through new Third Republic legislation, such as the regulation of the wet-nursing industry by the Roussel Law of 1874 and a revised French child labor law in 1874, may also explain this rise in parental action.[45]

Considering most mid- to late nineteenth-century parents and guardians in Paris had little to no medical expertise and the mortality rates at Sainte-Eugénie ranged between one-eighth and one-sixth of the total patient population for this period (depending on particular epidemics, such as cholera), families saw patient removal as a potentially life-saving, not self-defeating, course of action. Parents and guardians removed children from the hospital for several reasons, and a combination of factors likely played some role in their decision. Sainte-Eugénie register entries offer clear indications that a removal occurred, with such statements in the margins of the notes section as "removed by parents," "taken on the express demand of the mother," and "father took child home." While an incomplete picture of these family-initiated removals, a collective analysis of these entries, combined with notes on exceptional paying patients, yields some general impressions of the reasoning behind these parental choices. Considering age range, medical conditions, and family backgrounds for patients at the hospital, along with specific examples and some degree of speculation, French working-class parents removed their children from the hospital against doctor's orders due to the patient's young age, the loss of a child's economic contribution to the family unit, a parent's fear of a child's contracting a contagious disease in the ward, dissatisfaction with care or treatment options, a family's unwillingness to risk a child's dying in the institution, or a combination of these factors.

At Sainte-Eugénie the age of the patient seems to have had the greatest influence on whether a parent or guardian took the child home against the hospital's advice. Of the forty removals in the sample, half of early release requests involved children under the age of five years.

This rate suggests that for these families, separation from a young patient was challenging. Even a short-term hospital stay likely took an emotional toll on parent and child, especially children under the age of three who were still dependent on their mothers and aware of the separation. As the admission records indicate, younger patients were more likely to die from a medical condition than their older counterparts, having less-developed immune systems and more easily contracted life-threatening childhood diseases, such as diphtheria, measles, and whooping cough. If a toddler contracted an infectious disease in the ward, as many children did, it could prove fatal. As soon as a patient showed any sign of improvement, parents might remove the child to protect him or her from further contagion.[46]

For older patients, family-initiated removals may have been motivated by financial need as much as emotional attachment or dissatisfaction with a medical outcome. For these families, the loss of the child's work earnings endangered the family's economic survival. Despite increasing regulations on child labor and the move toward free and compulsory education in France during the second half of the nineteenth century, working-class children under the age of fifteen regularly contributed to the household economy.[47] Sainte-Eugénie's registers listed male and female patients as young as ten who were working apprentices to florists, jewelers, printers, and masters of other trades. Certain details in the admissions register suggest that some patients played a supporting role in keeping the family afloat. For example, eight-year-old Jules Violet's mother removed him from the hospital after a week-long stay for a fracture of the left radius.[48] His father, a handyman (*homme de peine*), may have needed his son to accompany him on odd jobs, and Jules may even have obtained his injury working alongside his father. Since the young boy was old enough to contribute to the family income—even while suffering from a tubercular condition—the family may have decided that the hospital stay was not worth the cost of the child's labor.

Even if they did not earn wages, children contributed to the family in other ways. Especially girls as young as five or six were expected to mind the younger children and do domestic chores.[49] In the case of eleven-year-old Marguerite Lauer, the Sainte-Eugénie patient whose father denied her an elbow operation, the young girl's removal from the hospital may have been related to her duties at home. Her father, a widower, may have relied on Marguerite to manage the house and, if she had younger siblings, to be their caretaker. Mothers also relied on their young daughters to run the house and mind the babies, enough so that losing a daughter for an extended time was too difficult to bear. Domestic exigencies of working-class life could take precedence over a child's hospitalization and procedures, especially when these medical conditions and their consequences for lack of treatment were little understood by families.

Mothers and Fathers

A gender analysis of parental involvement at Sainte-Eugénie demonstrates that mothers and fathers wielded influence in distinct ways. While both mothers and fathers figured prominently at Sainte-Eugénie, mothers of Paris-born patients especially played an active role at the time of discharge. The admissions registers frequently indicated when one or both parents or another family member demanded to take the child home or picked up the child after he or she was discharged. In the sample of 770 patients, mothers were the overwhelming majority of family representatives who demanded the removal of a patient, took custody of a discharged patient, or both. In 1872, of the thirty-five patients in the register sample, six were removed from the hospital; three were taken by "express demand of the mother." The other three patients were removed by the stepmother (*belle-mère*), a female cousin, or an unnamed member of the family, further suggesting patient removal at the Parisian children's hospital was an overwhelming female responsibility. In the sample for 1875, twelve patients were removed from the hospital, including two by "express demand of the mother"; ten patients simply "left with the mother," and two patients left with their father, one of whom "wanted to take him." In a sample from 1876, of the thirteen hospital discharges, two involved mothers who "insisted" on taking the patient home, and one was removed by "formal demand" of the father. Interestingly, out of all the express demands for a patient's removal, only one involved a single parent (a widow), and of the discharges handled directly by the mother, only one involved an unmarried mother (no father listed in the register).

The strong presence of poor mothers at the children's hospital underscores the agency that women had within poor Parisian families, not just inside the household but in family interactions with welfare institutions. As a public welfare institution, the children's hospital might be considered a state instrument to police the health of poor children, but mothers were agents in their child's health care, not simply "state-approved nurses" or submissive subjects of direct surveillance.[50] Furthermore admission policies at Sainte-Eugènie were based more upon verifiable and objective factors such as socioeconomic need and residency than moralistic concerns over family structure or social conventions. In contrast to British children's hospitals that wrestled with cultural concerns about the "deserving" and "undeserving" poor, Paris hospitals accepted all Paris-born and paying or subsidized nonresident children regardless of whether they were an orphan or half-orphan, a child born of a legal marriage or the natural child of an unwed mother.[51]

At Sainte-Eugénie, French mothers also dominated hospital requests concerning *autorisations exceptionnelles*. As mentioned, mothers wrote more letters than fathers to l'Assistance publique requesting respite from their financial obligations. As the cases of Elisa Robardy and Eugénie Choquet demonstrate, mothers initiated formal requests to l'Assistance publique for a reduction in hospital fees, sometimes more than once. For example, Louise Nolin wrote to the administration in 1855 and in 1856 to renegotiate the daily rate for her son Eugene's stay at the hospital.[52] The family was Parisian, therefore in domicile, but was not considered indigent, and initially her son, who suffered from several chronic skin conditions, was admitted as a paying patient. Madame Nolin's first letter, in late 1855, instigated a new inquest into the family situation, and when hardship was discovered the daily rate was reduced. A few months later she wrote a similar letter, but with the opposite effect. Her son's rate increased to 55 centimes per day due to the new information. As this example shows, while their requests might or might not pay off, determined working-class mothers in Paris worked hard to keep the hospital fees down.

Conclusion

Some working-class family members—particularly Parisian mothers—navigated the ins and outs of the children's hospital of Sainte-Eugénie, negotiating with hospital and public assistance administrators and demanding what they believed was best for their children. In this sense they navigated the domain of social medicine, ensuring their child's right to public health care yet also exercising their own right as parents or guardians to permit treatment or remove their child from hospital care. From a nineteenth-century medical standpoint, their actions and choices did not always serve the best interests of the child: some went without operations, further treatments, or proper convalescent time. When in doubt about a procedure or course of treatment, families of patients at Sainte-Eugénie often removed the child from the hospital. Family members in these examples, however, had other alternatives: not to take their child to the hospital in the first place, or in extreme cases, abandon their child to the institution. Judgment aside, patients' families had choices; they discovered the options available to them and made their decisions, for better or worse.

The choices that families faced and the sphere of action available to them depended on several factors. At Sainte-Eugénie strict policies for patient eligibility based on geographic domicile and vigilant attempts to serve the local needy population translated into greater obstacles for families from outside the Department of the Seine seeking medical care for their child at the Paris children's hospital. While fixated on the bottom line—finances and economy—Sainte-Eugénie was a large state institution predicated on the notion of a poor child's "right" to medical service. Under the supervision of a centralized umbrella organization, Sainte-Eugénie's administrators deferred to the power of l'Assistance publique in matters of family financial responsibility. If a parent formally requested its aid, the administration would usually concede for what they considered to be medically in the best interest of the child, since such an action also contributed to the state's interests in fostering the health of French children. Despite the centralized attempts by l'Assistance publique and the Paris children's hospital to regulate and monitor their populations, some parents—especially mothers residing in Paris—worked hard to get their child's needs met on their own terms.

The examples here demonstrate that some families of patients in nineteenth-century children's hospitals were not passive recipients of state-funded hospital care and actively asserted their rights as guardians. These families had choices and faced a range of dilemmas: how to obtain hospital care for their child, how to pay for it, and even when hospital care was freely provided, whether to trust the medical establishment or to remove their child from the hospital altogether. All of these decisions also highlight the risks inherent in nineteenth-century children's hospital care: the risk of imperfect medical knowledge and procedures, the risk of the child's contracting another infection in the ward, and the risk of the child's dying in the hospital without family members at the bedside. The life-or-death stakes at the children's hospital were different for families than for doctors or institutional administrators. Even for the most compassionate doctor, a young patient was a "case," a success story or another tragic loss of life, and even for the most concerned administrator, a young patient was a number in the register, a statistic in the annual report, or another poor child whose parents couldn't pay the daily fee. Many working-class families did not have the luxury of reason, objectivity, or perspective; their choices about their children's medical care were subjective, intimate, and permanent.

Notes

1. Michel Foucault's *Discipline and Punish: The Birth of the Prison* (New York: Vintage, 1995), part 3, "Discipline," 135–69, explores social control of individual bodies through disciplinary institutions, such as the school, the military, the asylum, and the hospital, and the process of accessing, disciplining, and regulating individuals through specific medical-legal technologies and practices within those institutions. Jacques Donzelot's *The Policing of Families* (Baltimore: Johns Hopkins University Press, 1977) expands on Foucault's theory and identifies specific "tutelary complexes"

that discipline the behavior of families and allow the state to govern families. Donzelot's "government through the family" argument focuses on a range of social welfare institutions and statutes, including the Paris foundling hospital, but does not discuss the general children's hospitals.

2. For a general history of the Paris hospitals, see Erwin H. Ackernecht, *Medicine at the Paris Hospital, 1794-1848.* (Baltimore: Johns Hopkins University Press, 1967); for Paris as the premier location for medical training, see Thomas N. Bonner, *Becoming a Physician: Medical Education in Great Britain, France, Germany, and the United States, 1750-1945* (New York: Oxford University Press, 1996); and for the Paris hospital's place in the history of medical specialization in Europe, see George Weisz, *Divide and Conquer: A Comparative History of Medical Specialization* (Cary NC: Oxford University Press, 2005).

3. Ann La Berge, *Mission and Method: The Early Nineteenth Century French Public Health Movement* (Cambridge, UK: Cambridge University Press, 1992); Philip Nord, "The Welfare State in France, 1870–1914," *French Historical Studies* 18, no. 3 (1994): 821–38.

4. Ackernecht, *Medicine at the Paris Hospital*, 155; La Berge, *Mission and Method*, 310.

5. Marc Dupont, *L'Assistance publique / Hôpitaux de Paris: Organisation administrative et médicale*, (Paris: Vélizy, 1998).

6. L'Assistance publique, Circulaire 14 mai 1856, Archives de l'Assistance publique-Hôpitaux de Paris (hereafter AP/HP) 9L 154. This centralization of public hospital care under state supervision was unique to France, as in Great Britain and the United States hospitals were voluntary institutions.

7. Lee Shai Weissbach, *Child Labor Reform in Nineteenth-Century France: Assuring the Future Harvest* (Baton Rouge: Louisiana State University Press, 1989); George D. Sussman, *Selling Mother's Milk: The Wet-Nursing Business in France, 1715-1914* (Urbana: University of Illinois Press, 1982); Sylvia Schafer, *Children in Moral Danger and the Problem of Government in the Third Republic* (Princeton NJ: Princeton University Press, 1997).

8. Eduard Seidler's "An Historical Survey of Children's Hospitals," in *The Hospital in History*, ed. Lindsay Grandshaw and Roy Porter (London: Routledge, 1989), 181–97, is a brief overview of European children's hospitals. For nineteenth-century British children's hospitals, see Elizabeth Lomax, *Small and Special: The Development of Hospitals for Children in Victorian Britain* (London: Wellcome Institute for the History of Medicine, 1996); Andrea Tanner, "Choice and the Children's Hospital: Great Ormond Street Hospital Patients and Their Families, 1855-1900," in *Medicine, Charity and*

Mutual Aid: The Consumption of Health in Britain, c. 1550–1950, ed. Anne Borsay and Peter Shapely (London: Ashgate, 2007), 135–61. Luc Passion and Michel Sorin's chapter "L'Invention du patient: L'hôpital et l'enfant à Paris au XIXe siècle," in *Les Maux et les soins: Médecins et maladies dans les hôpitaux parisiens au XIXe siècle*, ed. Francis Demier and Claire Barille (Paris: Action Artistique, 2007), 191–200, is a broad survey of the Paris children's hospitals and patients. No scholarly study of Sainte-Eugénie exists.

9. Elinor A. Accampo, Rachel G. Fuchs, and Mary Lynn Stewart, eds., *Gender and the Politics of Social Reform in France, 1870–1914* (Baltimore: Johns Hopkins University Press, 1995); Seth Koven and Sonya Michel, eds., *Mothers of a New World: Maternalist Politics and the Origins of Welfare States* (New York: Routledge, 1993).

10. Rachel G. Fuchs, *Abandoned Children: Foundlings and Child Welfare in Nineteenth-Century France* (Albany: State University of New York Press, 1984) and *Poor and Pregnant in Paris: Strategies for Survival in the Nineteenth Century* (New Brunswick NJ: Rutgers University Press, 1992).

11. Lydia Murdoch, *Imagined Orphans: Poor Families, Child Welfare, and Contested Citizenship in London* (New Brunswick NJ: Rutgers University Press, 2006); Ellen Ross, *Love and Toil: Motherhood in Outcast London, 1870–1918* (New York: Oxford University Press, 1993).

12. The magnitude of the admissions registers for Sainte-Eugénie required a random sampling of thirty-five patient entries per year, for every year from the 1855 to 1876, totaling 770 sample patient register entries.

13. Chirurgie: plan du rez-de-chaussée; médecin: plan du 1er étage; scrofuleux: plan du 2e étage; teigneux: plan du 3e étage, AP/HP, 793 FOSS 56/7.

14. Sainte-Eugénie, Registres d'entrées, 1855–71, AP/HP. During this period, the children's hospital admitted a total of 50,138 patients.

15. Administration générale de l'Assistance publique, *Renseignements statistiques sur la population indigente de Paris d'après le recensement opère en 1869* (Paris: Paul Dupont, 1871), 10, Archives de Paris (hereafter AdP), Collection Husson, D6z/4.

16. Note relative a l'annexion des nouveaux arrondissements, AdP, Husson Collection, D6z/3.

17. These three arrondissements recorded between 3,000 and 4,000 indigent families for the years 1861, 1863, 1866, and 1869. AdP, Husson Collection, D6z/3, 6.

18. For example, fourteen of thirty-five (or 40 percent of) patients in 1855 were residents of the old 8th arrondissement, and between one third and one half of patients after 1860 were residents of the 11th or 12th

arrondissements (former 8th arrondissement). Sainte-Eugénie, Registres d'entrées, sample for 1855, 1860–76, AP/HP.

19. S. Borsa and C.-R. Michel, *Des hôpitaux en France au XIXe siècle* (Paris: Hachette, 1985), 69–72. For the connection between medicine and infant health and hygiene, see Pierre Huard and Robert La Plane, *Historie illustrée de la puériculture: Aspects diététiques, socioculturels et ethnologique* (Paris: Roger Dacosta, 1979).
20. L'Assistance publique, Circulaire 14 mai 1856, AP/HP, 9L 154.
21. Passion and Sorin, "L'Invention du patient," 193. Out of 770 sample patient register entrées, 738 indicated that the patient resided in the Department of the Seine and did not include mention of payment.
22. L'Assistance publique, Circulaire de 19 mars 1855, AP/HP, 9L 154.
23. Registre d'entrées, L'hôpital Sainte-Eugénie, SainteEugenie (1Q 2/1–1Q 2/11), 1855–76, AP/HP.
24. L'Assistance publique, Circulaire 14 mai 1856, AP/HP, 9L 154.
25. Letter from l'Assistance publique to Sainte-Eugénie, May 18, 1871, AP/HP, 9L 155.
26. Circulaire de 19 mars 1855, AP/HP, 9L 154.
27. Registre d'entrées, L'hôpital Sainte-Eugénie, SainteEugenie (1Q 2/1–1Q 2/11), 1855–76, AP/HP.
28. Letter from l'Assistance publique to the hospital director of Sainte-Eugénie, June 28, 1858, AP/HP, 9L 155.
29. These occupations roughly constituted a similar working-class socioeconomic stratum based on Armand Husson's published works on working-class and indigent occupations in Paris. See Tableau synoptique des professions, no. 2. n.d., AdP, Husson Collection, D6z/3.
30. Registre d'entrées, L'hôpital Sainte-Eugénie, 1865–67 (Sainte-Eugénie 1Q 2/6), entries #338 (Gustave Scheppe) and #722 (Gustave de Bardel), AP/HP.
31. Throughout the sample entries for this study, only three *étrangers* appeared. Registre d'entrées, L'hôpital Sainte-Eugénie, 1865–67 (Sainte-Eugénie 1Q 2/6), entries #289 and #290: Lucie and Lucette Galland (twins) admitted for impetigo on February 2, 1866, AP/HP. The other nonresident was Clarise Beauvallet, daughter of a farmer from Loiret, admitted with eye disease on November 17, 1861, entry # 2517 (Sainte-Eugénie 1Q 2/4), AP/HP.
32. Recueiles des arrêtes, instructions, et circulaires de l'Assistance publique, AP1J5, Circulaire de 19 juillet 1873, AP/HP.
33. Letter from Central Administration de l'Assistance publique to Directeur de l'hôpital Sainte-Eugénie, January 11, 1869, AP/HP, 9L 155. In this letter l'Assistance publique allowed admission to a child from Marne for

a specialty operation and informed the hospital that the child would be placed in the care of Dr. Marjolin.

34. Letter from Central Administration de l'Assistance publique to Directeur de l'hôpital Sainte-Eugénie, July 23, 1873, AP/HP, 9L 155. L'AP gave *autorisation exceptionnelle* for the young Balaud boy, and the parents agreed to make two payments: one for the *l'obturateur de la voute palatine* (the closing/sealing of the site) if necessary, and the other for the hospital stay. Since the letter mentioned that Dr. Thorin asked for the specialty surgery in Paris, his request may have carried some weight with the Paris administration.

35. Weisz, *Divide and Conquer*, chap. 1, "The Rise of Specialties in Nineteenth-Century Paris."

36. Linda Pollock, *Forgotten Children: Parent-Child Relationships from 1500–1900* (Cambridge, UK: Cambridge University Press, 1995) 133–34, 140–41.

37. Letter from l'Assistance publique to Directeur de l'hôpital Sainte-Eugénie, November 1864, AP/HP, 9L 155.

38. Letter from Central Administration de l'Assistance publique to Directeur de l'hôpital Sainte-Eugénie, January 18, 1866, AP/HP, 9L 155.

39. Letter from Central Administration de l'Assistance publique to Directeur de l'hôpital Sainte-Eugénie, September 18, 1855, AP/HP, 9L 155.

40. Letter from Central Administration de l'Assistance publique to Directeur de l'hôpital de Sainte-Eugénie, May 9, 1859, AP/HP, 9L 155.

41. Registre d'entrées, L'hôpital Sainte-Eugénie, 1861–62 (Sainte-Eugénie 1Q 2/4), patient record #1099, May 1861, AP/HP.

42. Letter from Central Administration de l'Assistance publique to Directeur de l'hôpital de Sainte-Eugénie, July 11. 1874, AP/HP, 9L 155.

43. Registre d'entrées, L'hôpital Sainte-Eugénie, 1855–70, AP/HP. Three patients were over the age of ten, one patient was three years old, and one was twenty months.

44. Registre d'entrées, L'hôpital Sainte-Eugénie, 1871–76, AP/HP.

45. For the Roussel Law, see Sussman, *Selling Mother's Milk*. For the revised child labor law, see Weissbach, *Child Labor Reform*.

46. Registre d'entrées, L'hôpital Sainte-Eugénie (Sainte-Eugénie 1Q 2/9), 1873–74, AP/HP. For example, in November–December 1872 four patients were removed from the hospital expressly to convalesce at home.

47. Peter Mandler, "Poverty and Charity: An Introduction," in *The Uses of Charity: The Poor on Relief in the Nineteenth-Century Metropolis*, ed. Peter Mandler (Philadelphia: University of Pennsylvania Press, 1990), 6. In nineteenth-century capitals like London and Paris, women and children's

labor was particularly in demand, where upper classes needed domestic servants and finished luxury goods, and opportunities for delivery work and scavenging were available (6). Also see Colin Heywood, *Childhood in Nineteenth-Century France: Work, Health and Education among the "Classes Populaires"* (Cambridge, UK: Cambridge University Press, 2002); Weissbach, *Child Labor Reform.*

48. Registre d'entrées, L'hôpital Sainte-Eugénie, 1865–67 (Sainte-Eugénie 1Q 2/6), patient record #658, March 1866, AP/HP.

49. Ross, *Love and Toil*, 135, 154.

50. In this sample of patients, the recorded involvement of mothers in family-initiated removals provides a revisionist interpretation to these specific arguments about mothers made in Donzelot, *The Policing of Families*, 31.

51. For discussions of British hospitals and charity, see Keir Waddington, *Charity and the London Hospitals, 1850–1898* (London: Boydell and Brewer, 2000), 28, 116.

52. Letter from Central Administration de l'Assistance publique to Directeur de l'hôpital de Sainte-Eugénie, June 25, 1856, AP/HP, 9L 155.

5

Illustrations as Good as Any Slides

Women's Activist Social Novels and the
French Search for Social Reform, 1880-1914

JEAN ELISABETH PEDERSEN

In 1912 the feminist activist Louise Compain published her third novel, *La vie tragique de Geneviève*, the story of an orphan girl who moves to Paris with an illegitimate child, struggles to survive as a domestic piece worker in the garment trades, experiences such poverty and desperation that she tries to kill herself and her children, and ultimately finds hope at the end of the story with the possibility of working to establish living wages for female workers. The political economist Charles Gide, who reviewed the new novel for *Le christianisme social*, highlighted not only its literary merit but also its political value when he recommended it to the particular attention of contemporary French activists against the "*sweating system* [emphasis in the original]." "All those who have to give lectures on the woman worker and home industry," he concluded with approval, "should find illustrations here that are as good as any slides."[1]

Lynn Hunt has identified the far-reaching political significance of eighteenth-century French and British novels in the creation of the "imagined empathy" that encouraged individual readers to "relate beyond their immediate families, religious affiliations, or even nations to [the] greater universal values" that eventually encouraged successive generations of readers, writers, revolutionaries, and reformers to support new political causes such as women's rights, workers' rights, and other forms of national and international human rights.[2] Mary Poovey's "history of the modern fact" and Joshua Cole's study of "the power of large numbers" both identify the subsequent nineteenth century as a period when predominantly male policymakers increasingly put their trust in the apparent objectivity and rationality of statistical science as they sought to address the new "social question" of how to respond to the social and economic consequences of industrialization among the laboring classes.[3] Marie-Emmanuelle Chessel has suggested, however, that the same female social reformers who participated in the creation of the modern social sciences when they conducted inspections among the urban poor may also have challenged those same social sciences by turning from sociology and statistics to fiction and photography to convey the significance of their results.[4] The encounter between Louise Compain and Charles Gide further underscores the continuing power of both novels and visual images for the social reformers of the French Third Republic.

Most historians who have written about late nineteenth- and early twentieth-century French feminism, female activism, and the search for social reform have tended to overlook women's literary productions in favor of a focus on the study of their newspapers and pamphlets, their organizations and demonstrations, and their interactions with national party leaders and parliamentary politicians.[5] As the case of Compain and Gide demonstrates, however, French activists could also fight for social change by exposing social problems and suggesting political solutions in the pages of the books that their contemporaries identified as "social novels" or "thesis novels," novels that combined realistic settings with melodramatic plots to make powerful activist points. As Jean Charles-Brun explained in his study of the significance of such novels in 1910, "Along with the theater, the novel is the most widespread genre, the one whose action can be, if not the strongest . . . at least the most [widely] diffused."[6]

This chapter explores the complex relationships among the use of fact, the use of fiction, and the search for social reform by focusing on the work of three pioneering women who practiced different combinations of these three activities during the first half of the French Third Republic: the school inspector Pauline Kergomard (1838–1925), the consumer activist Elise Chalamet (1848–1925), and the feminist journalist Louise Compain (1869–1940). Kergomard's *Heureuse rencontre* (*Happy Meeting*, 1895) highlights the work of the Union pour le sauvetage de l'enfance, the organization Kergomard founded with Caroline de Barrau in 1887 to rescue abused or abandoned children. Chalamet's *Petite bonne* (*Little Maid*, 1905) exposes the difficult living conditions of the female domestic servants whose lives Chalamet tried to improve by working with Henriette Brunhes's Ligue sociale d'acheteurs and associated networks of social reformers and socially conscious consumers to survey buildings, publicize lists of acceptable accommodations, and encourage architects to design better servant apartments. Compain's *La vie tragique de Geneviève* (*The Tragic Life of Geneviève*, 1912) supports not only the national campaign for a living wage for domestic piece workers but also a range of other initiatives that Compain also supported, including the legalization of paternity suits to help single mothers care for their illegitimate children and the creation of sewing cooperatives to improve the conditions of employment for women in the garment trades.[7]

Pauline Kergomard and *Heureuse rencontre*

Pauline Kergomard is especially well-known today both as one of the founders of the modern French nursery school and as one of the most important female school inspectors of the late nineteenth and early twentieth centuries. She earned her initial teaching certification from a private institution in Bordeaux in 1856, moved to Paris in 1861, and started her influential career in the French national educational establishment by passing the state certifying exam to direct nursery schools in 1877, earning a post as general delegate for nursery school inspection under Jules Ferry in 1879, and converting this to a new post as general inspector for nursery schools as part of the national initiative that she organized to transform the original *salles d'asile* (day care centers with limited instruction) into real *écoles maternelles* (nursery schools with a more extensive curriculum) in 1881. In 1886, five years into her forty-year career as a school inspector, she also became the first woman to win a seat on the board of the Conseil supérieur de l'instruction publique, the elected council that served as an advisory body to the Ministère de l'instruction publique, the Ministry of Public Instruction.[8]

Kergomard complemented her paid work as a school inspector with a combination of philanthropic and activist initiatives to help abused and abandoned children, to fight for women's rights, and to support adult education. In 1887, for example, she worked with Caroline de Barrau to create the child-rescue organization that still exists today under the name of the Union française pour le sauvetage de l'enfance; in 1897 she started contributing a column on education for Marguerite Durand's new feminist weekly, *La Fronde*; in 1898 she founded a new *université populaire* to provide continuing adult education in the 14th arrondissement of Paris; in 1899 she helped to organize the international Congrès des oeuvres et institutions féminines that highlighted women's participation in charitable works and institutions as a justification for improvements in women's social condition and legal status; in 1900 she attended both the second Congrès des oeuvres et institutions féminines and the Congrès de la condition et des droits des femmes, two complementary international conferences that assembled overlapping groups of female philanthropists and feminist activists to fight for further improvements in women's rights; and in 1905 she joined the board of the Conseil national des femmes françaises as the chair of its Education section, where she advocated for related reforms that included coeducation and sex education.[9] Kergomard highlighted the work of the Union française pour le sauvetage de l'enfance when she published *Heureuse rencontre*, the 1895 novel that she dedicated to the six grandchildren of her Union cofounder, Caroline de Barrau, the friend and fellow philanthropist whom Kergomard described in the text of the dedication as "a woman who passed over the earth doing good."[10]

Kergomard and de Barrau cofounded the Union française pour le sauvetage de l'enfance in 1887 as the Union française pour la défense ou la tutelle des enfants maltraités ou en danger moral, the French Union for the Defense or the Guardianship of Mistreated Children or Children in Moral Danger.[11] They started their operations in 1888, lobbied French senators and deputies to approve a parliamentary proposal that would allow the French state to remove children from the familial care of those it deemed to be unsuitable or irresponsible, and then used the resulting Roussel Law of July 24, 1889, to work with Union members, family members, community members, and the courts to find new homes for children whose parents abused, overworked, or abandoned them.[12] In 1900 the Union took in 402 children; in 1901, 437; in 1902, 493; in 1903, 602. By 1904 the leaders of the group projected a budget of roughly 200,000 francs to fund a comprehensive set of programs that provided room and board, clothing, medical care, apprenticeships for the boys, training in domestic arts and needlework for the girls, and dowries for the children of both sexes who came under their care.[13] Their work continues today.[14]

De Barrau and Kergomard used their organization to collect money, but they strongly believed that finding money was only one part of the solution to the social problem they were seeking to address. As they explained in the flyer that they used to recruit new members, "Giving an annual subscription is very good. That is not enough. Each one has the duty to come to the aid of the unfortunate children in whose favor our charity has been founded in some personal manner."[15] Kergomard's 1895 novel *Heureuse rencontre* publicizes the work of the group and stresses the significance of individual engagement when it tells the story of the titular "happy meeting" between Marius, a beggar boy, and Madame Lucyol, an elegant society woman who volunteers with the Union.[16]

At the beginning of the novel Marius's father is dead of unemployment and alcoholism, his mother is dead of poverty and anxiety, and his sister, Louise, is missing. When Marius faints from hunger while he is carrying Madame Lucyol's parcels in exchange for the price of a meal, Madame Lucyol takes him into her home, replaces his rags with some of the good used clothes that she regularly collects from her friends, sets him up as the apprentice to a shoe manufacturer, and promises to search for his sister. When Madame Lucyol finds Louise in a house where the employer forces children to beg for a living, she brings the girl home and places her with the Union, where the organizers first send her to a Union sanatorium in the countryside to cure her cough and then find a place for her in another Union member's private home in Pau. At the end of the novel Marius and Louise are reunited in Paris at the Union's annual Christmas party.

The novel serves to publicize the work of the Union by identifying Madame Lucyol as a member of the group, by describing the many kinds of children that the group accepts, and by explaining the rationale behind Madame Lucyol's decision to seek an independent apprenticeship for Marius and a Union sponsorship for Louise. It also publicizes de Barrau and Kergomard's belief in the importance of individual engagement by showing that Madame Lucyol's money is not enough for Marius without the power of her good example and his desire to make her and his new employer proud. At the end of the novel Marius compares his own situation with the fate of one of his former friends, a young boy who has just been caught with a group of older house burglars and sentenced to ten years of detention. "I would be with him," says Marius, "enveloping Madame Lucyol with a look full of gratitude" in the last line of the novel, "if you had not met me in time."[17]

The first edition of the novel appeared with eighteen engraved illustrations that served to highlight some of the text's major messages. The first illustration in this edition, for example, introduces Marius and Madame Lucyol at their initial meeting in the cold winter streets around Les Halles over the caption "Madame Lucyol looks at the beggar." Another illustration emphasizes the perilous situation of Marius and Louise when it shows them discovering their mother's death in their fatherless family's small attic apartment over the caption "We found our poor mother at the foot of her bed." The final illustration in the first edition rounds out Marius's story and stresses the ideal relationship of affection between the boy and the family that has been housing him during his Union-sponsored apprenticeship when it shows him rushing into M. Tournier's open arms while Madame Lucyol looks on over the caption "First it was the worthy M. Tournier."[18]

Four out of the fifteen remaining engravings in the first edition appear in an uninterrupted sequence that serves to support the parallel plot of Madame Lucyol's successful search for Louise. The first of these, for example, shows the poverty and squalor of the neighborhood where Louise has been living among other abandoned children on a street with the ironic title "La rue des Bons Gîtes," the Street of Good Lodgings. The two subsequent illustrations in the group show two different views of Arcachon, the seaside town where Madame Lucyol takes Louise to recover her health after her rescue: "Arcachon: the beach" and "Arcachon: the winter village." The fourth illustration in the sequence rounds out Louise's story and stresses the beneficent work of the Union with the image of a healthy, happy Louise reading a book in the company of a teacher and several other children grouped under a tree in the garden of a comfortable house over the caption "Louise was placed in the temporary shelter [of the Union]."[19]

Kergomard published her novel in one of the Librairie Hachette's first series aimed at children and their parents, the Bibliothèque des écoles et des familles, in 1895.[20] By 1912 the book had gone through seven editions over a period of seventeen years, a republication record that suggests there were a number of readers who were interested in the story she had to tell. One early Union historian, Jean Aninard, reported in 1928 that the Union had designed a series of special campaigns to encourage parents, teachers, and schoolchildren to donate funds for the Union's work, and it is possible that Kergomard's novel worked to encourage her readers' engagement with the Union in similar ways.[21] When "A.S." reviewed *Heureuse rencontre* for the daily national newspaper *Le temps* shortly after the initial appearance of the novel in 1895, he both grouped it in the general category of fictional works that served as "good actions . . . to affect our egotism, to inspire us with sympathy, and to serve a great healthy and patriotic cause" and praised the volume itself in more specific terms as a book that "simply wants to let us know that there is a great and good society in Paris that calls itself the 'Sauvetage d'enfance' and that accomplishes . . . the best and most urgent social work."[22]

Elise Chalamet and *Petite bonne*

The life and work of Elise Chalamet offer a similar combination of authorship and activism with a different primary philanthropic focus: the provision of clean, safe, inexpensive housing for domestic servants, especially for the many young women who came from the countryside to the capital in search of work. Marie-Emmanuelle Chessel has identified Chalamet's work as a particularly good example of the "mix of genres" that she finds in the work of female reformers, and the combination of circles in which Chalamet participated also serves as a good example of what Christian Topolov has characterized as the "reform nebula" of the French Third Republic."[23] When Chalamet died in 1925 her obituary in *Le temps* described her as a woman of "generous social preoccupations" who founded the first Froebel-style kindergarten in France, participated in the Université populaire movement that sought to provide adult education to working-class men and women in Paris and across the country, and became the "passionate animator" of the Université populaire's associated Maisons universitaires, the residences that one of her biographers described as centers that existed "to procure for young workers, including intellectual workers, meeting places and residences [that would be] well-appointed for study [and] well-suited to develop the taste for being at home and encouraging social culture."[24]

Chalamet began her campaign for domestic servants in 1897 by placing an open letter to the members of the Union pour l'action morale in the pages of the group's primary periodical, the *Bulletin de l'Union pour l'action morale*, that they published every three weeks. Paul Desjardins had just founded the Union five years earlier to encourage interested men and women from different religious, political, and socioeconomic backgrounds to devote themselves to the cause of self-examination and the search for social reform.[25] Chalamet used her letter to alert *Bulletin* readers to the problem she identified as "the question of the sixth floor," the need to find cleaner and safer alternatives to the tiny apartments where French domestic servants lived in crowded conditions under the rooftops of the otherwise luxurious apartment buildings that marked the modern Parisian cityscape. Introducing herself and her fellow campaigners as "a group of individuals ... who have resolved to occupy ourselves actively, methodically, and in a practical fashion with the question of lodging for domestics in Paris," she outlined their plans to improve servants' living and working conditions by engaging "the triple collaboration" of servants' employers, "especially the mistress of the house"; "domestic servants themselves"; and "property owners and architects."[26] She signed her letter with the masculine penname Jean Rozane, a name that she had already used to publish one of her early novels.[27]

Chalamet's open letter to the Union proposed to "facilitate, simplify, and focus—above all focus!—the exchange of ideas" among those who were interested in the work of her new group by sending out "a brief questionnaire" for them to complete before attending a meeting in person.[28] In 1905 she began working on a second series of questionnaires, this time in the interest of working with Henriette Brunhes's Ligue sociale d'acheteurs and its active membership of social reformers and socially conscious consumers to establish a list of buildings that could provide acceptable housing for domestic servants by offering clean apartments with working windows, good light, regular heat, appropriate ventilation, and, whenever possible, a location on the same floor as the apartment of the family for whom they worked.[29] In the same year she directed additional public attention to her concern over servants' living conditions when she published a serial novel on the front pages of the national daily newspaper *Le temps* that addressed the topic under the alternate penname of Jacques Naurouze.[30]

Chalamet's literary alter ego Naurouze was already well-known to the readers of the Belle Epoque as the author of an award-winning seven-volume series of historical novels about the shifting fortunes of the Bardeur-Carbansane family.[31] *Petite bonne*, the short novel that she published in six installments in *Le temps* from May 27 through June 4, 1905, focuses less on the romance of the French past, however, than on the problems of the French present. The main character is Marie Estran, a peasant girl from the Cévennes who comes to Paris to find work after her mother dies, her father loses his livelihood and descends into alcoholism, and her godmother dies unexpectedly without remembering her in her will.[32] Marie manages to find successive positions as a maid of all work, a nursery maid, and a ladies' maid and also to guard her virtue against the servants, local tradesmen, and older and younger male relatives of her employers, all of whom want to take advantage of her vulnerable position far from home. She loses her last and best job when she falls in love and sleeps with her fiancé; he dies in an accident before they have a chance to celebrate their wedding; she discovers that she is pregnant with his child; and her employer fires her and sends her away. In the final installment of the novel, Marie dies just after giving birth to a baby boy.

The novel highlights Chalamet's concern with servants' living accommodations by describing Marie's changing situation in a series of five different urban households. When Marie gets her first job in Paris, for example, the thing that makes her the happiest about having found the new position is the chance to trade her "sordid" hotel room in a "slum" for "a clean room" where she can live "in safety."[33] After she finishes a long, hard day on the new job, her biggest disappointment is the discovery that her room will be all the way up on the sixth floor of her new building, accessible only by a separate stairway from that of her new employers. The corridor is dark, the landing is cold, and the room itself is a wreck: "A stupefying odor welcomes her on the threshold, her head almost hits a low rafter, [and] her feet bump up against a heap of trunks, boxes, broken pieces of old furniture."[34] She cannot open the windows because the rain will come in the skylight; she cannot open the door because there is a terrifying man with a pale face and blackened teeth waiting for her in the hallway right outside; and she cannot even get help from her fellow servants because the majority of them carry on affairs, embezzle from their employers, and try to intimidate or entice her into their own promiscuous and larcenous lifestyle.

Although the novel does not mention any specific philanthropic initiatives or legal reforms that might help Marie out of her difficult circumstances, it offers a different kind of activist appeal in the words and behaviors of Marie's final employers, Mme Biennal and Mme Biennal's daughter, Marthe. When Marie confesses her pregnancy to Marthe, Marthe expects that Mme Biennal will let Marie stay with the Biennal household. When Mme Biennal proposes to fire Marie instead, Marthe comes to Marie's defense as if she were "her sister," compares Marie's feelings for her lover with her own feelings for her husband, and begs her mother to change her mind. When Mme Biennal persists in her plan, Marthe brings Marie to live in the new household that Marthe has just established as a result of her recent marriage. When Marie dies, Marthe and her husband follow the coffin from the hospital to the church, and Mme Biennal cries at the funeral service. If Marthe's speech in sympathy with Marie's difficult situation gives voice to Chalamet's own political perspective on the linked problems of servant misery and single motherhood, then Mme Biennal's eventual expression of grief after Marie's death suggests that Mme Biennal may have come to regret her earlier indifference to Marthe's pleas on Marie's behalf and also that Mme Biennal and others like her might even one day adopt Marthe's generous attitude and seek similarly to alleviate the suffering of domestic servants.[35]

Chalamet's novel appeared in serial installments on the front page of *Le temps*, the daily newspaper that the historian Christophe Charle has described as one of the four "quality papers" of the French Third Republic, "destined for a bourgeois public," "especially interested in [the news of] foreign countries, economic questions, and financial questions," and willing to "leave a large place for literary or fashionable society rubrics" that "attract[ed] cultivated and well- to-do readers."[36] Each one of the six episodes of *Petite bonne* had the potential to reach every single one of the paper's thirty-five thousand to thirty-six thousand readers, an audience that may have been especially sympathetic to Chalamet's work because the journal was the only one of the four journals that Charle has grouped together as members of "the Parisian bourgeois press" to represent what he has characterized as a "center left" political position."[37] When Chalamet died in 1925 the obituary the journal's editors included in *Le temps* made special mention of the "several novels" she had contributed to their pages. While the anonymous author of the piece diminished her achievements as a writer by saying that "she was in no way a woman of letters," the same author nevertheless praised her for her literary work as "entirely an apostle" of social reform.[38]

Louise Compain and *La vie tragique de Geneviève*

Louise Compain, a freelance writer and feminist activist who built herself a reputation as a woman of letters with a social reform agenda, participated in both Kergomard's and Chalamet's networks in many different ways. Like De Barrau and Kergomard, she took an interest in abandoned children, and she worked for their Sauvetage de l'enfance as an inspector. Like Kergomard and Chalamet, she supported adult education for working-class men and women when she served on the founding board of the Société des universités populaires.[39] Compain also participated in Paul Desjardins's Union pour l'action morale, whose *Bulletin* published Chalamet's open letter about the need to reform the living conditions of French domestic servants. In 1905 she joined the founding board of Desjardins's new organization, the Union pour la vérité, and in 1908 and 1909 she and Kergomard participated in the Union's series of roundtables on women's social and legal condition.[40] By the time Compain stood for election to the board of the Conseil national des femmes françaises in 1911, she and Kergomard also shared a commitment to women's suffrage.[41]

Compain combined her work as an activist with work as a journalist and with work as a novelist. By the time she published *La vie tragique de Geneviève* in 1912, she had produced dozens of articles on many different aspects of women's changing legal and economic situations. The list of progressive newspapers and journals that published her work included not only Jane Misme's feminist weekly *La Française* and Alfred Lechatelier's republican monthly *Les idées modernes* but also *La grande revue*, *La revue socialiste*, and *La petite République*.[42] When Lucien Maury contributed a lengthy retrospective on Compain's work to the prestigious *Revue bleue* in 1914, he focused especially on what he saw as her distinctive ability to combine fact and fiction in the service of progressive struggles for social change: "Mme Compain publishes investigations on 'women in workers' organizations'; she investigates and her witness is authoritative. One does not always know whether it is the novelist one is listening to or the social apostle, but their united efforts hold our attention, and we are grateful to this distinguished woman of letters for her double attempt, and for the skillful dosage that prolongs our pleasure at the moment where our zeal for difficult reading might [otherwise] ease up."[43]

Like Kergomard and Chalamet, Compain incorporated her research into her novels and used the results to press for social reform. In 1907, for example, she participated in the feminist campaign to legalize paternity suits by publishing a six-part series in *La Française* on the progress of the relevant parliamentary proposals that included her analysis of the benefits and drawbacks of each of them.[44] In 1912, when she published *La vie tragique de Geneviève* just a few months before paternity suits finally became legal under certain limited circumstances, she gave voice to feminists' criticisms of the impending legislation by including a conversation in which a sympathetic lawyer had to tell the abandoned Geneviève why she would not be able to expect any financial assistance from her daughter's natural father "even if the law and its proposed amendments passed tomorrow."[45]

From 1910 to 1911 Compain published a series of ten articles on "feminine trades and their wages" in *La petite République*.[46] In 1912, when she published *La vie tragique de Geneviève*, she created a whole series of minor characters to practice many of these feminine trades and compared her main characters' incomes to their expenses using the same kinds of concrete sums that she had uncovered in her earlier investigations. Compain's newspaper series, which focused on the futile search for manual trades in which women could make a living wage, included articles on the long working days, difficult labor conditions, and generally insufficient average incomes of dressmakers, feather workers, and artificial-flower makers. Her novel takes up the same themes and topics when it introduces Geneviève's new urban neighbors, characters such as Clémence, who already suffers from lung problems at the early age of twenty-three as a result of her exposure to the feathers she once used for trimming women's hats; old Mother Hardouin, whose eyes are going after sixty years of all-night sewing sessions; and their building's anonymous concierge, "an ageless little brown-haired woman," who has to supplement her housekeeping income by painstakingly turning thousands of paper petals into decorative sprigs of artificial myosotis.[47]

Compain took a consistent interest in the difficult lives of French working-class women whether she was writing as a journalist or a novelist, and French newspapers and magazines rewarded her research on this topic by printing not only her original articles but also excerpts from the novel that it inspired. In 1911, for example, *La petite République* carried Compain's editorial report on the unintended consequences of a new law that had tried to end the exploitation of working women by forbidding night shifts in factories. In 1912 *La Française* and *Les annales politiques et littéraires* both reprinted an extended section from the first part of *La vie tragique de Geneviève* that made a similar political point when it showed how poverty could still force women to defy the law by bringing raw materials home to work overtime at night in their own apartments instead.[48]

When Geneviève's flighty neighbor Marcelle observes, "I hear that they have gotten rid of night work," Marcelle's serious sister, Rose, thinks to herself that the only result of the "recent law that had gotten rid of night work in workshops" has been that "everyone left at eight, women worked late at home, and nothing had changed."[49] Echoing in her fiction the political concerns that she had already expressed in her investigative reporting and associated editorials, Compain closes the chapter with the "buzzing" sound of Geneviève's sewing machine, which "escapes like a sob from the badly connected walls of the old house where so many women are exhausting themselves [in the effort] to avoid death." The last sentence of the chapter, which is also the last sentence of the excerpt, alerts novel readers and newspaper readers alike to the need for immediate action on behalf of women in such situations: "The sigh crossed the courtyard, increased in volume with other similar sobs, and went away . . . without having awakened Justice!"[50]

For those readers who came across the novel independently or purchased a copy after reading a newspaper excerpt that had aroused their interest, Compain used the rest of the work not only to expose the social problems that she saw but also to suggest ways that interested readers might act to address them. In the second part of the novel, for example, Compain shows how the provincial lawyer's daughter Marguerite Varenne has acted "to ease suffering" and combat "human injustices" by moving to Paris in search of her lost illegitimate half-sister, enrolling as a medical student, reading social novels and sociology to familiarize herself with "new information on women's trades and salaries," studying the various laws and "individual initiatives" that seek to alleviate female poverty, and practicing at a hospital that serves working-class women. Compain uses this same section of the novel to incorporate the results of her own earlier journalism on the perils of women's piecework and the need for a minimum wage by highlighting Marguerite's growing interest in "a cooperative store where starvation wages were abolished" and where "a certain number of *ouvrières* were already employed."[51] In the third part of the novel Compain offers further inspiration for reform-minded readers by describing the cheerful interactions of the workers and clients in this cooperative sewing workshop, by identifying the workshop with the existing initiative of the real-life feminist labor activist Gabrielle Duchêne by giving it the same name as Duchêne's own cooperative workshop project, and by placing that name on its own line of type in capital letters: "L'ENTR'AIDE," mutual assistance.[52]

The final chapter of the final part of the novel draws special attention to the importance of women's social reform work in solidarity with other women when Geneviève herself begins to entertain the possibility of campaigning against women's sweated labor by speaking out to convince female shoppers that they should purchase only those clothes and other consumer products that have been made by women who earn living wages. In the last three pages of the novel, the progressive lawyer Raymond Valdier gives voice to Compain's own political beliefs by hailing the significance of Geneviève's new mission in a way that stresses women's work together both within and across class lines. "You are right, madame," he tells Geneviève, acknowledging the importance of her new project by addressing her as a social equal, "it is essential to have a voice to tell women about the sufferings of other women. . . . To those [women] who enjoy themselves, you will explain the ills of the needle-workers; to those [women] who suffer you will speak of the agreement and the association for struggle that will emancipate them." The final word of the novel is "hope," and Compain emphasizes its importance by following it with an exclamation point.[53]

Compain's publishers, her reviewers, and as a result perhaps also her general readers all seem to have especially appreciated her ability to combine a good story with solid research and progressive politics. Notices in two of the most important Paris daily papers hailed the new novel as "both a sad love story that makes you cry and a thesis that makes you think." "There is so much emotion in these pages quivering with life," proclaimed these short announcements in *Le Figaro* and *Le temps*, "that this novel is read with passion by women and by men."[54] Although "L.D.," who reviewed *La vie tragique de Geneviève* for *La semaine littéraire*, admitted that "certain circumstances, [and] certain encounters necessary to the progress of the novel can seem a bit conventional and even improbable," he nevertheless insisted that "the basis of the tale is always interesting and often poignant." Directing special attention to Compain's central chapters on women's domestic piecework, which he praised as "sober, tragic pages, as oppressive as some of the scenarios of Dante's *Inferno*," he concluded, "One feels them to be faithful, absolutely true, we were going to say lived."[55] Even Marcel Lebon, who warned the readers of the conservative Catholic *Romans-revue* that *La vie tragique de Geneviève* was "evil or dangerous" because it treated Geneviève's convent education with a "disdainful manner," still had to admit that the book was "not without merit" offering as it did "a salutary lesson" that worked to "denounce, with a vigorous indignation, the miserable situation of the Parisian working woman as much from the moral perspective as the material one."[56]

The solidarist economist Charles Gide, who had chaired a monthly series of roundtable conversations on women's work in which Compain participated at the Union pour la vérité, contributed a review of *La vie tragique de Geneviève* that was particularly clear on the nature of Compain's acute social observations and the potential political impact of her work in the service of women's labor reform, which he compared to the significance of Harriet Beecher Stowe's *Uncle Tom's Cabin* in the earlier American fight for slave emancipation. "The central part of the book," he observed to the readers of *Le christianisme social*, ". . . is moving because it is alive. It is easy to see that the author, if [s]he has not lived this life, has at least observed it closely, and that, if [s]he has not shared the suffering, [s]he has taken part in the just anger that it incites."[57] Wilfred Monod, a Protestant pastor who worked with Gide at the head of the cooperative movement and reprinted passages from Compain's new novel for the social Christian weekly *La vie nouvelle*, stressed Compain's authority and expertise in similar terms. "Mme Compain knows her sad subject from the ground up," he wrote, "and in *La vie tragique de Geneviève* . . . she puts statistics and firsthand documents to good use." In the final sentence of his review, Monod testified further to the potential power of the social novel by recommending the book's "sincere and ardent pages" for the effective conversion of female shoppers from unconscious consumers into committed participants in the struggle for social reform.[58]

Conclusion: Social Science, Social Novels, and Social Reform

When the literary historian Victor Cazamian wrote his study of the social novel in 1904, he defined it as "a novel with a social thesis, [a novel] that wants to act directly in whole or in part on the relationships among men."[59] Jean Charles-Brun, who offered two series of lectures on "the social action of literature" in the period from 1906 to 1908, demonstrated the connections that he and his contemporaries saw among social fiction, social science, and social reform when he published his resulting book on "the social novel in France in the nineteenth century" as the tenth volume of a series of "economic and social studies" and dedicated it to Paul Deschanel, the president of the Collège libre des sciences sociales, the Free College of the Social Sciences. Presenting himself both as a literary scholar and as a sociologist, Brun concluded, "It is fairly striking to note . . . the translation of public ideas into books and, in exchange, the translation of books' ideas into facts or laws."[60]

Cazamian's study of the British social novel focused special attention on the works of Charles Dickens, and Brun's subsequent study of the French social novel gave similar attention to the work of romantic writers such as Georges Sand and Victor Hugo. While activist authors such as Kergomard, Chalamet, and Compain clearly drew on both realist and romantic literary traditions when they wrote their new social novels, they also offered a range of distinctive portrayals of women, their social situations, and their social reform work that differed in several important ways from the typical series of "women in love, mothers that are admirable models of devotion, and ... [female] victims" that the historians Marie-Hélène Zylberberg-Hocquard and Slava Liszek have identified as the majority of the female character types in nineteenth-century French novels.[61] Where Hugo had identified the promise of social reform with the work of male characters such as the reformed convict Jean Valjean and the idealistic revolutionary Marius Pontmercy, for example, Kergomard, Chalamet, and Compain consistently identified the cause of social reform with the efforts and achievements of female characters that included the Union volunteer Madame Lucyol in Kergomard's *Heureuse rencontre*, the compassionate observer Marthe Biennal in Chalamet's *Petite bonne*, and the urban doctor Marguerite Varenne in *La vie tragique de Geneviève*. Even when Compain introduced the male character of the progressive lawyer Raymond Valdier as an advisor to the female character of the exploited seamstress Geneviève, she nevertheless still closed her novel by putting Geneviève herself at the head of a new social reform movement to improve the lives of working women by encouraging them to band together to help themselves.

While men as well as women wrote social novels that made political points, women's activist social novels may have served a particularly important purpose in a society where women could not vote or run for political office in their own right. The individual cases of Kergomard's *Heureuse rencontre*, Chalamet's *Petite bonne*, and Compain's *La vie tragique de Geneviève* show how social novels could attract attention not only in literary magazines but also in national newspapers and the periodical publications of social reform organizations from across the religious and political spectrum. The reviewers of these three novels and the many others like them that appeared under the Third Republic included not only novelists and literary critics but also teachers, professors, social scientists, political activists, lawyers, priests, and pastors. Serial novels created their own publicity networks by virtue of their standard location on the front pages of national newspapers, and even novels that appeared only as books might receive broader publicity and additional audiences both when they served as the subject of written reviews and when newspaper editors chose to reprint key passages in their papers.[62]

Regardless of where they appeared or what specific causes they supported, these activist women's social novels all worked to gain audience support in similar ways through similar strategies. First of all, they all took a broad sociological approach to the presentation of urban life, its difficulties, and its dangers. Kergomard, who founded the Union pour le sauvetage de l'enfance, incorporated her observations of Parisian poverty into her portrayal of Union member Mme Lucyol's observations of the Rue des Bons Gites in *Heureuse rencontre*. Chalamet, who publicized, distributed, and administered surveys for the housing section of the Ligue sociale des acheteurs, incorporated the results of her labors into her descriptions of Marie Estran's successive servant apartments in *Petite bonne*. Compain, who devoted her journalistic energies to the support of women's rights and the investigation of women's working conditions, received special attention for the scenes of women's sweated labor that she incorporated into *La vie tragique de Geneviève* when reviewers praised the work for providing "illustrations . . . as good as any slides" in the service of social reform and for "put[ting] statistics and firsthand documents to good use" in the construction of her story.[63]

Beyond providing authoritative witness to the difficulties of urban life, however, these activist authors also hoped to gain readers' support for social reform by encouraging them to sympathize or empathize across class lines. The title, opening illustration, and frame story of Kergomard's *Heureuse rencontre* all turn around the importance of the "happy meeting" where the elegant Mme Lucyol reaches out to help the ragged Marius. The final episode of Chalamet's *Petite bonne* features a key scene where the privileged Marthe Biennal criticizes her mother's decision to fire her pregnant maid for preparing to bear a child out of wedlock and takes Marie Estrans into her own home. The plot of Compain's *La vie tragique de Geneviève*, which features numerous scenes of working women's difficult lives in the flower, feather worker, and textile trades, culminates with the alliance between the lawyer Raymond Valdier, the doctor Marguerite Varenne, and the newly socially conscious worker activist Geneviève. When the leaders of the Ligue sociale d'acheteurs obtained Compain's permission to include an excerpt from *La vie tragique de Geneviève* in their trimestrial *Bulletin*, they highlighted its potential to appeal to new audiences, claimed it would be "impossible to open it [Compain's book] without being seized by all the fibers of one's heart and without feeling oneself invaded by an immense pity for the unhappy needle workers whose miserable life appears to us with an impressive precision," and expressed the hope that the passage they had selected would "inflame the consciences" of readers who were not already moved by the power of "dry surveys" and "cold statistics" alone.[64]

From one perspective, novels such as these may seem sentimental in their appeal to emotion, melodramatic in their reliance on improbable plot twists, and even moralizing in their common assumption that the ideal family for rich and poor alike will always feature a working father, a loving mother, and a series of healthy legitimate children. From another perspective, however, they also convey a series of progressive ideals in their consistent refusal to blame the main characters themselves for their difficult situations, in their keen identification of a range of structural problems as the root cause of urban poverty, and in their implicit or explicit commitment to a number of different philanthropic and legal reforms that would improve the lives of women and children. Kergomard's *Heureuse rencontre* presents Marius's temporary turn to theft as the result of bad company rather than bad character. Chalamet's *Petite bonne* presents Marie's initial interest in the man who later becomes her lover as a result of urban loneliness rather than original sin. Compain's *La vie tragique de Geneviève* even works to convince readers to pardon Geneviève's role in the death of her two children by presenting a scene where the jury of the Cour d'assises acquits Geneviève of infanticide on the grounds that "she was not a great criminal: she was only a poor honest woman who had tried to feed her children by her labor and who, desperate [to the point of attempting suicide], had tried to bring them with her into death," a victim of severe social injustice rather than a voluntarily murderous mother.[65]

Female social reformers and feminist political activists such as Kergomard, Chalamet, and Compain worked for public laws and private initiatives that would improve French women's and children's lives across the socioeconomic spectrum. Kergomard, for example, not only supported legislation that would protect children from abandonment and abuse but also campaigned to increase the number of women who served as school inspectors, to allow women to inspect coeducational classrooms as well as single-sex girls' classrooms, and to grant women the right to vote.[66] Chalamet worked to provide better housing options for university students and domestic servants of both sexes, and she also designed a program that would make it easier to organize among working-class women by attracting them to participate in the Coopération des idées, the founding branch of the *université populaire* movement that supported workers' continuing adult education in Paris and across the country.[67] Compain campaigned for women's suffrage with the Union française pour le suffrage des femmes, encouraged the creation of women's unions, and supported women's labor struggles.[68]

Novels like Pauline Kergomard's *Heureuse rencontre*, Elise Chalamet's *Petite bonne*, and Louise Compain's *La vie tragique de Geneviève* combine vivid descriptions of realistic urban scenes with the creation and presentation of imaginary working-class characters whose sufferings give greater import to the difficulties of urban life. Reflecting the politics of their authors and the preoccupations of their times, they created a space in which readers could imagine acting to solve the social problems that these novels helped them to identify. Regardless of how we ourselves respond to the literary and political merits of these stories and others like them, their appeal for the audiences of the fin de siècle and the Belle Epoque indicates the potential importance of women's activist social novels as a source for the further study of the politics, political culture, and public policy debates of the French Third Republic.

Notes

1. Charles Gide, "Le salaire des femmes," *Le christianisme social*, November 1912, 676–77.
2. See Lynn Hunt, *Inventing Human Rights: A History* (New York: Norton, 2007), esp. 32. Benedict Anderson makes a similar argument about the power of novels and the newspapers that he describes in novelistic terms as "one-day best-sellers" in the creation of the "imagined communities" that enabled individual readers to see themselves as members of a greater nation. See Benedict Anderson, *Imagined Communities* (London: Verso, 1983), esp. 26–36.
3. Mary Poovey, *A History of the Modern Fact: Problems of Knowledge in the Sciences of Wealth and Society* (Chicago: University of Chicago Press, 1998); Joshua Cole, *The Power of Large Numbers: Population, Politics, and Gender in Nineteenth-Century France* (Ithaca NY: Cornell University Press, 2000). For work on the history of the professions that suggests the simultaneous development of the related preference for objectivity over emotion, see, for example, Terry N. Clark, *Prophets and Patrons: The French University and the Emergence of the Social Sciences* (Cambridge MA: Harvard University Press, 1973); Donald N. Levine, *Visions of the Sociological Tradition* (Chicago: University of Chicago Press, 1995); Peter Novick, *That Noble Dream: The "Objectivity Question" and the American Historical Profession* (Cambridge, UK: Cambridge University Press, 1988); Dorothy Ross, *The Origins of American Social Science* (Cambridge, UK: Cambridge University Press, 1991). On the gender implications of this shift, see, for example, Jacqueline Carroy et al., eds., *Les femmes dans les sciences de l'homme (XIXe–XXe siècles): Inspiratrices, collaboratrices, ou créatrices?* (Paris: Editions Selie Arslan, 2005); Joan Wallach Scott, *Gender and the Politics of History*, 2nd rev. ed. (New York: Columbia University Press, 1999); Bonnie G. Smith, *The Gender of History: Men, Women, and Historical Practice* (Cambridge MA: Harvard University Press, 1998); Marynel Ryan Van Zee, "Shifting Foundations: Women Economists in the Weimar Republic," *Women's History Review* 18 (2009): 97–119; Marynel Ryan Van Zee, "'Womanly Qualities' and Contested Methodology: Gender and the Discipline of Economics in Late Imperial Germany," *Gender and History* 22 (2010): 341–60.
4. Marie-Emmanuelle Chessel, *Consommateurs à la Belle Epoque: La Ligue sociale d'acheteurs* (Paris: Presses de la Fondation nationale des sciences politique, 2012), esp. 149–77. For additional work on the messy relationship between fact and fiction in the emerging social sciences, see, for example,

Wolf Lepenies, *Between Literature and Science: The Rise of Sociology*, trans. R. J. Hollingdale (Cambridge, UK: Cambridge University Press, 1988); Judith Coffin, "Social Science Meets Sweated Labor: Reinterpreting Women's Work in Late Nineteenth-Century France," *Journal of Modern History* 63 (1991): 230–70; Judith Coffin, *The Politics of Women's Work: The Paris Garment Trades, 1750–1915* (Princeton NJ: Princeton University Press, 1996); Eveline Pinto, ed., *L'écrivain, le savant, et le philosophe: La littérature entre philosophie et sciences sociales* (Paris: Publications de la Sorbonne, 2003).

5. For one recent review of the scholarship on the history of French feminism, see Jean Elisabeth Pedersen, "French Feminisms, 1848–1949," *French Historical Studies* 37, no. 4 (2014): 663–87.

6. [Jean] Charles-Brun, *Le roman social en France au XIXe siècle* (Paris: V. Giard et E. Brière, 1910), 46. For a more recent survey of the French social novel and its development over the course of the nineteenth and twentieth centuries, see Sophie Béroud and Tania Régin, eds., *Le roman social: Littérature, histoire, et mouvement ouvrier* (Paris: Les éditions de l'Atelier/Editions ouvrières, 2002). On the related topic of social theater, see Armand Kahn, *Le théâtre social en France de 1870 à nos jours* (Paris: Librairie Fischbacher, 1907); Jean Elisabeth Pedersen, *Legislating the French Family: Feminism, Theater, and Republican Politics, 1870–1920* (New Brunswick NJ: Rutgers University Press, 2003).

7. These novels thus make a particularly appropriate focus for this chapter because their topics so often overlap with the topics that Rachel G. Fuchs herself explored in her histories of abandoned children, single mothers, women and work, gender and poverty, the struggle for paternity suits, and other aspects of French social history and the French fight for social reform. See Rachel G. Fuchs, *Abandoned Children: Foundlings and Child Welfare in Nineteenth-Century France* (Albany: State University of New York Press, 1984); Rachel G. Fuchs, *Poor and Pregnant in Paris: Strategies for Survival in the Nineteenth Century* (New Brunswick NJ: Rutgers University Press, 1992); Elinor A. Accampo, Rachel G. Fuchs, and Mary Lynn Stewart, eds., *Gender and the Politics of Social Reform in France, 1870–1914* (Baltimore: Johns Hopkins University Press, 1995); Rachel G. Fuchs, *Gender and Poverty in Nineteenth-Century Europe* (Cambridge, UK: Cambridge University Press, 2005); Rachel G. Fuchs and Victoria E. Thompson, *Women in Nineteenth-Century Europe* (Houndmills, UK: Palgrave Macmillan, 2005); Rachel G. Fuchs, *Contested Paternity: Constructing Families in Modern France* (Baltimore: Johns Hopkins University Press, 2008).

8. See "Pauline Kergomard," Dos KER, Bibliothèque Marguerite Durand, Paris; Linda L. Clark, *The Rise of Professional Women in France: Gender and Public Administration since 1830* (Cambridge, UK: Cambridge University Press, 2000), 48–60; Eric Plaisance, *Pauline Kergomard et l'école maternelle* (Paris: Presses universitaires françaises, 1996); Geneviève Poujol, *Un féminisme sous tutelle: Les protestantes françaises, 1810-1960* (Paris: Les éditions de Paris, 2003), 223–24.

9. See Clark, *Rise of Professional Women in France*, 69–73; Laurence Klejman and Florence Rochefort, *L'égalité en marche: Le féminisme sous la Troisième République* (Paris: Presses de la Fondation nationale des sciences politiques et Des femmes, 1989), 154, 157; Plaisance, *Pauline Kergomard*, 10–12; Poujol, *Féminisme sous tutelle*, 224.

10. Pauline Kergomard, *Heureuse rencontre* (Paris: Librairie Hachette, 1895).

11. Their statutes defined "children" as minors under sixteen. "Mistreated children" were children who suffered "habitual or excessive mistreatment," children who were "habitually deprived of care because of the criminal negligence of their parents," children who made a "habitual practice of begging or vagabondage," children who were employed in "dangerous trades," or children who were "materially abandoned." Children in "moral danger" were the children of parents who "live[d] in notorious and scandalous misconduct," who were "habitually drunk," who "live[d] by begging," or who had been condemned for "crimes," "theft," or "outrages against good morals." See *Bulletin de l'Union française pour le sauvetage de l'enfance* no. 1 (April 1891): 1.

12. For some of the Union's early appeals, see "Caroline de Barrau," Dos BAR, Bibliothèque Marguerite Durand, Paris; "Pauline Kergomard," Dos KER, Bibliothèque Marguerite Durand, Paris. For more comprehensive histories of the Union, see Jean Aninard, *Le problème de l'enfance délaissée: Etude sur l'oeuvre de l'Union Française pour le Sauvetage de l'enfance* (Marseille: Imprimerie Marseillaise, 1929); Annick Parent, *Cent ans d'action et de réflexion en faveur de l'enfance* (Paris: Union française pour le sauvetage de l'enfance, 1988). On the origins, implementation, and implications of the Roussel Law, see Sylvia Schafer, *Children in "Moral Danger" and the Problem of Government in Third Republic France* (Princeton NJ: Princeton University Press, 1997).

13. See *Bulletin de l'Union française pour le sauvetage de l'enfance* 14, no. 33 (1904): 1–9. For more extensive descriptions of the Union's programs and detailed tables of its expenses from 1892 to as late as 1928, see Aninard, *Le problème de l'enfance délaissée.*

14. Their website is http://sauvetage-enfance.org/.
15. "Programme de l'Union française pour le sauvetage de l'enfance," bound in with *Bulletin de l'Union française pour le sauvetage de l'enfance* no. 1 (April 1891).
16. Kergomard, *Heureuse rencontre*.
17. Kergomard, *Heureuse rencontre*, 192.
18. Kergomard, *Heureuse rencontre*, 7, 23, 180.
19. Kergomard, *Heureuse rencontre*, 91, 98, 101, 107.
20. On the history of French children's publishing, see Penny Brown, *A Critical History of French Children's Literature*, 2 vols. (New York: Routledge, 2008).
21. In 1890, for example, the Union convinced the minister of public instruction to send a circular that encouraged his inspectors to spread the word of the program among their primary school students; in 1892 a second circular directed them to encourage high school students to respond as well. The Union also published a monthly bulletin filled with stories about needy children as another way of encouraging schoolchildren to share what they had with those who had nothing. See Aninard, *Le problème de l'enfance délaissée*, 18-20.
22. A.S., "*Heureuse rencontre*, par Mme Kergomard," *Le temps*, October 7, 1896.
23. Chessel, *Consommateurs à la Belle Epoque*, 175; Christian Topolov, ed., *Laboratoires du nouveau siècle: La nébuleuse réformatrice et ses réseaux en France, 1880-1914* (Paris: Ecole des hautes études en sciences sociales, 1999).
24. "Nécrologie," *Le temps*, February 13, 1925; Raoul Gout, *L'apostolat intellectuel et social d'Elise Chalamet, 1848-1925* (Alençon: Imprimerie Corbière et Jugain, 1949), 20; Odette Autrand, "Elise Chalamet (1848-1925): Une pédagogue aux racines protestantes et à la ferveur républicaine," *Mémoire d'Ardèche et temps présent* 79 (August 15, 2003): 35-38.
25. See François Beilecke, *Französische Intellektuelle und die Dritte Republik: Das Beispiel einer Intellektuellenassoziation* (Frankfurt: Campus Verlag, 2003); François Chaubet, *Paul Desjardins et les Décades de Pontigny* (Villeneuve d'Ascq: Presses universitaires du Septentrion, 2000); Anne R. Epstein, "Gender, Intellectual Sociability, and Political Culture in the French Third Republic, 1890-1914," PhD dissertation, Indiana University, 2004; Anne R. Epstein, "Women on the Margins? Intellectual Sociability and Citizenship in Belle Epoque France," *International Review of Sociology: Revue internationale de sociologie* 20 (2010): 273-90; Anne R. Epstein, "Gender and the Rise of the Female Expert during the Belle Epoque," *Histoire @Politique: Politique, culture, société* no. 14 (2011), www.histoire-politique .fr; Jean Elisabeth Pedersen, "The Gender of Truth: Men and Women as Public Intellectuals in France, 1890-1920," book in progress.

26. Elise Chalamet, writing as Jean Rozane, "La question du sixième," *Bulletin de l'Union pour l'action morale*, November 15, 1897, 56–60, reprinted in "La question du sixième," *Bulletin de la Ligue sociale d'acheteurs*, 2nd trimester (1908): 68–71.

27. The novel told the unhappy story of a mismatched marriage, and Chalamet apparently adopted the new pen name Jean Rozane to distinguish the work from the three historical novels on lighter themes that she had already published over the pen name Jacques Naurouze. See Jean Rozane, *Maldonne* (Paris: Armand Colin, 1895); Gout, *L'apostolat intellectuel et social d'Elise Chalamet*, 17; and, for further information on Chalamet's historical novels over the name Jacques Naurouze, see note 31.

28. Chalamet, writing as Rozane, "La question du sixième," 70.

29. See Chessel, *Consommateurs à la Belle Epoque*, 175–77. For Chalamet's own description of her work on this survey, see Rose-Elise Chalamet, *Les ouvrières domestiques*, ([Paris]: *L'action populaire*, pamphlet no. 184, [1908–9]).

30. See Chessel, *Consommateurs à la Belle Epoque*, 175–77.

31. Specific volumes: 1. *La Mission de Philbert* (1889); 2. *Les Frères d'armes* (1891); 3. *A travers la tourmente* (1893); 4. *L'Otage* (1896); 5. *Séverine, 1814–1815* (1896); 6. *Autour d'un drame* (1896); 7. *Fils de bourgeois* (1899); 8. *Myrielle, jeune fille de France* (1926). See further Gout, *L'apostolat intellectuel et social d'Elise Chalamet*, 14–16.

32. See Jacques Naurouze, "Feuilleton du *Temps*: Petite bonne," published in six installments on the front page of *Le temps* on May 27, May 28, May 30, May 31, June 3, and June 4, 1905.

33. Naurouze, "Feuilleton du *Temps*: Petite bonne," May 28, 1905.

34. Naurouze, "Feuilleton du *Temps*: Petite bonne," May 30, 1905.

35. Naurouze, "Feuilleton du *Temps*: Petite bonne," June 5, 1905.

36. Christophe Charle, *Le siècle de la presse, 1830–1939* (Paris: Editions du Seuil, 2004), 157–59.

37. Charle, *Le siècle de la presse*, 160. For circulation figures, see Claude Bellanger, Jacques Godechot, Pierre Guiral, and Fernand Terrou, eds., *Histoire générale de la presse française* (Paris: Presses universitaires de France, 1972), 3:355.

38. "Nécrologie," *Le temps*, February 13, 1925.

39. See "Comité d'administration," *Bulletin des Universités populaires*, no. 1 (March 15, 1900), inside front cover.

40. See Jean Elisabeth Pedersen, "'Speaking Together Openly, Honestly, and Profoundly': Men and Women as Public Intellectuals in France in the Twentieth Century," *Gender and History* 26, no. 1 (2014): 36–51.

41. For brief biographies of Louise Compain, see "Elections au Conseil national des femmes," *La Française*, December 24, 1911; Steven Hause and Jennifer Waelti-Walters, eds., *Feminisms of the Belle Epoque: A Historical and Literary Anthology* (Lincoln: University of Nebraska Press, 1994), 94, 133–34, 201; Rachel Mesch, "Louise Compain," in *Le dictionnaire universel des créatrices*, ed. Béatrice Didier, Antoinette Fouque, and Mireille Calle-Gruber (Paris: Editions des femmes, 2013), 1023–24. For a range of literary critical approaches to Compain's novels, see Jennifer Waelti-Walters, *Feminist Novelists of the Belle Epoque: Love as a Lifestyle* (Bloomington: Indiana University Press, 1990), 126–37; Juliette Rogers, *Career Stories: Belle Epoque Novels of Professional Development* (University Park: Pennsylvania State University Press, 2007), 79–111; Rachel Mesch, *Having It All in the Belle Epoque: How French Women's Magazines Invented the Modern Woman* (Stanford CA: Stanford University Press, 2013), 123–43.

42. For one especially important collection of her articles on working-class women, see L.-M. Compain, *La femme dans les organisations ouvrières* (Paris: V. Giard et E. Brière, 1910).

43. Lucien Maury, "Les lettres: Oeuvres et idées," *Revue bleue*, April 25, 1914, 535.

44. See Louise Compain, "La recherche de la paternité," a series of first-page articles in *La Française* that ran from November through December 1907. For the larger history of the campaign itself, see Fuchs, *Contested Paternity*, chap. 3; Pedersen, *Legislating the French Family*, chaps. 4 and 5.

45. Compain, *La vie tragique de Geneviève* (Paris: Calmann-Lévy, 1912), 190–92.

46. See Louise Compain, "Métiers et salaires féminins," a series of first-page articles in *La petite République* that ran from September 1910 through October 1911.

47. Compain, *La vie tragique de Geneviève*, 110–12, 118–36, 140–59, 224–33, 260–62.

48. See Louise Compain, "La loi sur les veillées, est-elle observée?," *La petite République*, April 11, 1911; "Feuillets de livres: La vie tragique de Geneviève," *La Française*, October 26, 1912; "La vie féminine: La vie tragique de Geneviève," *Les annales politiques et littéraires*, May 19, 1912, 443–44.

49. Compain, *La vie tragique de Geneviève*, 141–42.

50. For the excerpts, see "Feuillets de livres: La vie tragique de Geneviève," *La Française*, October 26, 1912; "La vie féminine: La vie tragique de Geneviève," *Les annales politiques et littéraires*, May 19, 1912, 444; for the original, Compain, *La vie tragique de Geneviève*, 152.

51. Compain, *La vie tragique de Geneviève*, 218. See further note 52.

52. For Compain's earlier journalistic description and editorial praise of Duchêne's work, see Compain, *La femme dans les organisations ouvrières*, 115–17; L.-M. Compain, *En feuilletant les catalogues* (Paris: Union pour la vérité, 1910), 18–21. For Compain's successive mentions of L'entr'aide in her novel, see Compain, *La vie tragique de Geneviève*, 218, 260–61, 326, 333–34.

53. Compain, *La vie tragique de Geneviève*, 333–34.

54. See "Vient de paraître," *Le Figaro*, May 20, 1912; "Librairie," *Le temps*, May 20, 1912.

55. L.D., "Bulletin bibliographique," *La semaine littéraire*, September 21, 1912, 458.

56. Marcel Lebon, "Les romans," *Romans-revue: Guide général de lectures*, July 15, 1912, 542, 546.

57. Charles Gide, "Le salaire des femmes," *Le christianisme social*, November 1912, 676–77.

58. Wilfred Monod, "Revue des livres: *La vie tragique de Geneviève*," *La vie nouvelle*, August 24, 1912, collected in the papers of Abbé Houtin, NAF 15696, Bibliothèque nationale de France, Paris.

59. Victor Cazamian, *Le roman social en Angleterre (1830–1850)* (Paris : Société nouvelle de librairie et d'édition, 1904), quoted in Charles-Brun, *Le roman social en France*, 55.

60. Charles-Brun, *Le roman social en France*, title page, dedication, 348.

61. Marie-Hélène Zylberberg-Hocquard and Slava Liszek, "*Marie-Claire* ou la voix des couturières: Marguerite Audoux," in Béroud and Régin, *Le roman social*, 38. For additional work on French women's fiction of the nineteenth and twentieth centuries, see the works in note 41, and see also Margaret Cohen, *The Sentimental Education of the Novel* (Princeton NJ: Princeton University Press, 1999); Alison Finch, *Women's Writing in Nineteenth-Century France* (Cambridge, UK: Cambridge University Press, 2000); Diana Holmes, *French Women's Writing, 1848–1994* (London: Athlone Press, 1996); Diana Holmes, *Romance and Readership in Twentieth-Century France* (Oxford: Oxford University Press, 2006); Diana Holmes and Carrie Tarr, eds., *A "Belle Epoque"? Women in French Society and Culture, 1890–1914* (New York: Berghahn Books, 2007); Rachel Mesch, *The Hysteric's Revenge: French Women Writers at the Fin de Siècle* (Nashville TN: Vanderbilt University Press, 2006); Timothy Unwin, ed., *The Cambridge Companion to the French Novel: From 1800 to the Present* (Cambridge, UK: Cambridge University Press, 1997).

62. On the history of readers and reading under the Third Republic, see James Smith Allen, *In the Public Eye: A History of Reading in Modern France, 1800–1940* (Princeton NJ: Princeton University Press, 1991); Anne-Marie

Thiesse, *Le roman du quotidien: Lecteurs et lectures populaires à la Belle Epoque* (Paris: Le Chemin Vert, 1984).

63. Gide, "Le salaire des femmes," 677; Monod, "Revue des livres."

64. *"La vie tragiqe de Geneviève* par Mme Louise Compain," *Bulletin des Ligues sociales d'acheteurs*, 4th trimester (1912): 171–72.

65. Compain, *La vie tragique de Geneviève*, 311. This brief description is from Compain's introduction to the chapter on Geneviève's trial. For Marguerite Varenne's and Raymond Valdier's more extensive legal testimony on Geneviève's behalf, see 317–25.

66. See Clark, *The Rise of Professional Women in France*, 56–60, 69–73; and, more generally, the biographical works in note 8.

67. See Gout, *L'apostolat intellectuel et social d'Elise Chalamet*, 19–21; untitled announcement, *Bulletin de l'Union pour l'action morale*, April 15, 1901, 22; and, more generally, the biographical works in note 24.

68. See "Elections au Conseil national des femmes"; and, more generally, the biographical works in note 41.

6

French Girls Are the Most Desired

*Organizing against the White Slave
Trade in the Belle Epoque*

ELIZA EARLE FERGUSON

"French girls are the most desired," a legal scholar wrote in 1903, "the most in demand for their esprit and their grace in all the countries of the world."[1] Although France would not abolish its system of legal prostitution until 1946, it surprisingly became the leader in the international movement against the white slave trade after the turn of the twentieth century.[2] The French government sponsored a series of meetings that resulted in an international legal convention against the white slave trade and the unprecedented coordination of laws and criminal procedures among fifteen nations by 1910. France's contradictory position on the international stage—endorsing legal prostitution while opposing international sex trafficking—was the fruit of ongoing domestic battles linking white slavery with a variety of other social issues, from women's wages and women's rights to abolitionism and moral uplift. This chapter investigates the social and institutional networks that produced the many-faceted French campaign against the *traite des blanches*. Across the political and religious spectrum, women and men created an interlocking web of private and public initiatives aimed at protecting girls from sexual exploitation. The proliferation of voluntary organizations formed to assist working-class girls constituted a significant terrain of activity for women in Third Republic civil society. Social networks encompassing reformers and politicians enabled the transfer of philanthropic women's strategies into national and international policies. Ultimately the networks created through these philanthropic activities resulted in access to the nascent apparatus of the welfare state as well as direct influence on the first international legal framework created to combat trafficking.

Analyzing French leadership in the fight against the international white slave trade illuminates a key moment in the international history of feminism that has been little studied. Scholars have richly documented the collaboration, inspiration, and challenges shared among feminists organizing across national boundaries in the nineteenth and twentieth centuries.[3] Yet while activism against the white slave trade is certainly not ignored in international feminist histories, the articulation between women's organizations and state-sponsored actions in the international political arena remains unexplained.[4] How exactly did female activists lacking full civil and especially political rights manage to shape a new international agenda around the traffic in women at the turn of the twentieth century? In France an exceptionally propitious environment for women's activism in voluntary associations combined with widely held ideas about French national identity and the vulnerability of working-class girls to produce government action at the international level. Historians have explored the significance of women's participation in voluntary associations and clubs in other national contexts, emphasizing how they provided a vast field for women's civic engagement and a training ground for eventual participation in politics.[5] In France women would seize the opportunities opened by new laws governing the right to association in the late nineteenth century, claiming real if limited powers to define key social problems and implement programs aimed at solving them. Denied political rights, French women leveraged social capital in the public sphere and effectively set the agenda for government action against the white slave trade.

For French politicians and reformers, gendered ideas about French national identity gave *la traite des blanches* a special resonance. The legendary beauty and allure of French women made them particularly desirable both at home and abroad. "The pimps of the whole world come to Paris to provision themselves," declared an article in *Le Matin* in 1910. "Veritable export agencies exist in our capital."[6] Better to keep French women in France to be available to French men. A few authors did not conceal their disgust in imagining French women in the arms of foreigners. A former police commissioner painted a vivid picture of the fate awaiting the "charming *midinette*" or "trusting provincial girl": "Both girls, without defense, poor wounded birds, find themselves in the same brothel in Buenos-Aires or Vladivostok" required to "lend themselves to the caprices of some bestial Argentine peasant or some Cossack drunk on vodka."[7] Despite the racist tone of this quote, discourse about French women trafficked to French colonies and territories abroad is hard to find, at least until the interwar era.[8] An article in *Le Matin* asserted that France supplied the majority of the women trafficked to the United States.[9] Reportedly in Cape Town, French women were so numerous among the ranks of prostitutes that "French lady" and "French girl" were used as synonyms for "prostitute."[10] This was not the international reputation France wanted. As the social reformer and Republican senator Ferdinand Dreyfus proclaimed in 1905, "Our country must appear once again as the protector of the disinherited and the defender of justice."[11] If French women were especially valuable as commodities in the international sex trade, it was also the special mission of France as a nation to protect them. Jules Lenoble began his 1900 doctoral dissertation on the white slave trade by invoking the legacy of the Revolution: "The Revolutionaries of '89, in a beautiful flight of generosity, put an end to servitude and proclaimed aloud the great principles of liberty, equality, and brotherhood," but he warned, "Slavery even more shameful than the old one, piracy even more odious, still exist today. And it is precisely among the most civilized people that this slavery exerts its ravages. The institution . . . to which I allude, is the shameful traffic in women, and above all in young girls, which is carried on in our capitals, at the door of our churches, a stone's throw away from our tribunals."[12] In the frequent comparisons like this one between the white slave trade and the trade in enslaved Africans, French writers tended to insist that the white slave trade was worse precisely because they, the contemporary, civilized French, should know better. The trade in "ivory" was more shameful than the trade in "ebony" not because the slave was *other* but because the slave was *us*. A proper distinction between the French and other people depended on restoring the image of France as a nation of freedom.

The national interest in protecting French girls from trafficking sprang equally from a new focus on the *jeune fille* as a social problem and new social and legal possibilities for association. The *jeune fille* was an unmarried young woman in her teens or early twenties, whose potential to achieve economic and sexual autonomy was perceived as a source of social disorder. Unlike in other countries at the time, when French reformers and philanthropists talked about young women's labor, they assumed that it was a necessity. France had a higher proportion of women working for wages than other European countries in this era, due in part to its important industries in fashion, lingerie, and accessories. As technological changes rendered women's labor in rural areas obsolete, they migrated to cities in search of work, often without marketable skills.[13] In France it was not a question of whether young women should work, but how best to provide them with conditions that could enable them to make a living. Reformers recognized the economic vulnerability of young women as the root cause of their sexual vulnerability. Although reliable statistics on actual victims of the *traite des blanches* do not exist, activists framed every girl traveling in search of work as a potential victim.

Stories of victims of the white slave trade repeated in the press reinforced the idea that victims were not bad girls who succumbed to temptation but good girls who were just trying to make a living. In 1890 the liberal feminist newspaper *Le Droit des Femmes* reprinted a report from *La Lanterne* concerning the methods used to recruit girls into prostitution in New York.[14] There were the male procurers who sought out girls "dying of hunger" in cheap cafés, bought them a good meal, offered them some kind of contract, and sent them off to Le Havre. Then there were the female procurers, the *racoleuses*, who, the author notes, were even more dangerous, "since they addressed themselves to honest working women" who wanted nothing more than a job. They posted fake job announcements (amid the legitimate ones) on the walls of Saint-Eustache near Les Halles, or the town hall. "Hiring young girls between 20 and 30 years old. Easy work." Then, when pretty girls came to inquire about the position, the *racoleuse* offered them a job as a domestic servant in some grand house in New York. "If the woman looking for a job is at the end of her resources, if for many months she has worked day and night to earn barely a crust of bread, she accepts the position, signs a contract, receives an advance, and embarks. Once she has arrived in New York and she understands what kind of house she has been sent to, it is too late to refuse." Girls could be tricked and trapped by similar methods to supply brothels in France, as in the story of Marie, an apprentice seamstress living with her sister in Paris, who trusted in false promises of a job and ended up in brothel in Troyes.[15] In 1902 *Le Matin* reported on the arrest of two individuals named Beaucourt and Hayum, who had been rounding up girls to perform as singers in a café-concert in Cape Town. Of course there really was no theater, only bars full of rowdy, drunken English soldiers, and the only job available was prostitution.[16]

Rather than being lost to international sex work, girls' productive and reproductive capacities were essential to revitalizing the French nation and race. They were of particular interest in the Belle Epoque because the Third Republic had finally provided for girls' secondary education (1880) and required the secularization of schools (1881–82). Catholic girls' schools were closed, and nuns were removed from teaching in state-run schools. Just as the government sought to instill republican values in its schools, the Catholic Church sought other means to keep girls in its fold. As a result of these economic and ideological factors, new charity organizations for working-class girls proliferated enormously as the century drew to a close. One type of organization was the neighborhood *patronage*, founded in the thousands by Catholics, Protestants, and even a few republicans to provide girls with moralizing recreational activities on Thursdays and Sundays, when school was not in session and working girls had time off. Female teachers in state-run schools offered extracurricular courses for girls when school was out. One author asserted there were 966 courses offered in 1894, and by 1912 there were 15,354 courses serving 174,000 students.[17]

Many of these courses offered training in useful skills such as stenography or cooking, while more informal clubs for female graduates of primary schools sought to entertain them with singing, games, and other wholesome entertainment.

Catholics avidly promoted *patronages* and other organizations for girls, which could "complete and correct" the education girls received in state-run schools.[18] The Catholic *Oeuvre générale des patronages de jeunes filles* specifically promoted the creation of patronages run by *dames patronesses*, rather than nuns, starting in 1880. By 1898 they claimed to have 950 *dames patronesses* assisting 20,000 girls in Paris.[19] To be sure, religious charities for girls had existed for centuries, such as those run by the Filles de la Charité de Saint-Vincent de Paul, but even long-established organizations took new turns toward the end of the nineteenth century. Once they lost the right to run schools, the Filles de la Charité converted many of their abandoned instructional facilities into residences for working girls age sixteen to twenty-five known as the *Bonnes-Gardes*. A Catholic author described daily life for girls in the *Bonnes-Gardes*: "All day they are in the store, at the workshop, given to the hard labor that the struggle for life imposes on them, and to the much otherwise hard work of keeping intact their faith and their honest life of a young girl, in the midst of the dangers that surround them. In the evening, at the family home they rediscover an atmosphere of affection and devotion that gives them courage again for tomorrow's struggle."[20] Shelters like the *Bonnes-Gardes* aimed to replace the lost paternal home and preserve the virtue of working girls.

Jewish philanthropies to assist young girls also grew in this era.[21] In his analysis of Jewish involvement in the white slave trade, the historian Edward Bristow has found that Jews were overrepresented as victims and as traffickers in the late nineteenth and early twentieth centuries, due in large part to social upheaval and persecution in Central and Eastern Europe that sparked massive Jewish migration.[22] France was a major destination of displaced Jews from the East. However, Bristow found that French Jews were reluctant to engage in public discourse on white slavery, "in keeping with the very defensive posture of the community there during the aftermath of the Dreyfus case."[23] Nonetheless

Emily Machen has found that French Jewish women were active in denominational philanthropies to assist poor, single young women, and they founded a girls' shelter called the Toit Familial.[24] One contemporary author asserted that the Alliance Isréalite de Paris saved many girls from prostitution through its mission of education and job training.[25] Members of the Rothschild family frequently appeared on lists of donors to charities created to protect girls.

Political conditions in France made this proliferation of philanthropic organizations possible, opening fertile terrain for women's civic activism. As power in the Third Republic shifted to the republicans in the late 1880s, the government became more amenable to the creation of voluntary associations, not only to promote its ideology among the needy recipients of charity but also to promote the exercise of liberal rights among its citizens.[26] In addition, the Republic needed the assistance of private organizations to implement its social policies. As the state expanded its efforts to provide the poor with medical care, decent housing, and a basic standard of living, it created partnerships with voluntary associations new and old, a crucial step in the eventual creation of the welfare state. It was thus a political necessity for republicans to liberalize French laws on association. Ever since the Le Chapelier law of 1791 banning guilds, French laws governing the creation of associations of all kinds had been highly restrictive. Until the end of the nineteenth century, any group of more than twenty people required government permission at the municipal level to meet regularly.[27] Moreover associations could not hold property or receive bequests without the status of *utilité publique*—being designated as beneficial to the public good—which required an onerous bureaucratic process. Finally, after dozens of proposed bills since the founding of the Third Republic, a law permitting true freedom of association was promulgated on July 1, 1901. Now, upon a simple declaration to the prefect, an association could become a legal entity (*personne morale*) able to receive gifts and own property. This was a crucial development for voluntary associations to ensure their financial security and longevity.

Organizations across the political spectrum, many led by women, immediately took advantage of this new legal framework. On the left, radicals and republicans were motivated by their philosophy of solidarism, which promoted cross-class cooperation to improve the well-being of all citizens, creating programs informed by social scientific study of poverty and crime.[28] On the right, Catholics received a new impetus toward social engagement with the publication of *Rerum Novarum* in 1891. Both ends of the spectrum were aiming to undermine the appeal of revolutionary socialism by improving social conditions and creating relationships across class lines.[29]

Scholars have investigated the differential impact of these developments on philanthropies dominated by women and by men in the nineteenth century. Providing charity was an integral part of bourgeois class identity for both genders.[30] In Bonnie Smith's classic analysis, bourgeois women exercised charity as an extension of their Catholic *caritas*, economic status, and reproductive roles.[31] However, since women's charities were often deeply identified with Catholicism, they did not fare as well when Republicans started making more money available to fund social welfare programs toward the end of the nineteenth century. As Smith notes, funds were diverted from organizations like *crèches* dominated by Catholic women in favor of newer republican ventures founded to help indigent women and children on scientific principles.[32] Sarah Curtis has demonstrated the vast scope of women's charitable activity through the Dames de la Charité and the Filles de la Charité in Paris, arguing that "the philanthropic activities of women became as central to the structure of welfare provision in France as they were to the restoration of a Catholic social order."[33] When the Republic eliminated support for Catholic charities, Curtis finds, work by the Dames de la Charité continued unabated with financial support from the faithful.[34] But tensions arose not only between the secular state and religious organizations. Timothy Smith has documented ongoing tensions between (male) notables who ran local charitable institutions such as municipal charity hospitals, and the centralizing aspirations of the Republic.[35] It was not until the financial and demographic catastrophe of the Great War that local notables conceded the necessity of state funding and with it surrendered some of their autonomy.

In the tug-of-war between religious and republican values and local and national control, philanthropies that aimed to protect girls from the white slave trade were in a unique position that would enable them to take advantage of state funding when it became available. Because all of these organizations—whether Protestant, Catholic, Jewish, or secular—shared essentially the same tactics in assisting girls, the state could endorse their activities without seeming to promote any religious ideology. Indeed all of them shared compatible ideas about the status of girls and why they merited protection. The problem of white slavery was understood from the beginning as one that could not be solved at the local level alone. Whether migrating from countryside to city or across international borders, it was the movement of young girls in search of work that made them particularly vulnerable.

Organizations created to combat the white slave trade were thus expansionary by design. They purposefully created networks of individuals in locales throughout France and abroad and cultivated formal links with other institutions. These social and institutional networks provided the scaffolding for personnel, ideas, and strategies to cross from philanthropy to policy, from female activists to male politicians. Certain activists found this state of affairs to be a natural expression of a gendered division of labor. As Madame de Schlumberger explained in a speech to the Association pour la répression de la traite des blanches in 1901, "An important part of the administrative, diplomatic, and official work cannot be done except by men, whose charitable spirit inspired them to fight against this terrible plague and help us to protect poor girls who are generally more innocent and imprudent than bad. We thank them with all our heart, especially our president [Senator René Bérenger], always ready to take on new burdens; but a large part of the task belongs to us, beginning with our heart, our true, loving heart." Women must not be deterred by a false sense of virtue, she explained: "Where women are concerned, it is *always* the duty of women to act."[36]

And act they did. The women ready to answer this call were usually wealthy, sometimes members of prominent families, and often endowed with impressive skills in writing, speaking, and organizing. It seems clear that France had far more philanthropic organizations dedicated uniquely to girls than other European nations did at the turn of the century, and the majority were run by women. In his report to the 1899 London conference of the National Vigilance Association, the scholar and social reformer Henri Joly noted that France had 1,350 orphanages for girls (as opposed to only 320 for boys), and in Paris alone there were 294 clubs and associations providing leisure activity for girls, numerous institutions offering professional training, and dozens of shelters for working-class girls.[37] None of the other national reports given at the conference came close to France's totals. Many newly founded institutions were small, unique establishments personally identified with their founders. Two homes for girls in Belleville were run by expatriates: the Swedish Madame Andersson de Meyerhelm's Abri de la fillette, which housed about a dozen girls, and the English Miss de Broën's Oeuvre de Bienfaisance de Belleville, which expanded to include a dispensary, an orphanage, an evening school for adults, a Sunday school, and a workshop serving thousands annually.[38] Madame Teutsch (wife of the reformer Jacques Teutsch) created her Maison du souvenir in Paris, which housed girls at risk. Women like these were praised for their dedication, charisma, and self-sacrifice—sometimes including the sacrifice of their personal fortunes in the interest of their charities.

As the nineteenth century waned, some charities founded by charismatic women created new branches and imitators, signaling a shift from the traditional *dame patronesse* to more modern institutional organization. The Oeuvre du Trousseau of Madame Béguin originated with a few girls sewing in her home in 1899 and by 1912 had thirty-three imitators.[39] Likewise the *Enseignement ménager* school founded by the Comtesse de Diesbach in Paris in 1903 spawned 195 schools in forty-nine French departments just six years after its founding, staffed by some of the 470 graduates of her certification program.[40] Inspired by Christian and nationalistic sentiments, the countess sought to change society through the *jeune fille*. "To go to her is to give a hand to the whole nation. In the thought of *l'Enseignement ménager*, the young girl of the people must serve the moral uplift of her class through the cares she will bring to the amelioration of the material life of the domestic foyer."[41] The purpose of the school was to train young women in the skills of running a household: lower-class girls learned how to cook, wash, and budget in preparation for their future roles as wives and mothers; upper-class girls learned to do the tasks in which they would eventually instruct their domestic servants; and other women earned the credentials to open schools of *enseignement ménager* themselves. The Comtesse de Diesbach specifically rejected a centralized structure for her organization, preferring to allow each new school the flexibility to adapt to local circumstances. "It was certainly the effacement of my personality," she explained. "But how can you think of yourself where the regeneration of a country is concerned? A *personal* charity is, by its very nature, destined to nullity since sooner or later it is called to disappear of necessity with the person who founded it."[42] She was an exceptionally active propagandist on behalf of her school, speaking at conferences and publishing a monthly bulletin as well as a veritable how-to manual on the functioning of her school.[43]

Expansion was part of deliberate strategies by philanthropists to spread public awareness of social problems as well as the solutions they devised to solve them. Philanthropic women and men actively created contacts with each other, giving speeches at each other's meetings, publishing articles in each other's specialized journals, and convening major gatherings to publicize their activities. The annual Conférence des oeuvres féminines, chrétiennes et philanthropiques, first convened in 1891 in Versailles by Sarah Monod, aimed "to see a moral link established among all the ladies [*femmes du monde*] who desire to work for the good and the progress of humanity in a spirit of Christian love."[44] This annual conference led to even bigger international gatherings. The Congrès international des oeuvres et institutions féminines was held twice in Paris, in 1889 and 1900, in connection with the Universal Expositions, plus a rival meeting of Catholic charities in 1900. A major activity at each of these gatherings was sharing details about the founding and functioning of different charities with the goal of expansion.

The career of Emilie de Morsier, the initiator of the 1889 conference of women's charities, can serve to highlight the personal and professional connections characteristic of this charitable milieu. Born to a

Protestant family in Geneva, she moved to Paris shortly after marrying a Frenchman. Her experience tending to the wounded during the Commune seems to have launched her into charitable works, but it was meeting Josephine Butler on the occasion of Butler's first speech in France in 1874 that gave direction to de Morsier's energies.[45] The two women worked together for decades, and de Morsier attended and spoke at numerous international meetings of Butler's International Abolitionist Federation. De Morsier's activism against prostitution and the white slave trade also led her to become involved with the Oeuvre des libérées de Saint-Lazare, a shelter for former inmates convicted of morals offenses, which she served as vice president from 1887 until her death in 1896.[46] De Morsier published articles about prostitution and the white slave trade in *Le Bien Public* and *La Femme* (publications of the Amies de la jeune fille), the *Bulletin Continental* (belonging to Butler's international organization), and *Le Droit des femmes* (Léon Richer and Maria Deraismes's feminist journal), as well as , *La Revue socialiste* (an organ of the SFIO), and *La Lanterne* (a republican, anticlerical daily paper). She spoke at meetings of the Ligue du droit des femmes in 1883 and the Congrès Pénitentiaire held in Paris in 1895, where she recounted a vivid story about women forced into prostitution who were traveling to service the sailors in Riga.[47] Finally, with the support of the minister of the interior and Yves Guyot, who was then a deputy from the Seine, de Morsier had the 1899 conference of women's charities officially affiliated with the Universal Exhibition. It brought together hundreds of women for one week to hear reports about charities run by and for women, to tour charities in Paris, and to discuss social issues, a tremendous networking opportunity for all involved.[48]

The major organizations established specifically to combat the white slave trade flourished in France's lively philanthropic milieu and receptive political environment.[49] The original was the Union internationale des amies de la jeune fille (hereafter the Amies), founded in Geneva in 1877; the French branch was established in 1884 and held its first national convention in 1895.[50] By 1900, it counted 8,170 members worldwide.[51] While its organizers were Protestant, the Amies aimed to protect "any young girl called to leave the paternal home to seek her living elsewhere . . . any young girl who is isolated or at risk [*mal entourée*], no matter what her nationality, religion, or occupation."⁵² Thus the focus was on the security of working girls. France was one of eight national committees, each with its shelters (called by the English term "homes"), placement agencies, train services, and networks of friends (*amies*) ready to provide information and assistance in hundreds of towns.⁵³ *Amies* awaiting travelers in train stations could be identified by their logo, a seven-branched star. Homes existed in such far-flung locales as Constantinople, Stockholm, and Pesth, and members were linked through the publication *Le Bien Public* (produced by the international headquarters in Neufchatel), an annual list of *amies*, and a booklet of information listing useful addresses (the *livret*). The Amies claimed they did not aim to proselytize the girls they assisted, a point that one otherwise friendly Protestant minister regretted.⁵⁴

Indeed the main rival of the Amies de la jeune fille was a Catholic organization founded quite explicitly in imitation of it. The Oeuvre international de la protection de la jeune fille (hereafter the Protection) was created in August 1897 at a meeting of Catholic philanthropists in Fribourg, Switzerland. As one author noted, girls were at risk of losing their faith as well as their honor if their rescue was left to Protestants: "The Amies are one of the best mechanisms of Protestant recruitment."⁵⁵ The international office remained in Fribourg, with subsidiary committees at the national, regional, and city levels. The Protection was envisioned primarily as a federation of charities, creating links among existing institutions, although it also instituted its own programs. Like the Amies, it aimed to protect young working-class girls through shelters or residences, placement agencies, a train station service, and a network of charitable ladies who could provide assistance. Representatives of the Protection could be recognized at train stations by their yellow and white ribbons, the colors of the pope. Members were linked through a monthly bulletin published by the central office, supplemented by a monthly bulletin on France, beginning in 1904. This publication circulated reports on local committees and numerous how-to articles for founding a local chapter, school of household management, or train station service. The steps listed in founding a local chapter in a 1904 article prioritized linking with the international organization and publicizing its program before actually establishing local services to help girls.[56]

The Protection grew and prospered through a deliberate and savvy strategy of publicity largely orchestrated by the formidable baronne de Montenach, longtime vice president and then president of the international organization. Frequently praised for her thrilling voice and inspirational speeches, de Montenach was a ubiquitous presence at philanthropic conventions of many kinds.[57] Speaking at the May 1903 meeting of the French branch, the baroness urged the attendees to advance their efforts at propaganda by sending representatives to all Catholic and interconfessional conventions and promoting the frequent publication of positive articles about the Protection in newspapers.[58] In other contexts, she urged participants in the organization to leverage existing Catholic networks, seeking the support not only of local parish priests but of bishops and cardinals. The organization even obtained a special papal blessing, and de Montenach was one of the founders who received an Order of merit from Pope Pius X.[59]

While the Protection was explicitly Catholic in nature, its actual activities come to focus on the economic rather than spiritual well-being of girls, just like the Amies. Writing in the Catholic publication *Le Patronage des jeunes filles* in 1906, de Montenach enumerated the threats working girls faced: "defective placement, insufficient salaries, unhealthy lodging, bad food, and seduction." In de Montenach's analysis, the best defense for working girls was "a precise profession. The good cook, the adroit laundress, the well-trained modiste, in a word, the woman worker who is truly the mistress of a specialty always finds . . . remunerative employment in a nearby locale."[60] De Montenach facilitated links with institutions that provided such potentially lucrative skills, and also promoted the Protection's placement agencies as a reliable source of trustworthy Catholic girls for domestic service.

The latest and only nonsectarian organization against the white slave trade grew out of the special meeting of the National Vigilance Association Meeting in London in 1899. The International Association for the Repression of the White Slave Trade drew together a new network of organizations specifically organized against the white slave trade and linked together in a federation, with headquarters in London.[61] The French branch of the Association pour la répression de la traite des blanches et la préservation de la jeune fille was founded in 1901 (hereafter the Association), with Bérenger serving as president and Ferdinand-Dreyfus as secretary general. Women served in other leadership roles and populated the rank and file.[62] Like the Amies and the Protection, the Association created a federated structure of local chapters, connected its members through a monthly publication, and sought to establish services for traveling girls, including shelters and a train station patrol. A brief summary of its activities can serve to illustrate how it exploited the contemporary legal and political context. As of 1905, Secretary General Ferdinand-Dreyfus reported that the process of achieving *utilité publique* was nearly complete, having been approved by the Ministry of the Interior and the Municipal Council of Paris.[63] The major institution the Association established was the Asile de Clamart, a shelter for girls overseen by Madame Oster, one of the vice presidents of the Association.[64] Located in a suburb southwest of Paris, the Asile de Clamart was a large family home equipped with a garden, rabbits, and chickens, where girls received good food, basic training in needlework, and the moralizing influence of the *directrice*. Originally leased for 400 francs annually, it was purchased in 1904 for the price of 35,900 francs.[65]

At the Association's general assembly of 1906, Madame Oster reported that the shelter had served fifty girls in 1905.[66] Only two of these girls were traveling in search of work (sent by the local committees in London and Marseilles); most of the others had been entrusted to the shelter through the judicial system.[67] Minors who were deemed delinquent or in "moral danger" could be consigned by the state to various disciplinary or reform institutions, and the cost of their room and board was paid by the government. In 1905 Madame Oster reported that the total costs for the Clamart shelter were 5,552 francs, or 111 francs annually per girl.[68] Major contributions to the organization in 1905 included 1,000 francs from the Ministry of the Interior and 500 francs each from the Baroness de Rothschild, the Prefect of the

Police, and the Jewish Colonization Association.[69] Thus a combination of private and public initiatives combined to protect young girls at risk of trafficking.

The Association is significant not only because it demonstrates the spread of similar strategies among philanthropists interested in combating the white slave trade, but also because it provided a crucial link between the largely female world of philanthropy and the male world of state politics, as some of its leaders were male politicians. Specifically the French delegation to the 1899 London meeting of the National Vigilance Association, where the Association was founded, set the agenda that led directly to the International Convention against the white slave trade. The key leader in this effort was the republican senator René Bérenger, popularly known as "Father Modesty" (Père la Pudeur). A tireless champion of moral rectitude, whether through legal reform or the numerous charitable organizations in which he was active, Bérenger considered himself a firm republican and a "very firm Catholic."[70] At the 1899 London conference he proposed a resolution that aimed to engage national governments in cooperation with existing charities. It was resolved to promote government-level agreements to punish "the procurement of women or girls by violence, fraud, abuse of authority"; to coordinate the criminal investigations of such crimes across national borders; and to create agreements among "philanthropic and charitable societies" in different countries to work together to protect women emigrants, a task that would be facilitated by the new Association.[71] Bérenger volunteered to persuade the French government to lead the effort for international legal reforms, and thanks to him, the French Foreign Ministry convened and funded three international conferences in Paris in 1902, 1906, and 1910.

Bérenger's proposed resolution was an extension of his work on the regulation—but not abolition—of prostitution in France, notably an 1895 law that aimed to punish those forcing an adult woman into prostitution through violence, fraud, or coercion. However, Bérenger's refusal to attack the basis of legal prostitution was highly controversial at the 1899 London conference. Reporting on the debates, his fellow French delegate Senator Camille Ferdinand-Dreyfus noted that many of the attendees were strongly in favor of a resolution proposing the elimination of all legal prostitution, given its obvious connections to the white slave trade. "It took all Monsieur Bérenger's presence of mind, all his practical wisdom, and all his personal authority to prevent the Congress from turning into the dead-end of suppressing regulation [of prostitution]," he wrote admiringly.[72] Bérenger and Ferdinand-Dreyfus knew well that countries like theirs with legalized prostitution were far from ready to abandon their systems, and thus persuaded the international gathering to adopt their limited agenda.

Given that prostitution was legal in France, politicians like Bérenger insisted that adult women must remain free to choose to participate in it. At the 1906 meeting in Paris for the repression of the white slave trade, Bérenger argued, "Adult women [*Les majeures*] can freely dispose of themselves, they are, if you like, free citizens; it is very difficult to impose anything on them that is against their will."[73] This view must not be mistaken as a progressive view of women's autonomy, however, for Bérenger continued, "They are prostitutes, vile creatures, who refuse to quit their odious profession, and in this sense they are worthy of little interest. But they are not any less their own mistresses."[74] For this reason, the resolutions of the 1902 conference stopped short of attacking the recruitment of adult women into international prostitution, except where effected by force or fraud, a point that was heavily criticized by social reformers and feminists. Writing in *Le Relèvement social*, Léon de Seilhac pointed out that false papers could easily turn a minor girl into an adult. Furthermore, once admitted to a brothel, an adult woman "no longer belongs to herself," trapped into virtual slavery by a system of debts.[75] It was a paradoxical kind of individual freedom that permitted selling oneself. The obvious solution was to end legal prostitution, but the French refused to discuss the issue at any of the international meetings, insisting that it would be too divisive in their own country.[76]

Even fulfilling Bérenger's more limited aspirations to protect girls from international trafficking was far from simple. States would not only have to revise certain elements of their criminal law codes but also create new procedures for working together across national borders to stop the crime. These were distinct tasks, which the leaders of the 1902 conference divided between two different official agreements addressing legal and bureaucratic reforms, respectively. First, the task of revising national law codes in order to make white slavery a crime depended on parliamentary procedures within each country. Reports from the 1902 and 1910 conferences were devoted to comparing the existing and proposed laws for each country, and the eight-year delay between the two meetings provided the time required for completing this process, which encompassed laws defining the ages of consent and of majority and the offenses of procurement, prostitution, and international trafficking. These legal changes were formalized in the Convention relative à la répression de la traite des blanches, proposed in 1902 and signed in 1910,[77] among the very first international agreements concerning persons not involved in warfare.

By contrast, the task of coordinating procedures to prosecute criminals and assist victims could largely be accomplished through administrative rather than parliamentary means. These reforms were accomplished much more quickly and with much more direct influence from women's charitable organizations.[78] They were enumerated in an Administrative Arrangement, signed in Paris in May 1904 by the attendees of the 1902 conference. This Arrangement required its signatories to create a centralized bureau of information about hiring women for debauchery abroad; to maintain surveillance of ports and train stations for female travelers in need of assistance or traveling with suspicious companions; to investigate foreign prostitutes living in their countries and repatriate them if they wished; to cover the expenses of repatriation if necessary; and to maintain surveillance of placement agencies.[79] It is significant that most of these actions were already being performed by private groups. Both the Amies and the Protection had submitted reports detailing their activities to the 1899 London conference, and the Amies submitted reports to the 1902 international congress detailing its history and activities, including surveillance of train stations and its networks of shelters for lone girls.[80]

Here Jacques Teutsch presented a report for the French delegation, proudly asserting that the French Oeuvre des Gares had already assisted more than two thousand young travelers since its founding a year earlier (October 1905).[81] Women were especially well suited to this work, Teutsch noted, because of the sensitivity it required. "To strike up a conversation with [a traveler], to inquire, without appearing indiscrete, to elicit confidences, to console and find the right words, which while comforting are also warnings; this is assuredly a task at which any woman would excel."[82] Such charitable ladies were not likely to lose their role with the adoption of the Administrative Arrangement; on the contrary, the Arrangement specifically invoked their continued participation, and official delegates congratulated themselves on their states' receiving such services for free. None of the official delegates to the 1902 or 1910 conferences was a woman, yet women successfully framed the problem of the white slave trade and its remedies in terms of protecting young girls who had to travel in order to make a living. Their strategies for patrolling train stations, monitoring placement agencies, and assisting travelers became in effect government policy.

The successful enactment of the International Convention Relative to the Repression of the White Slave Trade, together with its supporting Administrative Agreement, was ultimately a victory for French political leadership and the philanthropic women on whose shoulders they stood. When the republican politician and reformer Jules Simon gave the opening speech for the 1889 National Vigilance Association congress in London, he invoked an image of Paris depicted in the foreign press as the Great Babylon, "the greatest city of pleasures, but of dishonest pleasures," especially since the Franco-Prussian War. Perhaps France did have "the most seductive and most able" courtesans, he reflected, but he urged the women attending the congress to show the world a different kind of French woman. "Tell us what women have been doing for the past twenty years, women represented in foreign gazettes as thinking of nothing but trifles, ceaselessly attending balls and amusements. . . . Tell us about the schools, the orphanages, the charity bazaars, the hospitals, the unhappy people aided in their hovels, the sisters of charity wearing silk dresses and the great ladies who only count their wealth by the good it permits them to do."[83] This statement portrays elite French women philanthropists as the antidote to the pervasive international image of the French prostitute. Providing official approval as well as financial and legal frameworks to support them, male politicians facilitated their work. The French effort to end the white slave trade was thus not only a public-private partnership but a masculine-feminine partnership as well. With the enactment of the international Convention, the nationally specific characteristics of the *jeune fille* developed in Belle Epoque France helped to define the relationship of the state to young women in protective legislation adopted by France and fourteen other countries in the early twentieth century.

Activism against the white slave trade demonstrates the surprisingly great extent of French women's power, despite their status as second-class citizens. Yet it also brings the limitations of those powers into stark focus, as contemporary women were well aware. In a speech to the first annual meeting of the French national committee of the Amies in 1895, Madame de Courteville outlined an impressive list of her strategies for promoting awareness of the problem of girls' emigration. First, she made a speech to the Ligue de la moralité publique in Lyon, where she convinced Léopold Monod to draft a resolution against fraudulent placement agencies. The group's founder, Louis Comte, promised her a series of articles on the topic in the group's journal, *Le Relèvement social*, and M. Gaufrès promised to explain the problem to the Conseil des ministres, where Interior Minister Charles Dupuy also spoke favorably. Then she "knocked at many doors": the bishop wrote a pastoral letter to the curés of his diocese, the prefect sent a circular on the topic to all the mayors, the mayor reiterated an *arrêté* against bad placement agencies and authorized the Amies to open one of their own, and the police chief expressed willingness to be informed of the relevant facts by members of the Amies. Yet Madame de Courteville asserted that all this was not enough: "The best will, the strictest surveillance cannot eradicate this plague, a law is absolutely necessary."[84] But promulgating a law to penalize placement offices for sending girls abroad into the clutches of traffickers was not something that women could do directly. She urged the Amies to gather as much information as they could about girls leaving their districts: "In each city, in each town in the East, let devoted Amies ask about poor children who have already left, excite the zeal of the police, and exercise surveillance in the train stations . . . and all of a sudden one will be stupefied at the extent of the evil."[85] The Amies were to communicate any information they gathered to Georges Berry, a Catholic right-wing deputy from the Seine, who was interested in the protection of children and was amenable to propose a law concerning placement agencies. "How many [girls] enticed by the appeal of travel are lost for France, while they could have become good family mothers and given the fatherland honest citizens. It is up to us, mesdames, if we are truly 'Friends,' to prove that the evil exists, that it saps the vital forces of the county, and that our legislators can eliminate it, eradicate it. As women, as Christians, and as Frenchwomen, our duty is to work to accomplish this."[86] Madame de Courteville had a clear vision for how French women could define the problem of girls traveling abroad for fraudulent jobs and apply pressure to a complete array of men in authority, from the most local to the national level. Yet activist women like her had little more than the lever of moral authority to persuade—certainly not to compel—men in power to carry out her designs.

A dramatic example of this limitation on activist women's power occurred at the 1906 Paris conference, where women were permitted to participate as speakers. On the last day of the meeting, Ghénia Avril de Sainte-Croix got into a very extended if polite verbal scuffle with Senator Bérenger and Ferdinand Dreyfus over the question of when and how the congress should consider the relationship between legal prostitution and the white slave trade.[87] The men argued that the issue was too divisive and advised her to be patient. She warned them of the dangers of putting things off: "What I desire, is not to leave here without putting a heavy stone on each of your hearts. . . . This stone is the feeling of duty that is not yet fulfilled, of questions not yet resolved, of injustice that has not yet been uprooted."[88] Of course the injustice of legal prostitution would not be uprooted until 1946, perhaps not coincidentally the first year that French women voted in a national election. The heavy stone of unfulfilled duty was a weak metaphor compared to the power to participate fully in the political process.

Nonetheless Avril de Sainte-Croix spent the rest of her life working to eliminate legal prostitution in France as well as international trafficking. A founding committee member of the French branch of the International Abolitionist Federation as well as of the French branch of the Association, she was also the founder of the Oeuvre des Libérées de Saint-Lazare, which assisted former inmates of the notorious Parisian women's prison, often convicted prostitutes. She became a member of the Société française de prophylaxie sanitaire et morale, an organization dominated by male politicians and social hygienists, that frequently discussed prostitution as a matter of public health and moral order.[89] Her career is a shining exemplar of women's activism through voluntary associations in the Third Republic.[90] And in the interwar era, Avril de Sainte-Croix would go on to participate in the League of Nations' special Consultative Commission for the Battle against the Trade in Women and Children, and then its Committee on the Traffic in Women and Children.[91]

The foundations that activists like Avril de Sainte-Croix lay before the First World War created significant institutional and legal legacies. The League of Nations Committee initially included representatives from five international organizations, including the Protection and the Amies.[92] Despite discontinuities in the 1940s, similar work has continued under the auspices of the United Nations,[93] and today the wellspring of action against international human trafficking is not any one state, but an array of nongovernmental organizations that continue to promote awareness, aid victims, and hold governments to account. From this perspective, it is evident that activist women of the Third Republic helped create a transnational public sphere where their strategies of communication and forms of action have endured. As the political scientist Ann Florini has observed, "transnational civil society networks . . . tend to aim for broader goals based on their conceptions of what constitutes the public good."[94] Composed of NGOs operating across national boundaries, such networks may exercise only "soft" powers of argument and persuasion, yet they have proved highly effective in shaping norms and policies, often by influencing public perception of problems.[95] In other words, participants in transnational civil society deploy their moral authority to bring about change. This is precisely the modus operandi of nineteenth-century French women's organizations against the white slave trade. Though not unique to them (crucial precedents were set by the international movement to abolish slavery), it is important to note that women deployed these strategies to make the most of the limited options available to them for political action. Denied political rights, they still enjoyed civil rights permitting lively participation in voluntary associations and the freedom to write and speak about their issues, and they exercised these rights to inform a new consensus on the causes and solutions for the *traite des blanches*. From this perspective, the national context of Third Republic France became a proving ground for women's activism in emerging transnational civil society.

Notes

1. Paul Appleton, *La Traite des blanches: Thèse pour le doctorat* (Paris: Rousseau, 1903).

2. On the system of prostitution in France, see Alain Corbin, *Women for Hire: Prostitution and Sexuality in France after 1850*, trans. Alan Sheridan (Cambridge MA: Harvard University Press, 1990); Jill Harsin, *Policing Prostitution in Nineteenth-Century Paris* (Princeton NJ: Princeton University Press, 1985).

3. Margaret McFadden, *Golden Cables of Sympathy: The Transatlantic Sources of Nineteenth-Century Feminism* (Lexington: University Press of Kentucky, 1999); Karen Offen, *European Feminisms, 1700–1950: A Political History* (Stanford CA: Stanford University Press, 2000); Leila Rupp, *Worlds of Women: The Making of an International Women's Movement* (Princeton NJ: Princeton University Press, 1997).

4. A clear example of this kind of omission (in a text that does aim to highlight activism around sexuality) is Nitza Berkovitch, *From Motherhood to Citizenship: Women's Rights and International Organizations* (Baltimore: Johns Hopkins University Press, 1999), 41. Berkovitch skips directly from the 1899 London conference resolutions to the signing of an international convention in 1910. The most complete international histories of activism against the white slave trade around the turn of the century focus on Jewish efforts: spurred by pogroms in the Russian Empire, Jewish women were especially at risk as they sought to immigrate to other countries. See Nora Glickman, *The Jewish White Slave Trade and the Untold Story of Raquel*

Lieberman (New York: Routledge, 1999); Edward J. Bristow, *Prostitution and Prejudice: The Jewish Fight against White Slavery, 1870-1939* (Oxford: Clarendon Press, 1982). Elisa Camiscioli has examined policies against the white slave trade in the interwar era. See *Reproducing the French Race: Immigration, Intimacy, and Embodiment in the Early Twentieth Century* (Durham NC: Duke University Press, 2009).

5. A rich field of scholarship documents women's voluntary associations in the United States and Britain. For instance, the enduring legacy of African American women's clubs in the United States attests to the possibilities such institutions have provided women in the absence of full civil and political rights. See, for example, Deborah Gray White, *Too Heavy a Load: Black Women in Defense of Themselves, 1894-1994* (New York: Norton, 1999); Floris Loretta Barnett Cash, *African-American Women and Social Action: The Clubwomen and Volunteerism from Jim Crow to the New Deal* (Westport CT: Greenwood, 2001); Michelle Rief, "Thinking Locally, Acting Globally: The International Agenda of African American Clubwomen, 1880-1940," *Journal of African American History* 89 (Summer 2004): 203-22. By contrast, scholarship on Germany suggests why women's voluntary associations developed much more slowly; see Rita Huber-Sperl, "Organized Women and the Strong State: The Beginnings of Female Associational Activity in Germany, 1810-1840," *Journal of Women's History* 13 (Winter 2002): 81-105.

6. "Les Trafiquants de la chair blanche," reprinted in *Le Relèvement social, Organe de la Ligue française de la moralité publique*, March 15, 1910, 3.

7. René Cassellari, *La Traite des blanches et le vice, étude sociale et révélations* (Paris: Librairie spéciale du "Detective magazine," 1914), 3-4.

8. At a 1905 general assembly of the Association pour la répression de la traite des blanches et la préservation de la jeune fille, the group's vice president, Madame Vincent, reported that women were trafficked on a "grand scale" between cities in Algeria and the Midi, though she also emphasized that many European prostitutes were from Spain. *Rapports présentés à l'Assemblée générale*, Paris, 1905, 4. In the 1930s, police in Bordeaux documented several registered adult French prostitutes who sailed for Dakar, but they were not, strictly speaking, part of the *traite des blanches*. See, for example, Archives Départementales de la Gironde, 4 M 431 Traite des blanches, Commissaire spécial to Prefect of the Gironde, February 5, 1932.

9. Reprinted in "La Traite des Blanches," *Le Relèvement social*, January 15, 1910, 3.

10. "La Traite des blanches," *Le Relèvement social, Organe de la Ligue française de la moralité publique*, June 15, 1902, 4. He was speaking at the 1905 general assembly of the Association pour la répression de la traite des blanches.

11. Association pour la répression de la traite des blanches et la préservation de la jeune fille (Paris), *Rapports présentés à l'Assemblée générale*, Assemblée générale du 12 mai 1905 (Paris: Association pour la répression de la traite des blanches et la préservation de la jeune fille, 1905–36), 18.

12. Jules Lenoble, *La Traite des blanches et le congrès de Londres de 1899, étude sur la protection de la jeune fille en France et à l'étranger* (Paris: Librairie de la Société du receuil général des lois et des arrêts, 1900).

13. On migration in nineteenth-century France, see Leslie Page Moch, *Paths to the City: Regional Migration in Nineteenth-Century France* (Beverly Hills CA: Sage, 1983); Leslie Page Moch, *The Pariahs of Yesterday: Breton Migrants in Paris* (Durham, NC: Duke University Press, 2012); Paul-André Rosenthal, *Les Sentiers invisibles: Espaces, familles, et migrations dans la France du 19e siècle* (Paris: Ecole des Hautes Etudes en Sciences Sociales, 1999).

14. Leon Richer, "La Traite des Blanches à Paris," *Le Droit des Femmes: Revue internationale du mouvement féminin* 22, no. 383 (1890): 269–70.

15. Jeanne Mercoeur, "La Traite des blanches à Paris," *Le Droit des Femmes: Revue internationale du mouvement féminin* 19, no. 305 (1887): 196–98.

16. Reprinted in "La Traite des blanches," *Le Relèvement social*, June 15, 1902, 4.

17. Max Turmann, *Initiatives féminines*, 5th edition (Paris: Victoir Lecoffre, 1913), 63, citing statistics given by Léon Bourgeois.

18. Turmann, *Initiatives féminines*, 62.

19. Oeuvre du Patronage des jeunes ouvrières, *Rapport présenté à l'Assemblé générale du Congrès national catholique, le 1er décembre 1898, par M. L'Abbé Odelin, Vicaire général, directeur des oeuvres diocesaines, Directeur de l'oeuvre* (Paris: Secretariat de l'oeuvre, n.d.), 12.

20. Etienne Védie, *L'Eglise et les oeuvres sociales en 1900* (Paris: Librairie Ch. Poussielgue, 1901), 46.

21. Lee Shai Weissbach has argued that French Jewish elites had much the same motivations and interests as French elites in general in their philanthropic endeavors. See Lee Shai Weissbach, "The Nature of Philanthropy in Nineteenth-Century France and the Mentalité of the Jewish Elite," *Jewish History* 8, nos. 1–2 (1994): 191–204. The Association Isréalite pour la protection de la jeune fille published a pamphlet around the turn of the century, but archival information on the group's activity remains elusive. Association isréalite pour la protection de la jeune fille, *La Traite des femmes* (Paris: n.p., n.d.).

22. Edward J. Bristow, *Prostitution and Prejudice: The Jewish Fight against White Slavery, 1870-1939* (New York: Schocken, 1983). On Jews and the white slave trade, see also Nancy M. Wingfield, "Destination Alexandria, Buenos

Aires, Constantinople: 'White Slavers' in Late Imperial Austria," *Journal of the History of Sexuality* 20 (May 2011): 291-311.

23. Bristow, *Prostitution and Prejudice*, 216. He locates the most active centers of Jewish organization against white slavery in Germany under the leadership of Bertha Pappenheim (232).

24. Emily Machen, "Traveling with Faith: The Creation of Women's Immigrant Aid Associations in Nineteenth and Twentieth-Century France," *Journal of Women's History* 23, no. 3 (2011): 97. Bristow also mentions the Association pour la protection de le jeune fille (Section Israelite), citing the same document as Machen (*Prostitution and Prejudice*, 274). He sees it as a section of the Catholic Association for the Protection of Young Girls, whereas Machen sees it as "very similar" but not apparently affiliated ("Traveling with Faith," 109n53).

25. Vittorio Levi, *La Prostitution chez la femme et la traite des blanches* (Naples: Imprimerie Castiglione, [1912]), 93.

26. John H. Weiss, "Origins of the French Welfare State: Poor Relief in the Third Republic, 1871-1914," *French Historical Studies* 13, no. 1 (1983): 47-78.

27. Christine Adams, "In the Public Interest: Charitable Association, the State, and the Status of *utilitié publique* in Nineteenth-Century France," *Law and History Review* 25, no. 2 (2007): 292. An excellent overview of nineteenth-century government policies toward associations is in Carol E. Harrison, *The Bourgeois Citizen in Nineteenth-Century France* (Oxford: Oxford University Press, 1999), especially chapter 3. Harrison notes that there were forty-five thousand legally constituted associations in France in 1901 (33).

28. On solidarism and social reform in the Third Republic, see Judith Stone, *The Search for Social Peace: Reform Legislation in France, 1890-1914* (Albany: State University of New York Press, 1985).

29. Not surprisingly, I have found few traces of socialist programs aimed specifically at working-class women and girls, only "La Ruche," a cooperative boardinghouse in Paris. By and large, French socialists in this era prioritized (male) workers' liberation over women's liberation.

30. On women's charity, see Bonnie G. Smith, *Ladies of the Leisure Class: The Bourgeoises of Northern France in the Nineteenth Century* (Princeton NJ: Princeton University Press, 1981) On men's philanthropy, see Carol E. Harrison, *The Bourgeois Citizen in Nineteenth-Century France: Gender, Sociability, and the Uses of Emulation* (Oxford: Oxford University Press, 1999); Paul Seeley, "Catholics and Apprentices: An Example of Men's Philanthropy in Late Nineteenth-Century France," *Journal of Social History* 25, no. 3 (1992): 531-45.

31. Smith, *Ladies of the Leisure Class*, chapter 6.

32. Smith, *Ladies of the Leisure Class*, 156–57.

33. Sarah Curtis, "'Charitable Ladies': Gender, Class, and Religion in Mid-Nineteenth-Century Paris," *Past and Present* 177 (November 2002): 122.

34. Curtis, "Charitable Ladies," 153.

35. Timothy B. Smith, *Creating the Welfare State in France, 1880–1940* (Montreal: McGill-Queens University Press, 2003).

36. Mme Paul de Schlumberger, née de Witt, "La Traite des blanches," *Revue Philanthropique* 57 (1901): 303.

37. Henri Joli, "Report" and "Annex" in *The White Slave Trade: Transactions of the International Congress* ... (London: National Vigilance Association, 1899), 119–30.

38. Mme Andersson de Meyerhelm, "L'Abri de la Fillette," in *Deuxième Congrès International des oeuvres et institutions féminines*, ed. Madame Pégard (Paris: Charles Blot, 1902), 85–87; Miss J. de Broën, *Discours prononcé par Miss de Broën, fondatrice de l'oeuvre de bienfaisance de Belleville au Congrès International des oeuvres et institutions féminines* (Paris: E. Buttner-Thierry, 1891). She was moved to help the people of Paris when she visited the city just days after the defeat of the Commune, and she funded the charity with her own fortune. She reported that this amounted to 27,000 francs in 1888.

39. Turmann, *Initiatives féminines*, xvii.

40. Comtesse R. de Diesbach, *Enseignement ménager: La nécessité, la nature, le programme, la directrice, les résultats de cet enseignement*, 2nd ed. (Paris: P. Téqui, 1914), xxvi, 73.

41. Comtesse de Diesbach, "L'Enseignement ménager," in Action Populaire, *Françaises* (Paris: V. Lecoffre, 1906), 158.

42. de Diesbach, *Enseignement ménager*, xxx–xxxi, emphasis in original.

43. The school was also regularly featured in publications celebrating women's philanthropies. Paul Acker, *Oeuvres sociales des femmes* (Paris: Plon, 1908), 109–20; Action Populaire, *Françaises*, 139–65; Turmann, *Initiatives féminines*, 94–102.

44. Sarah Monod, "Allocution de Mlle Sarah Monod," *Journal La Femme* 13 (July 1, 1892), 102. Monod also directed a Maison de la jeune fille, established with a donation from Madame veuve Febaudy in 1897. It aimed to house office workers and teachers who were out of work, without regard to religion. *Revue Philanthropique* 11 (1897): 634.

45. Emilie de Morsier, *La Mission de la femme: Discours et fragments, procédés d'une notice bibliographique et littéraire* (Paris: Fischbacher, 1897), 139.

46. Edouard Schuré, introduction to de Morsier, *La Mission de la femme*, x.

47. de Morsier, *La Mission de la femme*, 187.

48. *Actes du Congrès international des oeuvres et institutions féminines: Publiés par les soins de la Commission nommée par le Comité d'organisation* (Paris: Société d'éditions scientifiques, 1890). De Morsier served as secretary of the congress and promoted a resolution (which was approved) against legal prostitution and for "one morality for the two sexes," the agenda of the Association (de Morsier, *La Mission de la femme*, 124).

49. Emily Machen offers a comparative analysis of these organizations in the context of travelers' aid. See Machen, "Traveling with Faith." See also Christine Machiels, "Dealing with the Issue of Prostitution; Mobilizing Feminisms in France, Switzerland, and Belgium (1875–1920) (work in progress)," *Women's History Review* 17, no. 2 (2008): 195–205.

50. It is not accidental that the major Protestant and Catholic charities organized against the white slave trade were founded in Switzerland, given the limited economic opportunities for young women in Switzerland and their valuable multilingual skills. The federated organizational structure of the Amies paralleled the federated structure of Switzerland and was easily translatable into an international framework.

51. Sarah Monod reporting to the 1900 Congress, in Madame Pégard, ed., *Deuxième Congrès International des oeuvres et institutions féminines* (Paris: Charles Blot, 1902), 56.

52. Sarah Monod, "Les Devoirs des membres de l'Union: Travail présenté par Mlle Sarah Monod," in Union international des amies de la jeune fille, *Première conférence nationale française tenue à Valentigney (Doubs) du 10 au 12 Septembre 1895* (Audincourt: Imprimerie Charles Jacot, 1895), 36.

53. The other national committees were in Germany, England, the Netherlands, Switzerland, Ireland, Argentina, and Italy (founded in 1896). Organizational structure described in "Rapport du Bureau Central présenté à la conférence national française à Valentigny, par la présidente Mlle Anna de Perrot, le 11 septembre 1895," in Union international des amies de la jeune fille, *Première conférence*, 71–81.

54. Tommy Fallot, *Une Noble entreprise: L'Union internationale des amies de la jeune fille* (Valence: A. Ducros, 1902), 71. Fallot, a protestant minister, was also secretary of the Ligue de la moralité publique.

55. The French national committee was initially headed by Madame la baronne de Buat. "L'Oeuvre Internationale Catholique," *Le Patronage des jeunes filles* (October 1899): 151. Although Catholics often published remarks along these lines, it was quite rare for organizers of the Amies to comment on any efforts or successes in creating converts. See also Hélène

Déglin, "Rapport du comité de Nancy," *Supplément français au Bulletin mensuel de l'Association catholique internationale des oeuvres pour la protection de la jeune fille*, July 1904, 3.

56. Bl. de Beauval, "Comment Etablir l'oeuvre en province," *Supplément français*, August–September 1904, 1–2.

57. See, for example, Hélène Déglin, "Protection de la jeune fille," in Action populaire, *Françaises* (Paris: V. Lecoffre, 1906), 61. Déglin was president of the Protection Committee in Nancy.

58. "Association catholique international de l'oeuvre de la protection de la jeune fille," *Le Patronage des jeunes filles*, July 1903, 107.

59. "La Protection de la jeune fille," *Le Patronage des jeunes filles*, March 1910, 41.

60. Baronne de Montenach, "La Protection internationale de la jeune fille," *Le Patronage de jeunes filles*, October 1906, 126, 127.

61. Association pour la répression de la traite des blanches et la préservation de la jeune fille (Paris), [*Rapports présentés à l'assemblée générale*] (Paris: Association pour la répression de la traite des blanches et la préservation de la jeune fille, n.d.) "Assemblée générale du 12 mai 1906," 12.

62. The creation of the Association had been envisioned at the summer 1898 meeting of the International Abolitionist Federation held in London. The French branch of the Abolitionist Federation was founded in 1897, with men and women on the national committee. Women attendees at the 1898 conference included Madames Bogelot, Schmahl, de Sainte-Croix, Vincent, and Schirmacher. A. de Morsier, "Impressions d'Outre-Manche," *Le Relèvement social, Organe de la Ligue française de la moralité publique*, August 1, 1898, 2.

63. Association pour la répression de la traite des blanches et la préservation de la jeune fille (Paris), [*Rapports présentés à l'assemblée générale*], "Assemblée générale du 6 mai 1905," 11.

64. All of the vice presidents were women, though men held the other offices and composed half the members of the governing council.

65. Association pour la répression de la traite des blanches, "Assemblée générale du 6 mai 1905," 1.

66. Association pour la répression de la traite des blanches, "Assemblée générale du 12 mai 1906," 7.

67. On the power of the state to intervene in the lives of children deemed to be criminal or at risk, see Sylvia Schafer, *Children in Moral Danger and the Problem of Government in Third Republic France* (Princeton NJ: Princeton University Press, 1997).

68. Association pour la répression de la traite des blanches, "Assemblée générale du 12 mai 1906," 8.

69. Probably Madame la baronne Edmond de Rothschild, who was a member of the governing council. Association pour la répression de la traite des blanches, "Assemblée générale du 12 mai 1906," 28.

70. Henri Joly, "René Bérenger," *Revue des deux mondes*, November 1, 1915, 58. "I belong to political and religious doctrines that are absolutely contrary; I am, I hope, a firm republican, while also conservative, and I intend to be and remain a very firm Catholic."

71. National Vigilance Association, *The White Slave Trade: Transactions of the International Congress on the White Slave Trade, Held in London on the 21st, 22nd and 23rd of June, 1899, at the Invitation of the National Vigilance Association* (London: Office of the National Vigilance Association, 1899), 16–17. See also 49, 54–55, for Bérenger's original proposal.

72. Camille Ferdinand-Dreyfus, *Misères sociales et études historiques: L'Enfance devant la justice repressive, la traite des blanches, la réforme du caisier judiciaire, mendiants et vagabonds, les juifs et la révolution, la décentralisation, Michelet* (Paris: Sociéte d'éditions littéraires et artistiques, 1901), 4.

73. *La Répression de la traite des blanches: Compte rendu du 3e congrès international, tenu à Paris les 22–25 octobre 1906 sous le haut patronage de M. le Président de la République et la présidence d'honneur de M. le ministre des affaires étrangères et de M. le ministre de l'intérieur* (Paris: Société anonyme de publications périodiques, 1907), 257. He argued along similar lines in 1899: "Respecting the free choice of the individual our law considers the adult woman as capable of defending herself against suggestions from [others]" (National Vigilance Association, *The White Slave Trade*, 47).

74. *La Répression de la traite des blanches*, 258.

75. Léon de Seilhac, "Interdiction absolue de la traite des blanches," *Le Relèvement Social*, November 1, 1902, 3.

76. Along similar lines, commenting on a sensational case where a Swiss girl jumped out of a window to escape a legal brothel in Geneva, one feminist noted, "It is not only in Geneva, it is everywhere that prostitution is 'authorized' that the unhappy inmates of public establishments are well and truly kept prisoner, despite their protests and their tears." Georges Bath, "La Traite des blanches," *Le Droit des Femmes* 20, no. 327 (1888): 176–77.

77. The Convention defined the offense of participating in the white slave trade. In 1902 it was accompanied by a "Protocol de Clôture," affirming the solemn recommendation of the delegates that their respective nations each take steps to comply with, and eventually ratify, the Convention itself. The signatories were Germany, Austria, Hungary, Belgium, Brazil, Denmark, Spain, France, Great Britain, Italy, the Netherlands, Portugal,

Russia, Sweden, and Switzerland. Norway had sent a delegation in 1902 but not in 1910. For the full text of the convention and the conference proceedings, see Ministère des Affaires Etrangères, *Documents Diplomatiques: Deuxième Conférence internationale pour la répression de la traite des blanches (18 avril–4 mai 1910)* (Paris: Imprimerie Nationale, 1910).

78. The law professor Louis Renault observed that private initiative had paved the way for public initiative in several other recent areas, citing the Union international pour la propriété industrielle, L'Union internationale pour la protection des oeuvres littéraires et artistiques, and even a private conference in Geneva in 1863 that led to the diplomatic conference that produced the famous Geneva Convention. See Louis Renault, *La "Traite des blanches" et la conférence de Paris au point de vue du droit international* (Paris: A. Pedone, 1902), 4–5.

79. Ministère des Affaires Etrangères, *Documents Diplomatiques: Conférence internationale pour la répression de la traite des blanches* (Paris: Imprimerie Nationale, 1902), 209–210.

80. Ministère des Affaires Etrangères. *Documents Diplomatiques: Conférence internationale*, 96–99.

81. Ministère des Affaires Etrangères. *Documents Diplomatiques: Conférence internationale*, 25–42.

82. Ministère des Affaires Etrangères. *Documents Diplomatiques: Conférence internationale*, 39.

83. *Actes du Congrès international des oeuvres et institutions féminines*, xiv.

84. "Emigration des jeunes fille, Rapport de Madame de Courteville," in *Union internationale des amies de la jeune fille, première conférence française tenue à Valentigney (Doubs) du 10 au 12 Septembre 1895* (Audincourt: Charles Jacot, 1895), 45.

85. "Emigration des jeunes fille," 42.

86. "Emigration des jeunes fille," 49.

87. *La Répression de la traite des blanches: Compte rendu du 3e congrès international, tenu à Paris les 22–25 octobre 1906 sous le haut patronage de M. le Président de la République et la présidence d'honneur de M. le ministre des affaires étrangères et de M. le ministre de l'intérieur* (Paris: Société anonyme de publications périodiques, 1907), 218–94.

88. *La Répression de la traite des blanches*, 285.

89. "Correspondance," *Bulletin de la Société française de prophylaxie sanitaire et morale*, September 10, 1902, 277.

90. For an overview of Avril de Sainte-Croix's work, see Karen Offen, "Madame Ghénia Avril de Sainte-Croix, the Josephine Butler of France," *Women's History Review* 17, no. 2 (2008): 239–55.

91. Ghénia Avril de Sainte-Croix, "Commission de la Société des Nations," *International Women Suffrage News* 9, no. 18 (1924): 142. On the continued controversy over abolitionism, see Jessica R. Pliley, "Claims to Protection: The Rise and Fall of Feminist Abolitionism in the League of Nations' Committee on the Traffic in Women and Children, 1919–1936," *Journal of Women's History* 22, no. 4 (2010): 90–113. Pliley finds that feminist women activists lost their influence on the committee when representatives from women's voluntary organizations were excluded in the 1930s (105).

92. Pliley, "Claims to Protection," 95.

93. The UN Inter-Agency Coordination Group against Trafficking in Persons would look very familiar to someone like Avril de Sainte-Croix (http://icat .network).

94. Ann Florini, introduction to *The Third Force: The Rise of Transnational Civil Society*, ed. Ann Florini (Tokyo: Japan Center for International Exchange and Carnegie Endowment for International Peace, 2000), 7. On the creation of the transnational public sphere, see also John A. Guidry, Michael Kennedy, and Mayer N. Zald, eds., *Globalizations and Social Movements: Culture, Power, and the Transnational Public Sphere* (Ann Arbor: University of Michigan Press, 2000).

95. Florini, introduction to *The Third Force*, 11.

7

Vérine, the Ecole des Parents, and the Politics of Gender, Reaction, and the Family, 1929–1944

CHERYL A. KOOS

In a 1932 article that appeared in the left-leaning social Catholic newspaper, *La Jeune République*, Madeleine LeComte reviewed a volume containing the proceedings of the Ecole des Parents' 1931 conference, titled "La Jeunesse" (Youth). While positively reviewing one essay by the noted child psychology expert André Berge, LeComte had harsh words for the rest of the presentations, which, according to her, were "only banalities." One of the most troublesome was a speech by the pronatalist leader General L. Borie that asserted the preeminence of French culture "at the head of civilization" and decried efforts to promote disarmament and peace. Calling Borie's ideas "dead," she asserted, "*Tant pis* for those who want to revive them; thus the Ecole des Parents should not be surprised at their failures."[1]

Obviously LeComte did not agree with the ultranationalist tone of the conference. She made her opinions clear: while she approved in theory of the purpose of the Ecole des Parents to promote better child rearing, she warned in the title of her article that it should not become "the school of nationalism."[2] If one were to examine the rest of the roster for the 1931 conference as well as those of its six conferences held between 1929 and 1935, one would find some of the most prominent nationalists of the 1920s and 1930s, including many natalist-familialists, like-minded legislators, and extreme rightists, as well as a host of Catholic nationalist educators and professionals.

Founded in 1929 by the social Catholic writer and activist Marguerite Lebrun, better known by her pseudonym "Vérine," and several of her associates who were concerned about diminishing parental authority, the Ecole des Parents was established as an entity that would educate parents of all social classes in their proper roles as the moral educators of their children. Lebrun, like many conservatives in France, was perplexed by the perceived moral laxity that pervaded the country following the Great War. A bourgeois Catholic wife and mother of several children, she was deeply troubled by what she viewed as a rampant individualism that had weakened the nation in many ways, leading men and women to forsake their God-ordained roles as fathers and mothers and thus compromising the nation's physical and moral integrity through a declining birthrate and the embrace of modernity. With the organization's philosophy as articulated by its primary founder and spokesperson, its ties to nationalist leaders within the natalist-familialist movement, and her later involvement in the promotion and crafting of Vichy family policy, however, the Ecole des Parents and Vérine became much more in the 1930s and early 1940s; they became vehicles for inculcating nationalist values throughout the country and among diverse social classes. As such, the Ecole acted as one of several bridges between social Catholic activists, many of whom were women, and a network of conservative, nationalist, and natalist-familialist male politicians, educators, and professionals, a bridge that would eventually help rally support for Vichy's National Revolution, which would embody many of the tenets that Vérine, her associates, and the Ecole des Parents would value and promote in the 1930s.

However, the relationship between Vérine, the Ecole des Parents, and nationalism does more than highlight the ways in which right-wing politics and gender intersected in the 1930s and 1940s. As scholars such as Anne Cova, Laura Lee Downs, Kevin Passmore, Magali della Sudda, and Caroline Campbell have discussed, conservative, often Catholic French women, like their overtly feminist counterparts, found myriad ways to engage politically in the public sphere while lacking formal voting rights.[3] Engaging in "practiced citizenship," as the other chapters in this volume demonstrate, enabled these women to craft meaningful social relationships outside the home, become political subjects, and exercise a modicum of political power and influence. Often the formation of and participation in organizations that focused on children, family structure and welfare, faith, or a combination of these areas, all within the orbit of acceptable definitions of traditional bourgeois Catholic womanhood, allowed these women to gain access to overwhelmingly male political networks, like that of the pronatalists and familialists of the early twentieth century, and become valued and honored for their activism by their male peers while exerting an influence on state policy.[4] Institutions such as the Ecole des Parents and the Union féminine civique et sociale became culturally and politically acceptable vehicles for women's social and political activism because their focus and work reinforced conservative formulations of gender roles and the family and, by doing so, furthered the policies of conservative and reactionary political parties and extraparliamentary leagues such as the Croix de Feu. Vérine and her female associates in the Ecole des Parents and Catholic social action demonstrate that these formulations were not solely the terrain of men who may have had a vested interest in upholding and cementing traditional gender roles in their political philosophies and policies, but that women also used and advanced acceptable notions of gender to expand their own personal scope of influence in these networks and state structures in concrete ways while reinforcing their own exclusion from formal participation in politics.

Indeed the formation of the Ecole des Parents in 1929 and Vérine and her compatriots' involvement in social issues did not happen in a vacuum. Following France's defeat in the Franco-Prussian War in 1871, the nation's political culture became obsessed with the decline in the French birthrate; after all, its plans for *revanche* against a newly unified Germany would succeed only if it had enough soldiers in the future to wage a successful war that would recapture the lost provinces of Alsace and Lorraine and restore French dominance in continental Europe. While politicians and cultural commentators on the left and the right campaigned against *dépopulation* and *dénatalité* with equal vigor prior to the Great War, the devastation to the French male population, resurgent nationalism, and a conservative political surge that accompanied the war's aftermath skewed the debate about these issues decidedly to the right. Conservative, predominantly Catholic men and women founded and joined radical extraparliamentary political leagues and issue-oriented social organizations to advance their vision of France, one that eschewed disruptive modern gender roles that gave women greater cultural and economic freedom and that were perceived to be accompanied by a shift in morality, valorized traditional gender hierarchies and family structures set forth by the nineteenth-century social theorist Frédéric Le Play, and condemned what they saw as the pernicious effects of over a century of republican individualism.[5]

According to organizational lore, Vérine founded the Ecole des Parents after one of the participants of a meeting on sex education cried out, "There should be a school for parents!"[6] Vérine and her associates Mme G. Jean Camus and Joseph Wilbois, though, did not form the organization out of a vacuum. Vérine and Camus were active members of the Catholic women's group, the Union féminine civique et sociale (UFCS), founded by the social Catholic activist Andrée Butillard in 1925. Like many organizations in the social Catholic and natalist-familialist milieu of the 1920s and 1930s, the UFCS railed against rampant individualism and sought to restore the family as the top priority of French politics and society.[7] Butillard shaped her organization with the help of social Catholic participants like Vérine and Camus who were concerned with increasingly pervasive secularism and "demoralization" throughout society. As the historian Susan Pedersen notes, the doctrine of female, particularly maternal self-sacrifice was central to the UFCS mission.[8] Echoing this sentiment, Vérine opined in 1925, "The wife, the mother is a 'person,' but a person who only finds her real identity in the most total and complete self-abnegation. . . . It is not law that has made us slaves. . . . It is Love. The one who says 'I belong to myself'" and not 'I belong to them,' that one is not worthy of being a woman and a mother. . . . Woman is not made by man, but she is made for man, for the child, for the home."[9] Based on Vérine's writings about motherhood and her public activism opposing sex education in *lycées*, Camus and her UFCS colleague, Mlle Hallette, recruited her to write a series of six articles on the subject for the UFCS newspaper, *La Femme dans la vie sociale*, all of which appeared between November 1927 and June 1928.[10]

As a result of her activity in the UFCS on the group's Public Morality Commission and her early books on child rearing that opposed sex education in state schools, Vérine became a sought-after speaker in a variety of venues. She was recruited by the banker Albert Kahn's think tank, the Comité National des Etudes Sociales et Politiques, to participate in a panel discussion with Abbé Jean Viollet and several physicians and psychologists on the importance of marriage, a meeting that was held on April 30, 1928 at the Cours de Cassation in Paris.[11] All conference speakers emphasized marriage as the "essential fundamental institution of society," with the essential goal of marriage being "procreating children and raising them" within the context of values and traditional morality.[12] Familiar to the world of medicine as both the daughter of a wealthy physician and the wife of the suburban Parisian pathologist Emile Lebrun, Vérine combined a stance on scientific education with one that expanded the issue to a social problem related to bourgeois modesty.[13] To circumvent the larger problems, she proposed that parents, particularly mothers, must be imbued with confidence in order to resume their function as the moral educators of their children. To that end she implored mothers to be brave and courageous in educating their sons and daughters about premarital chastity and the proper place of sex within marriage, saying that "conjugal happiness of sons and daughters is made possible from the cradle by [the mother's] education in self-control." She added, somewhat sarcastically, that the state could not feasibly begin sex education so early.[14] She concluded that it was marriage that made all this necessary work possible and, within that context, mandated that mothers teach other mothers about the education of the senses and feelings of their children and that the "veneration of the family, based on conjugal love, was the basis of individual happiness."[15] Encouraged by conference attendees to form an "école des parents" that would do just that, Vérine and her UFCS associate Camus, a member of the

Comité departemental de la natalité, president of the Association des Mères françaises, and mother of twelve, approached the UFCS president Butillard with the idea and received permission to found the Ecole des Parents as an auxiliary organization to the UFCS that would sponsor educational sessions to reach parents across social classes in a variety of venues.[16]

As evident in Vérine's early speeches and writings, the Ecole des Parents from its beginning intended to instill in mothers and fathers traditional and patriarchal values that they would then teach their children and thus make the French family a bulwark against what its founders perceived as the license and lax morality of the modern age. Its educational model was hierarchical and rational as well; experts in morality, religion, child development, organization, and a wide range of issues that affected the family would educate parents to provide a certain type of moral leadership in the home and to function as the primary educators of their children. To that end Vérine and Camus invited Joseph Wilbois, a committed social Catholic educator and the director of the Ecole d'Administration et d'Affaires, to join them as they launched the organization in January 1929.

That they asked Wilbois to join them illustrates Vérine's and Camus's connections to a larger world of Catholic social action and a network of technocratic experts that viewed the traditional patriarchal family as fundamental to social organization in the model of the influential social theorist Frédéric Le Play.[17] As the historian Jackie Clarke has shown, Wilbois was part of an extensive group of engineers, educators, and businessmen who were adherents of Henri Fayol, a French organizational science innovator and engineer turned management theorist.[18] Like Fayol, Wilbois focused on managerial efficiency and was particularly concerned with leadership development. As an educator who taught at the Ecole des Roches, a private boarding school founded on the English public school model by Edmond Demolins with connections to the scouting founder Robert Baden-Powell, he integrated Fayol's ideas into his own theories on leadership education.[19] At his Ecole d'Administration et d'Affaires, Wilbois offered courses that emphasized *administration de soi* (self-management) and the primacy of leadership; he fervently believed that "the leader's personality must 'penetrate the souls of his subordinates,' turning weak elements into strong ones."[20] By substituting "parent" for "leader" and "children" for "subordinate," Vérine echoed Wilbois's formulations in her own work; similarly his emphasis on "self-management" found voice in her advocacy of *maîtrise de soi* (self-control). By persuading him to join their enterprise and by enlisting his aid in publicizing their venture in his social and professional circles, Vérine and Camus concretized Wilbois's influence on their organization and capitalized on his connections, lending more credibility to their efforts.[21]

With Wilbois on board, the three quickly planned the new organization's first activities, which included a press event organized by Wilbois at Vérine's home and a series of five conferences focusing on *éducation morale* to be held at Wilbois's Ecole d'Administration, featuring Wilbois, Vérine, Camus, the physicians Henri Abrand and Maurice Monsaingeon, president of the Ligue des Familles Nombreuses de France. The first conference, in January 1929, featured Wilbois discussing the current state of the French family. In attendance was the noted natalist-familialist Paul Haury, the editor of the *Revue de l'Alliance Nationale pour l'accroissement de la population française*, who reported on the meeting in the organization's journal. According to Haury, Wilbois focused on five "conditions of modern life that put the family in danger": "popular theories on pleasurable love" that promoted birth control and eroded parental authority; the lack of solid principles or methods of education in an age when children were escaping the influence of their parents; economic conditions associated with the rise of industry in large cities that increasingly removed women and children from the family; the family being "weakened by the State," caught in the crossfire between the intrusive centralized republican state and the individual; and the material difficulties related to the moral and material consequences of the Great War that purportedly diminished the number of marriages and births. Wilbois concluded his speech by praising organizations that strengthened the family, "the most efficacious agent of a people's spiritual formation." Saluting the new organization's emphasis on encouraging mothers and fathers to become aware of their familial, social, and national responsibilities, Haury, an educator himself, applauded the Ecole des Parents' efforts to promote the mutual education of parents and teachers to combat the dangers that Wilbois identified.[22]

With the help of well-connected men like Wilbois, Haury, and Monsaingeon, Vérine and Camus sought to expand the scope and reach of the fledgling organization. On May 17, 1929, the two women met with the UFCS leadership, including President Butillard, to discuss plans to hold a large conference at the Musée Social, a Parisian hub of social reform activity since 1895.[23] The true purpose of the meeting, though, was to make the case for the independence of the Ecole des Parents, an "oeuvre familiale," from the UFCS, an "oeuvre catholique." They successfully argued that for the Ecole des Parents to be successful in its mission to "serve all," it needed to be viewed as neutral and not as an extension of a particular creed. Convinced of this, Butillard, Vérine, and Camus mutually and in a "friendly manner" agreed that the new organization would be autonomous from the UFCS.[24] Seven days later Vérine, Camus, and Wilbois, along with Drs. Monsaingeon, Abrand, and Pasteau, met at Vérine's home to formulate plans for the Ecole's first conference on the subject of childhood.

The organization's independence from the UFCS, however, came at a short-term cost, as the Ecole des Parents lost its headquarters and financial support; however, the situation lent itself to an association that would reap long-term benefits. To shore up such logistical support, Vérine convinced Camus to approach an existing strong organization to help them. After much deliberation, they decided that the Alliance Nationale, having, as Vérine described, "a formula that approximated theirs," would be the type of collaboration that the Ecole des Parents needed. To that end, in November 1929 Vérine met with Paul Haury, Alliance Nationale board member and propagandist, and proposed that, in exchange for financial support, the Ecole des Parents would add a new educative goal that would "complete [the Alliance Nationale's] pronatalist teachings, the birthrate being above all a problem of moral education." Haury agreed to advocate for the collaboration between the two organizations and set up a meeting with Vérine with Alliance Nationale's president, Paul Lefebvre-Dibon, its business manager, General Borie, and himself. At that meeting it was agreed that the Alliance Nationale would receive a portion of the Ecole des Parents' membership dues in exchange for advertisements in the Alliance's journal and office support. In addition Borie and Haury would join the Ecole des Parents' administrative council (Borie eventually becoming vice president) and Vérine became a frequent book review contributor to the Alliance Nationale's *Revue*.[25] Borie would also help the organization achieve official recognition by the Chamber of Deputies on February 6, 1930.[26] Additionally, as the minutes of the Alliance Nationale's administrative council would note, President Lefebvre-Dibon and longtime member Auguste Isaac would join the Ecole's sponsorship committee; Lefebvre-Dibon, in asking the council to authorize officially the collaboration between the two organizations, noted that the Ecole des Parents had the "same goals" as the Alliance Nationale, namely "the restoration of an *esprit familial* in France."[27]

The collaboration between Vérine, the Ecole des Parents, and the Alliance Nationale proved to be mutually beneficial to both organizations. The Alliance Nationale gave financial stability and legitimacy to the fledgling Ecole des Parents and provided Vérine access to its members, including a wide array of natalist-familialist politicians, organizational leaders, and professionals. The Ecole des Parents contributed forthrightly to the Alliance's efforts to reinforce its familialist credentials alongside its more firmly established pronatalist agenda and gave its claims to be both *nataliste et familiale* credibility. Indeed at the conclusion of the first major conference held by the Ecole des Parents, Vérine saluted Lefebvre-Dibon and Haury pointedly and asserted, "Far too many people think that the Alliance Nationale is only concerned about the birthrate; its directors are certainly all pronatalists but they are also *familiaux* and educators."[28]

Vérine and the Ecole des Parents, though, should be viewed as benefiting the most from this collaboration. Indeed their visibility in the network of natalist-familialist activists and organizations increased dramatically after joining forces with the Alliance Nationale and after the success of its first conference. The organization's all-encompassing motto, "To Unite, to Instruct, to Serve," echoed the missions of other natalist-familialist and social Catholic family-focused organizations and educational institutions throughout France. Its board of directors and its yearly conferences would come to boast impressive rosters of natalist-familialist leaders. For its first conference, held in December 1929, Vérine and Camus secured the participation of prominent figures such as Georges Pernot, recently named minister of public works; longtime deputy and familialist leader Auguste Isaac; Gaston Lacoin, vice president of La Plus Grande Famille; Georges Risler, president of the Musée Social; Professor Pierre Bazy, a member of the Académie de Médecine and the Institut; and Lefebvre-Dibon of the Alliance Nationale, among others. Following the success of that conference, Gustave Bonvoisin, the managing director of the Comité Central des Allocations Familiales and an Alliance Nationale board member; Paul Hunziker, president of the Fédération des Associations des Parents d'élèves des lycées et collèges; and Robert Garric, the founder of a social Catholic version of scouting called the Equipes Sociales, all participated on the Ecole des Parents' administrative council or conference planning committees.[29]

Much like its fellow natalist-familialist organizations would in the 1920s and 1930s, the Ecole des Parents' defense of parental rights and family-based education would become infused with a doctrine of nationalism that would solidify support for such organizations and political legislation on the political right. In fact the Ecole des Parents began this decided drift to the nationalist right not long after it began collaborating with the Alliance Nationale. Not only did many of its conference speakers come from a conservative religious, social, and/ or political orientation, but many, including but not limited to Borie, Haury, Pernot, Bonvoisin, Garric, and the educator Georges Bertier, also belonged to conservative political parties or the far-right leagues of the interwar period and/or would support in some way the Vichy government. Even Marshal Hubert Lyautey, a far-right military hero and eventual Alliance Nationale patron, would speak at the organization's second conference on adolescence about the national importance of scouting in combating the evil of individualism that, in his opinion, was plaguing France.[30]

Emblematic of this infusion of nationalism and educational theory that stemmed from its collaboration with the Alliance Nationale and its increased prominence in the natalist-familialist universe was the school's third annual conference program. Titled "La Jeunesse," the 1931 conference followed two previous meetings that focused on childhood and early adolescence. The roster of speakers, many of whom were staunch supporters of the Ecole des Parents from its inception, read like a who's who of nationalists and rightists who inhabited the world of the natalist-familialist movement. Indeed amid conference sessions that addressed career preparation ("La Jeunesse devant la Profession" [Youth in the Face of Work]), which included a talk by Paulette Bernège on women's professions and the household), cultural instruction ("La Jeunesse devant les Arts et les Plaisirs" [Youth in the Face of the Arts and Leisure]), and conjugal love ("La Jeunesse devant L'Amour" [Youth in the Face of Love]), were lengthy panels that were strongly nationalistic in tone and content.[31] The roster of conference participants included Vérine; Antoine Rédier, the founder of the Légion, considered by some to be the first fascist league of the 1920s; the social Catholic and nationalist legislator Georges Pernot; Robert Garric, an educator and social Catholic affiliated with the far-right league Croix de Feu; and Haury and Borie, ardent pronatalists and Ecole des Parents administrative council members.

The opening session, entitled "La Jeunesse devant le Devoir Social," addressed young men's and women's relationship to their social duties, which began, according to the panel chair Georges Risler, president of the Musée Social, with raising their future children. Risler opened the conference by asserting that it was necessary to teach young people how to rear their children because of the social ramifications to society and the nation if they did not. Particularly lower-class women, who were insufficiently schooled in housekeeping, according to Risler, created slums that then had an immediate effect on the health of the nation.[32] For a nation and a people to stay strong, they had to keep morality, moral education, and the means of this education, the family, among their primary concerns because "moral ideas appear to be the solid and indispensable base of civilization."[33]

Robert Garric, president of the Equipes Sociales and director of the *New Youth Review*, echoed these themes in his call for social rapprochement in French society. To Garric, the key to solving poverty and other social questions that divided the country was *éducation familiale*. Children, through their parents, must learn about and encounter the poor in order to become effective as the *classe dirigeante*. Only through this moral education could social problems be alleviated in the future.[34] The right-wing press, including the major Catholic daily, *La Croix*, along with *Le Figaro* and *L'Intransigeant*, saluted Garric's prescriptions and lauded his calls for parents to think of their children not as individuals but as "social beings" who would benefit from scouting and participation in charitable enterprises.[35]

While most of the ideas that Garric presented in his speech were not overtly nationalistic, his broader solutions for remedying the self-centered individualism in youth and society at large and for bringing the classes together were, as evidenced in his political beliefs and involvement. Not only was Garric the director and founder of the Equipes Sociales, which had as its goal to instill nationalism, Christian morality, honor, discipline, and a sense of teamwork in young men, but he was also on the board of the Travail et Loisirs section of the fascistic paramilitary league the Croix de Feu and was involved in its post-1936 parliamentary counterpart, the Parti Social Français.[36] Like Vérine, Garric sought to ameliorate social class conflict through a union of, as the Croix de Feu and later the Vichy regime would hold, *travail, famille, et patrie*.[37] Garric's Equipes Sociales and involvement in the Croix de Feu/Parti Social Français aimed to do just that: bring together the *classe dirigeante* and those who needed leading under this grand project of national and social reconciliation. As Garric emphasized in his speech to the conference audience, "Social, c'est pas de tout 'socialisme'"; class and social reconciliation rather than class antagonism and revolution, as first Catholic social action and then the Croix de Feu/Parti Social Français would maintain, would provide the way forward for France.[38]

Following Garric, Marie du Rostu, the general director of the youth association of the largest Catholic nationalist women's association, the Ligue Patriotique des Françaises, and partisan of the Action française, echoed Garric's call for instilling a sense of social duty into French youth.[39] While Garric had focused on the young men who would inhabit his *equipes*, she emphasized a similar formation for young women. There they would be exposed to similar ideas and develop, "as all young women should, a love of what is good" for the benefit of French society and the nation.[40] Rostu emphasized that this *amour du bien* should be developed throughout a woman's lifetime and that women should be focused on serving others through their true nature. Like Vérine, she maintained that young women more than ever needed help in developing the unique qualities that were innately part of women's nature. Rostu asserted that the current French educational system, combined with the pressures of modern life, had worked to divert girls' attention away from these duties; only guidance from wise older women and their mothers would steer them back to where they could rediscover these values: "their family, their children, and their family circle." She exhorted the women in the conference audience to help young modern women to "stay women, beings of devotion, generosity, and self-sacrifice." In doing so they would have fulfilling lives centered on an *amour du bien* for the good of all and the future of the nation.[41] The conservative Catholic newspaper *La Croix* noted that Rostu and Garric both received "long applause" from their audience for their insistence that young men and women fulfill their social duties.[42]

More overtly nationalistic was the presentation by General Borie. In "Le Devoir envers la Patrie," the World War I army hero asserted that it was necessary to inculcate a love of the *patrie* in young men in order to fight the "pernicious pacifistic sentiment" that was pervading all facets of French life. Raising the specter of the Soviet peril and Bolshevism, Borie proposed a two-pronged assault on the minds of young French men and women in order to fight for the soul of France and its survival: families should actively encourage in their children both patriotism and the duty to reproduce in order to preserve "the French soul."[43] To that end, he advocated, citing his Alliance Nationale colleague Fernand Boverat's 1913 book, *Patriotisme et Paternité*, that fatherhood should be assimilated into military duty and that the two, insofar as they related to men's national duty, could not be separated; it was the parents' responsibility to make this connection and to develop in their children a spirit of sacrifice for the greater community.[44] Echoing Garric's call for the development of social duty in young men, Borie praised the French Army for making men of great courage and strong will; being a "school of discipline," it was also a "school of patriotism and of the best virtues: solidarity, equality, altruism, and self-sacrifice."[45]

As with Garric, the right-wing press highlighted Borie's ideas with great force. *La Croix* praised him for "exalting *la patrie* in eloquent terms" and for underscoring the necessity of serving France "above all in the present hour." By having more children and rearing its young men to fear the dangers that "menace[d] our civilization and soil," the family could save the nation.[46] *Le Figaro* similarly saluted his ideas regarding the young Frenchman's national duty. It chose to underscore Borie's exhortation to inculcate a love of the land and soil so that young men would "eagerly defend it when called upon to do so," emphasizing that the army must be considered a vital instrument of security, not of conquest, and to this end children should be reintroduced to it positively and celebrate its elegance: "It is necessary not to confuse honor and misplaced pride."[47]

Vérine herself echoed the sentiments of her panelists in her closing address to the 1931 conference, reiterating their ardent nationalism, defense of traditional gender hierarchies and familial hierarchies, and the Ecole des Parents' intended goal to assemble a *union sacrée* for the French family.[48] It was no coincidence that she would invoke the notion of a "sacred union" to describe their work; for most active participants in the natalist-familialist movement, the battle they were fighting for the soul of France was a continuation of the Great War, one that had far-reaching implications for the future of the nation. The Ecole des Parents' yearly conferences and leadership would continue to reflect the predominantly conservative and at times far-right political composition of the movement.

Following the acclaimed 1931 conference, the organization experienced significant changes that affected its direction and future. While Vérine remained president, the Ecole's cofounder, G. J. Camus, the widow of Jean Camus, a noted physician and member of the Académie de Médicine, resigned from her position as secretary-general because of pressing family issues that had forced her to reduce her commitment to the organization. Camus's resignation coincided with a major change in the funding of the organization. At the Administrative Council meeting on April 9, 1932, in which Camus announced her resignation, the Alliance Nationale and the Comité d'entente: Natalité-Famille-Education, an umbrella group launched by Abbé Jean Viollet and Michel Goudchaux of the Confédération Générale des Familles that brought together most natalist-familialist organizations to better coordinate action and lobbying, announced that both entities would cease financial and material aid for the Ecole des Parents, which had joined the Comité d'entente in 1930.[49] The loss of financial and logistical support for the organization would result in long-term damage to the stability of the organization. From that point on the organization would run deficits that would result in the cessation of its annual conferences in 1935 and eventually force the reorganization of the Ecole, including the resignations of its most notable council members.[50] In the short term, though, the Ecole des Parents continued most of its operations, including its yearly conferences at the Musée Social and its provincial affiliate conferences. The connections that Vérine made through participation in the Comité d'entente provided invaluable help in sustaining the activities of the organization; shortly after hosting a meeting of the Comité d'entente at her home in June 1930, Gustave Bonvoisin, the managing director of the Comité Central des Allocations Familiales (CCAF), Robert Garric, and Paul Hunziker would all join the Ecole's administrative council.[51] Eventually Bonvoisin and his associate, Paul Leclercq, the editor of the CCAF's *Revue de la Famille*, would provide office space and material support for the Ecole's operations beginning in December 1933, following its departure from the Alliance Nationale's headquarters. Bonvoisin and Leclercq would assume major leadership roles in the organization as well, becoming vice president and secretary-general, respectively.[52]

Increasingly Bonvoisin, Garric, Hunziker, and Leclercq and members of the Comité d'entente, including Georges Bertier, the director of the Ecole des Roches and frequent Ecole conference participant, would assert more leadership in the organization's annual conferences, with the Comité providing funding for the fifth conference, titled "L'Education de l'Effort." In her opening remarks at the conference, Vérine publicly acknowledged the Ecole's debt to the Comité d'entente, thanked its leaders profusely, and saluted its "desire to coordinate the entities pursuing the same goal in order to avoid the dispersion and distressing scattering of its efforts."[53] Indeed the conference readily reflected the conservative moral and political goals and values of its organizers through the paradigm of "effort," with Vérine echoing writer Charles Péguy's call for a veritable "social revolution [that] will be moral or it will not be one" to impress upon her audience the need for a spiritual renewal of authority.[54]

Most presenters focused on this concept and spoke at great length as to why French children and youth should be educated in the importance of engaging actively in all aspects of life and be raised by their parents accordingly. To underscore the necessity of this goal, the conference opened with discussions on how physical and moral effort was a central component in the education of the youth of Hitler's Germany and Mussolini's Italy. While neither speaker explicitly compared France's young men with those of Germany or Italy, it was clear that France did not rate favorably in this regard. Citing Germany's emphasis on integrating the individual into his or her social role and its focus on outdoor education and group formations such as the Hitler Youth, the monarchist author Comte Jean de Pange lauded the cultivation of dynamism in its young men but was concerned about state control.[55] Similarly Philippe de Zara, secretary-general of the France-Italy Committee, highlighted positively the fascist educational system's emphasis on sports, discipline, and "education d'énergie" as cornerstones of its development of patriotism; he praised the way physical education was not divorced from the larger education of Italian young men, unlike in most of France.[56] Others used their presentations to argue for the need for French families, teachers, schools, and other institutions, including politics, to emphasize the necessity of effort, activity, and engagement in all facets of life. Implicit in their discussions was the need to persuade French youth to make the effort to overcome what they considered to be the distractions of modern life in order to reengage in timeless traditions and values.[57] Echoing these concerns, Vérine concluded the conference by exhorting the "honest men and women" in attendance to oppose the "moral baseness, the debauchery that promotes greed, hypocrisy, compromise and cowardice," urging them to react against "the wind of materialism, sensuality and the satanic wind that blows through the world and oppos[es] the spiritual forces that aid our efforts to promote the Good, the Beautiful, Intelligence, and Love."[58]

Even with her work at the heart of the natalist-familialist movement with both the Ecole des Parents and the Comité d'entente, Vérine's writings and speeches that continued to center on moral action, such as the one she gave at the closing of the 1934 conference, displayed her early roots in Catholic social action with the Morality Committee of the Union Féminine Civique et Sociale. While she and Camus began their journey into public activism within the female-only confines of the UFCS, their expansion of the Ecole beyond that world, yet rooted firmly in it, mirrored the paths of conservative Catholic women in the 1930s who ventured into the world of right-wing politics and social action. As Kevin Passmore and Magali della Sudda have argued, there was significant overlap in membership between women's and girls' Catholic social action organizations like the UFCS, Ligue Patriotique des Femmes, and Guides des France and the women's auxiliaries of far-right leagues and political parties such as the Croix de Feu/Parti Social Français (PSF) whose social work activities and organizations bore great similarity to earlier women's formations.[59] Given this relationship, it should not be surprising that in October 1937 Vérine approached the PSF's Social Service Office about the possibility of writing weekly columns for its newly acquired mass-circulation newspaper, the *Petit Journal*. Her close association with the PSF social service section chief, Robert Garric, gave her inquiry legitimacy among the women staffing the social services office, particularly Jeanne Garrigoux, the codirector of the office, who advocated on her behalf to Antoinette de Préval, the head of the Croix de Feu/PSF women's organization and social work programs.[60] Vérine submitted four sample articles that echoed her body of work with the Ecole des Parents as well as PSF principles. What stands out in these essays, though, is her invocation of the Croix de Feu/PSF's slogan, "Travail, Famille, Patrie," which, according to Vérine, a "healthy France will have for a motto." Similarly she focused on the PSF's fundamental tenet of class and social reconciliation in a manner common to the adherents and leaders of the PSF like de Préval, Garric, and the Croix de Feu/PSF leader, Colonel François de la Rocque.[61] While it is unclear if Vérine's articles were published, affinity between her strongly held beliefs and those of the PSF's leaders was clear, beliefs that were found throughout the spectrum of the nationalist far right and the natalist-familialist movement by the end of the 1930s.

As financial difficulties forced the Ecole des Parents to reorganize after 1937, Vérine maintained her connections with the conservative-reactionary political world in which she had become a fixture. As such she eventually became a vocal supporter and defender of the Vichy government soon after the 1940 defeat. With its slogan, *Travail, famille, et patrie*, the Vichy regime fused national, moral, and social revolution and renewal and embodied the values that Vérine, her natalist-familialist colleagues, and others on the political right and far right had lauded during the interwar period and on which she had modeled her own organization; Vichy's focus on traditional gender and familial hierarchies and roles, infusion of spiritual values and ardent national-ism, and anti-Marxist labor policies in the name of class reconciliation were hallmarks of her and the Ecole des Parents' conferences and publications. Aided no doubt by her considerable political connec-tions within natalist-familialist circles of the 1930s, she was appointed to the Commissariat Général à la Famille's Comité Consultatif de la Famille along with Ecole cofounder Camus, UFCS president Butil-lard, and many male associates from the Comité d'entente, Alliance Nationale, and CCAF.[62]

As she worked to reinvigorate the Ecole des Parents (which included the rechristening of the organization as the Ecole des Parents et Edu-cateurs), Vérine continued to be recognized as an expert on family issues.[63] As the codirector of the pro-Vichy journal *Education* along with CCAF managing director Bonvoisin and educator Georges Bertier, Vérine echoed the tenets of the *ordre nouveau* in her columns, ideas that did not differ from her earlier treatises.[64] As before, she insisted that parents had the duty and responsibility to inculcate into their children values such as work, family, fatherland, discipline, respect for authority, moral and social hierarchies, and order.[65] Signifying her status in the natalist-familialist milieu, she was also selected as the only female contributor to the official thematic manifesto of the National Revolution published by Pétain's supporters and various Vichy officials.[66] In her essay Vérine asserted the centrality of the family in the regime's *révolution nationale*; she condemned the changes occurring within the structure of the family over the previous two centuries, which had "violated eternal principles" and had "revolted against the laws of fertility, authority, purity, and love." As a result man "created his own hell" and made himself an animal.[67] She refused, though, to blame only "anti-family" policies that emphasized pleasure and leisure; "unfruitful and sterile men and women whose souls had been hardened by *égoïsme* and withered by materialism," who were not able to "think French" and did not know anymore how to "think family," were also at fault. As a result "disorder was the order of the day in France." According to Vérine, only France's rich moral and intellectual patrimony would be saved through "familial virtues that would revive [its] sluggish forces."[68] Indeed much of the focus of Vérine's and Ecole des Parents' activities during the 1930s and early 1940s was directed toward instructing parents in how to teach the principles of God, Work, Family, and Fatherland to their children and thus throughout France. To this end Ecole des Parents and its founder pressed its case for heightened paternal authority while also promoting an anti-democratic vision of governmental authority over the individual. The Vichy regime was the answer to Vérine's concerns about the pernicious influence of republicanism on the family.

The Ecole des Parents would depart from its overtly political agenda after 1945, when Vérine resigned from the presidency due to ill health. The organization would be led increasingly by child psychologists, education specialists, psychiatrists, and pediatricians and still exists as a state-recognized entity that promotes early childhood education.[69] For its first decade and a half of operation, however, the Ecole des Parents grew out of the networks of the social Catholic action and then operated squarely within the natalist-familialist movement and its alliance with conservative and reactionary politics. With rhetoric and a mission that particularly targeted mothers specifically and parents more generally, Vérine and the Ecole des Parents extended the reach of the natalist-familialist movement. In doing so they provided another avenue, one that because of its female leadership and focus on child rearing and the family seemed more benign than its organizational counterparts, that helped to create the ideological climate for the transition to the Vichy Regime and contributed to its early popularity and acceptance. Indeed Vérine's social and political activism, while enabling her and her female colleagues a place at the table in the interwar milieu of predominantly male natalist-familialist and Vichy politics and policy, cemented traditional gender hierarchies rather than challenging them, thus further reinforcing women's structural political marginalization at a crucial moment in France's history.

Notes

1. Madeleine LeComte, "L'Ecole des Parents ne doit pas être l'Ecole du nationalisme," *La Jeune-République* (1932?), Press Clippings scrapbook, Archives de L'Ecole des parents et éducateurs, Paris.
2. LeComte, "L'Ecole des Parents."
3. See Anne Cova, *"Au Service de l'Eglise, de la Patrie, et de la Famille"*: *Femmes catholiques et maternité sous la IIIe République* (Paris: L'Harmattan, 2000); Laura Lee Downs, "Each and Every One of You Must Become a *chef*: Toward a Social Politics of Working-Class Childhood on the Extreme Right in the 1930s," *Journal of Modern History* 81, no. 1 (2009): 1–44, and "'And So We Transform a People': Women's Social Action and the Recon-figuration of Politics on the Right in France, 1934–1947," *Past and Present* 225 (November 2014): 187–225; Kevin Passmore, "'Planting the Tricolor in the Citadels of Communism': Women's Social Action in the Croix de feu and the Parti social français," *Journal of Modern History* 71 (December 1999): 836–37; Magali della Sudda, "Gender, Fascism and the Right-Wing

in France between the Wars: The Catholic Matrix," *Politics, Religion, and Ideology* 13, no. 2 (2012): 179–95; Caroline Campbell, *Political Belief in France, 1927–1945: Gender, Empire, and Fascism in the Croix de Feu and Parti Social Français* (Baton Rouge: Louisiana State University Press, 2015).

4. For discussion of bourgeois Catholic women's gender roles in the nineteenth century, see Bonnie G. Smith, *Ladies of the Leisure Class: The Bourgeoises of Northern France in the 19th Century* (Princeton NJ: Princeton University Press, 1981). For a paradigm-shifting anthology of essays on the politics of gender in the public sphere, see Elinor A. Accampo, Rachel G. Fuchs, and Mary Lynn Stewart, eds., *Gender and the Politics of Social Reform in France, 1870–1914* (Baltimore: Johns Hopkins University Press, 1995).

5. For more extensive analysis of the nineteenth-century depopulation crisis and its political impact, see Joshua Cole, *The Power of Large Numbers* (Ithaca NY: Cornell University Press, 2000); Karen Offen, "Depopulation, Nationalism, and Feminism in Fin-de-Siècle France," *American Historical Review* 89, no. 3 (1984): 648–76. For the interwar period, see Mary Louise Roberts, *Civilization without Sexes: Reconstructing Gender in France, 1917–1927* (Chicago: University of Chicago Press, 1994); Cheryl A. Koos, "Gender, Anti-individualism, and Nationalism: The Alliance Nationale and the Pronatalist Backlash against the *Femme moderne*, 1933–1940," *French Historical Studies* 19, no. 3 (1996): 699–723, and "Fascism, Fatherhood, and the Family in Interwar France: The Case of Antoine Rédier and the Légion," *Journal of Family History* 24, no. 3 (1999): 317–29. For a summary of Le Play's influence, see Janet Horne, *A Social Laboratory for Modern France: The Musée Social and the Rise of the Welfare State* (Durham NC: Duke University Press, 2002), 41–45.

6. "Naissance et développement de l'Ecole des Parents," *L'Ecole des Parents* 5 (May 1969): 6.

7. For discussion on the foundation and activities of the UFCS, see Cova, *"Au Service de l'Eglise,"* 128–221; Susan Pedersen, *Family, Dependence, and the Origins of the Welfare State: Britain and France, 1914–45* (New York: Cambridge University Press, 1993): 393–94. For organizational histories of the UFCS and the activities and motivations of its founder, Andrée Butillard, see Thérèse Doneaud and Christian Guérin, *Les Femmes agissent, le monde change: Histoire inedité de L'Union feminine civique et social* (Paris: Editions du CERF, 2005); Henri Rollet, *Andrée Butillard and feminisme chrétien* (Paris: Spes, 1960).

8. Quoted in Susan Pedersen, "Catholicism, Feminism, and the Politics of the Family during the late Third Republic," in *Mothers of a New World*, ed.

Seth Koven and Sonya Michel (London: Routledge, 1993), 250. Translation by Pedersen.

9. Vérine, *La Femme et l'amour dans la sociéte de demain* (Paris, 1925), quoted in Pedersen, "Catholicism, Feminism, and the Politics of the Family," 250–51.

10. Procès-verbaux du Conseil d'Administration de l'Ecole des Parents, January 25, 1930, Archives de l'Ecole des Parents et Educateurs, Paris. Also cited in Francine Muel-Dreyfus, *Vichy et l'éternel féminin* (Paris Seuil, 1996), 181–82.

11. Procès-verbaux du Conseil d'Administration de l'Ecole des Parents, January 25, 1930, 3. For the text of this speech, see Comité national d'Etudes sociales et politiques, *Les Grands problèmes de la vie: Le Mariage, Communications de Abbé Viollet, Mme Lebrun (Vérine), et al. Séance du Lundi 30 avril 1928* (Paris: Comité National d'Etudes, n.d.), 9–15. Details concerning these events can also be found in Muel-Dreyfus, *Vichy et l'éternel féminin*, 181; André Isambert, *L'Education des Parents* (Paris: Presses Universitaire de France, 1960), 32. For her early writings that focus on sex education, see Vérine, "A une Mère: L'Education des Sens," *La Femme dans la vie sociale* 7 (December 1927): 3; "A une Mere: L'Education des Sens et Sentiments," *La Femme dans la vie sociale* 9 (March 1928): n.p.; *Le Sens d'amour* (Paris: Bossard, 1927); *Un problème urgent! L'Education des Sens* (Paris: Editions d'Association du Mariage Chrétien, 1928); and *La Mère initiatrice* (Paris: Spes, 1928); Comité national d'Etudes sociales et politiques, *La Famille française actuellement: L'esprit de famille diminue-t-il en France? Communications de Mmes Lebrun et Jean Camus; Séance à Strasbourg, du 15 Mars 1929* (Paris: Comité National d'Etudes, n.d.). For detailed information on Abbé Jean Viollet and his involvement in the natalist-familialist movement, see Mathias Gardet, *Jean Viollet et l'apostolat laïc: Les oeuvres du Moulin-Vert, 1902–1945* (Paris: Editions Beauchesne, 2005).

12. Comité national d'Etudes sociales et politiques, *Les Grands problèmes de la vie*, 1.

13. For information on Vérine's family background, see Muel-Dreyfus, *Vichy et l'éternel féminin*, 181; Isambert, *L'Education des Parents*, 30–31.

14. Communication de Mme Lebrun (Vérine) in Comité national d'Etudes sociales et politiques, *Les Grands problèmes de la vie*, 13. An extended version of this speech was later published as a sixteen-page brochure by Abbé Viollet's Christian Marriage Association; see Vérine, *Un problème urgent!*.

15. Comité national d'Etudes sociales et politiques, *Les Grand problèmes de la vie*, 15.

16. Procès-verbaux du Conseil d'Administration de l'Ecole des Parents, January 25, 1930. In his hagiographic account of Butillard's life, the historian

Henri Rollet asserts that Butillard initiated the idea with Vérine and Camus. See Rollet, *Andrée Butillard*, 83.

17. Horne, *A Social Laboratory for Modern France*, 41-45.

18. Jackie Clarke, *France in the Age of Organization: Factory, Home and Nation from the 1920s to Vichy* (New York: Berghahn Books, 2011), 14-15.

19. For more on the Ecole des Roches and its roots in the New Education movement, see Georges Bertier, *L'Ecole des Roches* (Juvisy: Les Editions du CERF, 1935). See also Nathalie Duval, "L'Ecole des Roches, phare français au sein de la nébuleuse de l'Education nouvelle," *Paedogogica Historica* 42, nos. 1-2 (2006): 63-75, and "Le *self-help* transpose en milieu français: L'Ecole des Roches et ses élèves (1899-2009)," *Histoire, Economie et Société* 28, no. 4 (2009): 69-84.

20. Clarke, *France in the Age of Organization*, 50-51. For Wilbois's formulation of this, see Joseph Wilbois, *Le Chef d'entreprise: Sa function et sa personne* (Paris: Alcan, 1926), 93, and *La Psychologie au service du chef d'entreprise* (Paris: Alcan, 1934), 219. See also his memoirs, *L'homme qui ressuscita d'entre les vivants* (Paris: Spes, 1928).

21. Procès-verbaux du Conseil d'Administration de l'Ecole des Parents, January 25, 1930.

22. Paul Haury, "L'Ecole des Parents," *Revue de l'Alliance Nationale pour l'accroissement de la population française* 199 (February 1929): 54-56. For more on Haury, see Cheryl A. Koos, "Engendering Reaction: The Politics of Pronatalism and the Family in France, 1914-1944," PhD dissertation, University of Southern California, 1996, chap. 3; Koos, "Gender, Anti-individualism, and Nationalism"; Cheryl A. Koos, "Gender, the Family, and the Fascist Temptation: Visions of Masculinity in the Natalist-Familialist Movement, 1922-1940," in *The French Right between the Wars: Political and Intellectual Movements from Conservatism to Fascism*, ed. Samuel Kalman and Sean Kennedy (New York: Berghahn Books, 2014), 112-26.

23. See Horne, *A Social Laboratory for Modern France*, 54-96.

24. Procès-verbaux du Conseil d'Administration de l'Ecole des Parents, January 25, 1930.

25. Procès-verbaux du Conseil d'Administration de l'Ecole des Parents, January 25, 1930, 2, 8-9.

26. See *Journal Officiel de la République Française: Lois et Decrets* 46 (February 23, 1930): 2039.

27. Procès-verbaux du Conseil d'Administration de l'Alliance Nationale pour l'accroissement de la population française, May 13, 1930, Alliance Nationale—Population et Avenir Archives, Paris.

28. Vérine, "Conclusion," in Ecole des Parents, *L'Enfance* (Paris: F. Lanore, 1930), 226.

29. Procès-verbaux du Conseil d'Administration de l'Ecole des Parents, May 3, 1930; October 4, 1930; and February 28, 1931.

30. Ecole des Parents, *L'Adolescence* (Paris: Lanore, 1931), 217–19. For Lyautey's involvement in the Alliance Nationale, see Procès-Verbaux du Conseil d'Administration de l'Alliance Nationale, December 7, 1931.

31. Ecole des Parents, *La Jeunesse* (Paris: Lanore, 1932), 3. For more information about Paulette Bernège, see Clarke, *France in the Age of Organization*, 73–88.

32. Ecole des Parents, *La Jeunesse*, "Presidence de M. Georges Risler," 10–11.

33. Ecole des Parents, *La Jeunesse*, 12.

34. Garric, "Les conditions d'un rapprochement social," 31–50.

35. See for example, *La Croix*, December 18, 1931; *Le Figaro*, December 1, 1931; *L'Intransigeant*, December 4, 1931.

36. For a discussion of the Equipes sociales, see Bernard Comte, "Les organisations de jeunesse," in *Vichy et les Français*, ed. François Bédarida and Jean-Pierre Azéma (Paris: Fayard, 1992), 410–11. For the connection of Robert Garric to the Croix de Feu, see dossier "Travail et loisirs 1936–40," sous-dossier, Robert Garric, Archives Nationales (hereafter AN), Paris, 451 AP 187. I am indebted to Kevin Passmore for alerting me to the connection between Garric and Vérine and to the existence of this dossier in the La Rocque papers. For discussion of the Travail et Loisirs section of the Croix de Feu and PSF, see Passmore, "'Planting the Tricolor,'" 836–37; Downs, "'Each and Every One of You,'" 1–44.

37. See for example, Robert Garric, "L'Esprit social," a lecture given for the Parti Social Français section Travail et Loisirs, June 3, 1937, AN 451 AP 187: dossier "Travail et Loisirs 1936–40," sous-dossier, Robert Garric.

38. Garric, "L'Esprit social," 6.

39. For discussion of the Ligue Patriotique des Françaises, see Magali della Sudda, "Right-Wing Feminism and Conservative Women's Militancy in Interwar France," in Kalman and Kennedy, *The French Right*, 97–111, and "La Charité et les Affaires: Le Cas de la Ligue Patriotique des Françaises (1901–1914)," *Entreprises et Histoire* 56 (September 2009): 11–29. Della Sudda identifies Rostu as a partisan of Charles Maurras's Action française; see M. della Sudda, "La Ligue féminine d'action catholique et les ligues de droite radicale (1919–1939)" in *A droite de la droite: Droites radicales en France et en Grande-Bretagne au XXe siècle*, ed. Philippe Vervaecke (Villeneuve d'Ascq: Presses Universitaires du Septentrion, 2012), 436–37.

40. Marie du Rostu, "La Jeune Fille et l'Amour," in *La Jeunesse*, 51–68.

41. Du Rostu, "La Jeune Fille et l'Amour," 67.

42. "Le IIIe Congrès de l'Ecole des parents," *La Croix*, December 18, 1931.

43. L. Borie, "Le Devoir de la Patrie," in *La Jeunesse*, 249–80.

44. Borie, "Le Devoir de la Patrie," 255.

45. Borie, "Le Devoir de la Patrie," 264.

46. *La Croix*, December 18, 1931

47. "Le Congrès des parents: La devoir national et international," *Le Figaro*, December 7, 1931.

48. Vérine, "Pour Vivre une Belle Vie", in *La Jeunesse*, 378.

49. Procès-verbaux du Conseil d'Administration de l'Ecole des Parents, April 9, 1932. For more on the Comité d'entente, see Gardet, *Jean Viollet et l'apostolat laïc*, 274–81.

50. Procès-verbaux du Conseil d'Administration de l'Ecole des Parents, January 6, 1937.

51. For the meeting of the Comité d'entente at Vérine's home, se Procès-verbaux du Conseil d'Administration de l'Ecole des Parents, October 4, 1930. Also in attendance at the meeting were Leclercq and Michel Goudchaux, the president of the Comité; both would later become Ecole des Parents administrative council members.

52. Procès-verbaux du Conseil d'Administration de l'Ecole des Parents, December 4, 1933.

53. "Allocution de Mme Vérine," in Ecole des Parents, *L'Education de l'Effort* (Paris: Lanore, 1934).

54. "Allocution de Mme Vérine," 24.

55. Jean de Pange, "L'Education de l'Effort dans la jeunesse allemande," in Ecole des Parents, *L'Education de l'Effort*, 43–54.

56. Philippe de Zara, "L'Education de l'Effort dans la jeunesse italienne," in *L'Education de l'Effort*, 60–61.

57. See Paul Haury, "L'entraînement à l'école en liaison avec la Famille"; Georges Bertier, "Comment concilier l'Intérêt et l'Effort"; Gustave Bonvoisin, "L'Effort social collectif"; and Robert Garric, "Le but de l'Effort: A la conquête de soi-même," all in Ecole des Parents, *L'Education de l'Effort*.

58. Vérine, "L'Effort vers l'Amour," in Ecole des Parents, *L'Education de l'Effort*, 294.

59. For the connection between women's social Catholic action groups and the far-right leagues and political parties, see Passmore, "'Planting the Tricolor," 819, 822, 831; della Sudda, "Gender, Fascism and the Right-Wing in France," 179–95; Downs, "'And So We Transform a People,'" 197–98. See also Caroline Campbell, "Building a Movement, Dismantling a Republic:

Women, Gender, and Political Extremism in the Croix de Feu/Parti Social Français, 1927–1940," *French Historical Studies* 35, no. 4 (2012): 698–700, and *Political Belief in France, 1927–1945,* 49–85.

60. See dossier "Travail et Loisirs 1936–40," PSF (Dossier Vérine), letter from Mme J. Garrigoux to Melle de Preval, October 21, 1937, AN 451 AP 187.

61. Vérine, "Le Billet de Vérine: Le Métier de parents," in dossier "Travail et Loisirs 1936–40."

62. For Vérine's involvement in Vichy's Comité Consultatif de la Famille (which became the Conseil Supérieur de la Famille in 1943) see Archives du service médical: Médicin-Commandant Sautriau, Médecin-Capitaine Petchot-Bacqué, Médicin-Commandant Mourot, Procès-verbal d'Assemblée Plénière du 7 decembre 1943, AN AG 605. See also Geneviève Poujol and Madeleine Romer, *Dictionnaire biographique des militants XIXe-XXe siècles: De l'éducation populaire à l'action culturelle* (Paris: L'Harmattan, 1996), 371.

63. For the renaming of the organization, see Procès-verbaux du Conseil d'Administration de l'Ecole des Parents, April 16, 1942. The Commissariat Général de la Famille and the Secours National subsidized the organization and the Alliance Nationale helped with office space and support. See also Procès-verbaux du Conseil d'Administration de l'Ecole des Parents, December 4, 1941.

64. Bonvoisin was a noted collaborationist during the Occupation and a member of the French-German Committee with Otto Abetz, the Nazi administrator in charge of Paris. For information on Bonvoisin's political activities and associations with the PPF and during the Vichy regime, see Dossier Gustave Bonvoisin, Police Nationale, AN F7 15287. I am indebted to Paul Dutton for initially alerting me to this information. For more on Bonvoisin's Vichy era activities and writings, see Muel-Dreyfus, *Vichy et l'éternal féminine*, 99–102.

65. See, for example, Vérine, "Les yeux qui s'ouvrent . . . ," *Education* 57–58 (January 1941): 12–14; "Climat familial 1942," in Georges Bertier et al., *Les Devoirs présent des éducateurs* (Paris: Editions Sociale Française, 1942), 3–15; *C'est dans les familles que se fait la France* (Paris: Editions Sociale Française, 1942); *La Famille Nouvelle* (Paris: Spes, 1944).

66. Vérine, "La Famille," in *France 41: La Revolution Nationale constructive, un bilan et un programme* (Paris: Editions Alsatia, 1941), 191–214. See also Muel-Dreyfus, *Vichy et l'éternal féminine*, 181.

67. Vérine, "La Famille," 193.

68. Vérine, "La Famille," 194.

69. Procès-verbaux du Conseil d'Administration de l'Ecole des Parents, July 5, 1945. For discussion of the Ecole's post-1946 composition within the context of its early history, see Annick Ohayon, "L'école des parents ou l'éducation des enfants éclairée par l'psychologie (1929–1946)," *Bulletin de Psychologie* 53, no. 5 (2000): 640–41. Contrary to what Ohayon says, Vérine died on September 10, 1959. See "Nécrologie: Madame Lebrun-Vérine," *Vitalité Française* 448 (August–October 1959): 59, and "Deux Disparues," *Nouvelles Litteraires*, September 9, 1959, clipping in Dossier Vérine, Bibliothèque Marguerite Durand, Paris.

5. Maria Vérone (*left*), Alva Belmont (*standing*), and Alice Paul (*right*) meeting at the American University Women's Club (now Reid Hall), 4 rue de Chevreuse, Paris, April 19, 1925. © World Wide Photo. Image from Schlesinger Library, Radcliffe Institute, Harvard University.

8

Politics, Money, and Distrust

*French-American Alliances in
the International Campaign for
Women's Equal Rights, 1925–1930*

SARA L. KIMBLE

On April 19, 1925, the French feminist lawyer Maria Vérone met with two American feminist leaders of the National Woman's Party (NWP), Alva Belmont and Alice Paul, to plot the next phase of the international women's rights movement. On that cool spring day Vérone was a guest of Belmont and Paul for tea at the American University Women's Club in Paris (fig. 5). Belmont made France, where she had been educated as a girl, her permanent home in 1924.[1] Paul arrived in Paris after a trip to London, where she had met with Emmeline Pethick-Lawrence, Lady Margaret Rhondda, and other suffrage leaders to form the International Advisory Committee for the NWP. Their meetings in Paris during the spring and summer of 1925 were designed to extend the reach of the NWP's international committee beyond its main London branch.[2]

The international expansion of the NWP grew from its political triumph with the passage of the Nineteenth Amendment to the U.S. Constitution (1920) that granted voting rights to U.S. women. In 1923 the NWP announced new goals to secure nationwide equality in the form of an Equal Rights Amendment (ERA) under the U.S. Constitution, and it pledged to internationalize its campaign for equality.[3] Belmont and Paul also called for an international parliament of women designed to bring together varied organizations as a united movement to end "present world-wide subjection of women" by facilitating women's autonomy "so that women shall control life as much as men control life."[4] They seemed convinced that unity of purpose could bring rapid results and prompt the "evolution" of modern law from antiquated laws, for the "relics of ancient customs and musty tradition" inherited from English common law and the Napoleonic Code needed eradication.[5] In practice the Americans' international action had several prongs, including providing support for women's suffrage campaigns in places like Puerto Rico and, as we shall see, in France.[6]

In the mid-1920s the French and the American leaders often met at the American University Women's Club to discuss how to promote women's rights.[7] With French as their common language, the Americans made alliances with the peace activist Gabrielle Duchêne, the suffrage leader Germaine Malaterre-Sellier, and elite women in publishing and the arts, namely Anthippe Couchoud and Fanny Bunand-Sévastos.[8] Maria Vérone, who arose from humble origins, was an intellectual powerhouse in this group, and she would prove to be one of the Americans' most valuable political allies in France.

Vérone's militant activism for women's suffrage and her career as both an activist lawyer and a legal journalist contributed to her reputation as an idealistic, incorruptible, articulate, and passionate feminist. In the early 1920s the NWP women eagerly applauded Vérone's exploits in the political press and promoted her activism in their newspaper, *Equal Rights*.[9] By the time of their 1925 meeting, Vérone's commitment to deploying international law to secure women's equal rights was already in evidence. Vérone was an experienced international negotiator, active with the International Council of Women (ICW) and the International Woman Suffrage Alliance (IWSA), and an advocate for the peace and disarmament movement and women's equality in employment. She claimed a revolutionary and antiroyalist family heritage, learned political skills as a teenager from her free-thinker father, and demonstrated for the anticlerical cause while working as a young teacher. Beginning in 1913 she had been involved in international women's rights through the IWSA, traveled within Europe and into French North Africa, eagerly engaged in international friendships.[10] She reportedly wore a button with the revolutionary motto *Vivre libre ou mourir*.[11]

Unlike the other contributions to this volume, this history does not directly engage with questions of social rights, but the primary figures in this Franco-American alliance were rooted in social thought and action. Campaigns for social rights were foundational in the political development of Maria Vérone and Alice Paul. Vérone's political youth was also steeped among mutualists and socialists from the 1890s through 1913. With these affiliations, she engaged with issues such as the quality of urban housing and corruption in city government and participated in consumer co-ops. Vérone experienced financial insecurity after the death of her father and again later, as a single mother.[12] After she joined the Ligue française de droits des femmes (LFDF) in 1904, her activism focused explicitly on women's socioeconomic needs, and political issues, including suffrage, societal respect for girls and mothers, state financial support for children born out of wedlock, reform of the juvenile justice system, expansion of women's employment opportunities, and equal pay.[13] Vérone's political and legal work aimed to undercut the structures that kept the patriarchal family form (male as breadwinner, female as dependent) in place. Her involvement in questions of married women's independent nationality indicated her willingness to disrupt notions of normative family life as she emphasized women's agency to form, dissolve, and remake the family unit.[14]

Alice Paul (1885–1977) studied at the School of Philanthropy (later merged with Columbia University) and had served as a social worker among immigrants in New York (1905–7) and in a British settlement (1907–10). She joined the Women's Social and Political Union (WSPU) after hearing a persuasive speech by Christabel Pankhurst on women's suffrage. Before 1914 both Vérone and Paul turned from direct involvement in socioeconomic problems and social rights to reform work on a larger, structural level, a process facilitated by their academic studies of law (Vérone) and sociology, economics, and law (Paul).[15] They wanted to emancipate women from a variety of dependencies (financial, civil, political, psychological) that were the conventional core of gender relations in the late nineteenth and early twentieth centuries.

The most ambitious campaign undertaken during the interwar era by this loosely connected international group of allies was in support of the Americans' Equal Rights Treaty, or ERT. The ERT contained one article: "The Contracting States agree that upon ratification of the Treaty, men and women shall have equal rights throughout the territory subject to their respective jurisdictions."[16] The ERT was a legal agreement modeled on the ERA, both "born of the same idea, namely that the whole sex must cast aside its bondage in order to secure equal opportunity for any woman anywhere."[17] The ERT was a means through which all "unequal laws will be made equal" within each nation.[18] It was designed for implementation by an international body, such as the League of Nations, to serve as the vehicle for overturning the gender-specific limitations on citizenship. The concept of the ERT appears to have been proposed by Lady Rhondda to Alice Paul in correspondence in 1926 and the precise terminology finalized in 1927.[19] Doris Stevens (1888–1963), the energetic paid NWP organizer, later explained the ERT's purpose in Paris: "We want the grand principle of human freedom [*liberté humaine*] to be accepted as a fundamental principle in international law."[20] Despite these lofty ideals, however, Stevens's leadership in this campaign for equality later in Latin America was plagued by her attitude of superiority, an uncritical view of imperialism, and an authoritarian style.[21] In what follows, I analyze the history of the ERT in France that preceded the Latin American venture.

The Equal Rights Treaty effort was important as an attempt to renegotiate the social and sexual contract using the power of supranational structures. Susan Becker argues that the NWP wanted to act in the international sphere due to an assumption that the status of women of all classes and all countries was interrelated. Moreover the NWP women were cognizant of the influence that male-dominated international bodies such as the International Labour Organization and League of Nations could have over women's positions, and they intended to revitalize the international women's movement.[22] Women's involvement in the League convinced official League representatives that "the position of women in society could be construed as a problem for international attention" and thus "irrevocably challenged the notion that the status of women was a purely 'national' issue," according to

Carol Miller.[23] Feminist agency gave substance to the international agreements that eventually came into effect, particularly with events such as the League's Committee on the Status of Women (est. 1933).[24] This history underscores the potential power of citizens to act in discursive and material ways despite their formal exclusion from political rights (in the French case) or international bodies (in the case of the Americans' marginalization at the League of Nations). The campaign for an ERT also reveals the value these early feminists placed on international law as a means to redress the imbalance of power between men and women. This example of women's political involvement during the interwar era was also part of the broader historical trajectory of private women's organizations demanding equal rights for women through international law.[25]

The French had an important relationship to concepts of universal equality and international action. The 1878 Congrès des femmes claimed equality for all women.[26] This equality was a universalization of rights based on a generalization of European women's experiences as normative, regardless of differences such as race, religion, or structures of colonial power. France cemented its reputation as a home for human rights with both political action and rhetoric, surprising the world with its Senate's refusal to grant women's suffrage.[27] Martin Thomas notes that by rejecting women's claim for voting rights, "Republican universalism excluded women from the centres of power just as systematically as it excluded colonial subjects."[28] French suffragists expected that they would see suffrage after the First World War, when so many women had sacrificed for the nation and many other nations had enacted this fundamental reform. Sîan Reynolds writes that French women, including Vérone, engaged with international political affairs at the League of Nations with a kind of "desperate energy" that correlated to their displacement from national politics within the hexagon.[29]

Women's rights advocates were among the supporters of the League, a logical extension of their commitments to peace and diplomacy and against war, militarism, and violent nationalism. Comprehensive legal action to advance women's rights was a core strategy. In Rome in

1923, at the IWSA conference, Maria Vérone and a Scottish barrister, Chrystal Macmillan, proposed a convention to secure the independent nationality of married women, one of the earliest treaties by women on behalf of women.[30] In Santiago, Pan-American women lobbied delegates at the International Conference of the American States and secured resolutions to study the means of abolishing women's legal incapacities, advance women's education, and incorporate female delegates in future conferences.[31] The potential for securing women's equality through constitutional law had been successfully demonstrated in the Soviet Union and Scandinavia in the 1920s, a strategy the NWP publicized and pursued.[32]

This chapter is devoted to exploring the activities, motivations, and limitations of the often fragile and uneven Franco-American alliance as its members pursued gender equality in law. The presented evidence highlights the importance of taking seriously a shifting place of equality and rights in the interwar period, changing power dynamics between the national and international bodies at the nexus of international law, where the definitions of citizenship and human rights were debated and hammered into new forms. Moreover this history of intertwined activity around women's rights reinforces the significance of intellectual exchange in the struggle for the expansion of *les droits de l'homme* to encompass a broader notion of the human political subject.

The ERT's history in the Pan-American women's rights movement in the 1930s has been documented, but not so its earlier history in France.[33] In 1928 Doris Stevens formally announced the ERT in February in Havana, then carried it to Paris in August for its European launch. Paul Smith finds "no evidence" that the connections between the NWP and the LFDF "went any further than" one meeting on October 30, 1928.[34] By contrast, I have found evidence of direct interactions between Vérone and NWP leaders Paul and Stevens from at least 1925 until Vérone's death in 1938. I have also discovered that Vérone had an important supporting role in the American demonstration on August 28, 1928, in Rambouillet but her actions were not as described by either the press or subsequent scholars.[35] Consultation with French- and English-language archival material in comparison with published sources provides the opportunity to establish greater precision for an analysis of the relationship between militant women's rights activists from the United States and France on their engagement with questions of gender in citizenship, political tactics, and international law in ways that begin to untangle the intertwined histories of women's rights movements.[36]

This analysis of women assumed to be similarly situated reveals multiple trajectories of power that illuminate the complex challenges of enacting seemingly unifying ideals in an economically and politically stratified world.[37] The differences between the French and the Americans mattered to their transatlantic partnership such that their plans to forge an international "sisterhood" appear driven by competition and mistrust as well as by idealism and intermittent cooperation. Nevertheless they promoted claims for gender equality, raising questions about its continued denial and paving the way for further debate and eventual reforms.

This chapter is divided into three main themes. First, there is a narrative of political activity by women who emerged from the United States and France for the express purpose of coordinating an effort to speak to political authorities about legal equality. Second, there are debates among these rights activists over definitions, ideas, and strategies for how to best challenge the system of male dominance and female subordination. In this context, female activists demonstrated their capacity to act as citizens—that is, as peers engaged in a public space—despite the fact that their nations denied them full rights.[38] Third, these historic actors participated in a movement of "feminist internationalism," as they demanded that international law serve to grant equal political and civil rights to women.[39] On the surface of this Franco-American collaboration effort, activists claimed a common pursuit of women's rights on the international stage. An examination of the way power operated in this alliance reveals fault lines at the nexus of liberal rights, nationalism, and capitalism just under the surface of equanimity.

1925–1926: Forging Transatlantic Alliances in Paris

In principle France was fertile soil in which to nurture an international campaign for women's liberal rights. The French enjoyed a historic affinity with human rights that was rooted in revolutionary events and enlarged through subsequent representations. Even so, this seemingly homegrown affinity benefited from international exchanges such as the inspirational influence of the American Revolution on the Marquis de Condorcet and *The Declaration of the Rights of Man and Citizen* (1789).[40] In turn, nationalism was the vehicle for advancement of *les droits de l'homme* where the universality of its meaning was tested repeatedly by differences in religion, race, and gender. The concepts within the slogan *liberté, égalité et fraternité* facilitated the advance of civil, religious, and political freedom through revolutionary reconstructions of the French government and society (in 1789, 1830, 1848, and 1871). In the history of French-American interwar alliances, we see profound tensions between assumptions of the universality of rights and the restraining power of cultural and national specificity.

To build the Paris branch of the NWP, Alva Belmont and Alice Paul contacted several of the most powerful local women's rights leaders, including Gabrielle Duchêne, Germaine Malaterre-Sellier, and Maria Vérone. Duchêne (1870–1954) was a pacifist, communist sympathizer, and advocate for women's equal political rights, concerned that women must shape the legislation that affected their lives as workers and mothers.[41] She also headed the 4,500-member French section of the Women's International League for Peace and Freedom, a "key player" in the antimilitarist, antifascist movement.[42] Malaterre-Sellier (1889–1967) was the head of the Paris chapter of the Union française pour la suffrage des femmes (UFSF), the principal organ of the suffrage movement, which boasted twelve thousand members within five years of its founding in 1914. She engaged internationally as the leader of the Alliance international pour le suffrage et l'action civique et politique des femmes, vice president of the Union féminine pour la Société des Nations (est. 1920), and a leader in the Alliance-affiliated federation of women's organization, the Conseil national des femmes françaises (CNFF).[43] In 1914 the CNFF included 100,000 members across a variety of associations.[44] Vérone (1874–1938) was president of the oldest women's rights association in France, the mixed-sex LFDF, founded in 1882. She became one of the first female attorneys in France, chaired of the voting rights division of the CNFF, and served as the leader on legal questions within the ICW and IWSA. These Frenchwomen had broad experience in international women's rights organizations, as well as political influence within France itself.

If the press can be believed, the Franco-American women's alliance of 1925 focused on "the equality between men and women in labor legislation as well as all other legislation" affecting public life and work.[45] In a preliminary action, Duchêne, Malaterre-Sellier, and Vérone authored a letter addressed to Carey Thomas, Bryn Mawr's president emerita, asserting their allegiance to legal equality with the statement: "Sex should never, in our opinion, be a basis for legislation."[46] This action was undoubtedly performed at the request of the Americans, and consequently the French were drawn into the controversial debate on strict gender equality that threatened to unravel the decades of protective labor legislation that shielded working women from some degree of exploitation, while re-entrenching gender differences. French laws had advanced protective labor legislation for women that restricted women's working hours (1892) and constrained other conditions of labor that "represented a nod to a more gendered vision of the industrial world wherein male work was the norm and women's deviant."[47] Many French women's rights organizations had advocated for "protective" legislation, especially for mothers, that was based, in part, on the affective vocation of women.[48] Solidarism and maternalism were ideologies that proved effective in France to justify the expansion of the state into the private sphere to provide social rights within the developing welfare state.[49] In order to align with these Americans the French were asked to publicly depart from their long-held positions.

The NWP's strict definition of equality alienated those who supported politics based in maternal protections and civic maternalism.[50] Any cementing of gender difference in law, based on women's inferiority and dependence, was precisely what the liberal feminists, including the NWP, opposed.[51] The radical goal of the ERT was the worldwide application of laws that treated men and women equally. While sidestepping questions of the application in colonial contexts altogether, the egalitarian activists insisted on the simple equality of men and women under the law in their nations, to place women under the same legal standards as those established for men.

1926: American Feminist Action in France

The NWP contributed to the fracturing of the international women's rights movement over the question of whether to pursue women's rights via strict gender equality or accept the reification of gender difference and the restrictions on women's economic choices that occurred when they secured "protective" rights. At the 1926 Conference of the International Alliance for Women's Suffrage and Equal Citizenship (henceforth, the Alliance), the congress split over a resolution calling for "no special regulations for women's work different from regulations for men." While a majority of the Alliance voted in favor of equality in principle, they were countered by a multinational dissenting minority group who insisted upon the necessity of developing "legislative protection for working mothers and their children."[52] At this meeting the NWP also lost its bid for formal affiliation with the Alliance in a vote of 123 to 48, due in part to the controversy over special protections.[53] The mainstream French press characterized the NWP as an "extremist" group whose definition of equality was so radical that they would even support "the accession of women to the priesthood."[54]

Unable to join the Alliance, Belmont turned to France as a site to demonstrate the NWP's power to effect political change.[55] She believed that the Americans could unite all French suffrage associations to win voting rights for women. Presumably Paris would then serve as a headquarters for future action within Europe.[56] Belmont imagined the creation of a "union mondiale des femmes" designed to realize equal rights for men and women. The NWP hoped to lead and "revitalize the international women's movement."[57]

NWP archival sources show that after the 1926 Alliance meeting, Belmont and her American associates attempted to launch a binational suffrage movement to secure voting rights for French women. Stevens, Belmont's industrious assistant, "ran herself ragged" attempting to locate a suitable place for headquarters in Paris from which they could "conduct work for suffrage for French women" at the head of a "federation of all French suffrage societies."[58] At the outset, however, one NWP member, Mary Winsor, gave critical misinformation to Stevens about the political strategies of several French suffrage associations that influenced decision-making on this union. Winsor urged that the influential organizations headed by Maria Vérone (LFDF) and Cécile Brunschvicg (UFSF) should be kept "away from any offer that Mrs Belmont might make" on the grounds that these French leaders "both disapproved of the street work."[59] Winsor recommended that the Americans find alternative suffrage associations such as Marthe Bray's Ligue d'action féminine pour le suffrage, an "action league" that used humorous propaganda to win working-class support.[60] They also considered the suitability of Elisabeth Fonsèque's Société pour l'amélioration du sort de la femme.[61] These two groups had modest memberships (estimates of five hundred for Bray's, one thousand for Fonsèque's), and thus these organizations were likely more agile than the venerable UFSF and LFDF.[62] Most importantly, Bray praised the Americans' militant political tactics as "un bel exemple" and called for the "necessity of action" by the French.[63] As reported by the NWP, Bray was ready "to take advantage of Mrs. Belmont's offer, and [was] dreadfully afraid it might fall thro'; because of the opposition of Vérone and Brunschvicg's societies."[64]

There were several potential reasons why the Americans wanted to align themselves with the most radical elements of the French suffrage movement even if they did not represent the largest organizations. The American NWP and the British Women's Social and Political Union were infamous in part because of their willingness to engage in street demonstrations and prison hunger strikes and other high-profile activities in an effort to sway the public. Both Bray and Vérone were attracted to these controversial publicity efforts.[65] The LFDF under Vérone's presidency (1919–38) embraced militant tactics that brought confrontation, arrests, and public attention.[66] Her militancy prompted police surveillance.[67] In 1922 Vérone became known by the moniker "Madame Quand-Même" after her outburst from the gallery, "Vive la république quand même," when the Senate voted 156 *contre* 134, rejecting the opportunity to debate women's voting rights.[68] Her political strategies were applauded by her American counterparts while they troubled her co-nationalists.[69]

By contrast, Brunschvicg was known for her *féminisme féminin*, meaning that she supported moderate political tactics designed to avoid alienating the modicum of pro-suffrage public opinion. Brunschvicg's arguments, like those of her feminine counterpart Marguerite Durand, valued gender difference and political alliances that disincentivized militancy.[70] The influential UFSF boasted a membership of perhaps 100,000 by 1928 and secured affiliation with the Radical Party. The UFSF supported pro-suffrage candidates, paraded in poster-decorated buses, and published a politically moderate newspaper, *La Française* (1906–34). Brunschvicg accepted a program of gradual enfranchisement (initially, only local suffrage) rather than hold out for equal voting rights.[71] Oddly enough, the Americans confused the French organizations and erroneously conflated Vérone's militant position with Brunschvicg's cautious one.[72]

Conflict over leadership may have been a more intractable problem. Belmont wished to unite the French under her authority, which seems to have been unlikely to accommodate French leaders' desires to command their own national movement. The French suffrage leaders themselves had difficult relations and failed to unify their political strategy.[73] These internal divisions disrupted the plan for the Paris headquarters and stalled the coordination efforts to confront the status quo.

The American proposal to unite French suffragists came at a critical time. In 1926 the French voting rights advocates attempted to overcome the intransigence of the senators who refused to debate or pass the voting rights bill approved by the Chamber of Deputies in 1919. Even a proposal for the municipal vote (approved in the Chamber in May 1925) was repulsed by the Radical Party–dominated Senate.[74] Obstructionism in the Senate was fueled by opposition to gender equality and a masculine definition of the abstract individual that excluded women from this seemingly universal category because of the "stubborn particularity of their sex."[75] Citizenship in France was gendered male in ways that limited the application of the Rights of Man to women.[76] Additionally republicans feared that women, many of whom had been educated by Church schools, would vote for Catholic interests and thus undermine the secular republic.[77] In an attempt to break the juggernaut in the French Senate, Belmont donated 50,000 francs to the French suffrage movement.[78] The funds arrived at a moment of national financial crisis due to skyrocketing inflation rates and immediately benefited the foundering pro-suffrage newspaper *La Française*.[79] This mainstream feminist newspaper subsequently survived another eight years.[80] Activists could not know then that the French Senate would obstruct every suffrage bill approved in the Chamber of Deputies (in 1928, 1932, and 1938).[81]

Belmont's donation brought the NWP closer to Vérone and the LFDF despite the fact that the money we know about benefited the UFSF. Vérone enlarged her relationship with the NWP by publicizing their activities in her newspaper columns, and inviting the Americans to join public events. In December 1926, for example, Stevens lectured on gender equality in the workplace at a high-profile LFDF event.[82] Stevens's egalitarian politics were well matched at the LFDF's meeting where resolutions were approved on gender equality in studies of occupational diseases, sick pay rates for women equivalent to their regular pay, and demands for the implementation of "equal pay for equal work."[83] Paul attested that the NWP activism in Paris resulted in "exceedingly good" publicity that subsequently bolstered their fundraising power among other Americans in France.[84] By contrast, *La Française* did not increase its scanty press coverage of American efforts.[85] The collaboration between Stevens and Vérone confirms Martha Davis's claim that the NWP preferred to align themselves with a "network of more radical and confrontational allies" as well as those with egalitarian sensibilities.[86] No evidence has yet been located, however, to confirm the establishment of an American-directed headquarters for political action in Paris that had been proposed in the summer of 1926.

The contribution of American money to the French parallels a larger tendency within interwar feminism by which privileged women acted out of a sense of sympathy, protectiveness, or responsibility for their "little sisters." Antoinette Burton argues that British women who took an interest in Indian women out of a sense of responsibility for their "colonial sisters," and thus participated in "imperial feminism," consequently reified the assumptions of the imperial culture in which they lived.[87] Marie Sandell finds that during the interwar period, women from enfranchised nations assumed a mentoring attitude and offered advice and even money to activists in other nations. In 1921, for instance, Indian women received $500 from a fund managed by Carrie Chapman Catt to aid their suffrage movement.[88] Sandell asserts that even as women's rights activists became more aware of inequalities worldwide, Anglo-Saxon and Nordic women wanted to maintain their dominance within the international organizations. Letters exchanged among ICW leaders reveal prejudice at the expense of the French and other so-called Latin countries characterized as "backward" in terms of societal development in comparison to their "Germanic" counterparts.[89]

The expressions of cultural superiority are also evident among the Americans of the NWP in some of their commentary on the French. In a published interview Belmont declared that women from "England, America, Sweden, [and] Norway" who were the "farthest along" in the women's movement "ought to help the women of nations less advanced."[90] This obligation required both money and labor, and it was tied to what Belmont and Paul considered a historic "evolution" away from national isolationism toward internationalism. One NWP member, Katharine Anthony, characterized the French women's rights movement as "lagging" in "vitality" due to defects in the supposed French national character and psychological weaknesses that, she claimed, had been observed by Mary Wollstonecraft in the eighteenth century. The "decorum" and lassitude of the French suffrage movement, Anthony asserted, were consequences of women's failure to ally themselves with other women due to a deference to "coquetry" and interest in the "opposite sex." Anthony claimed that the French lacked emotional unity as a class of women, a bond that served the English and Americans.[91] Moreover the Americans hoped to inspire Frenchwomen by their own stories of militancy so that the French would "devise equally effective measures for winning their own suffrage fight."[92] This also raises questions about the ways binary notions of superiority and inferiority influenced French-American alliances in international feminism. This thread of criticism, akin to victim-blaming, made the singular praise for women like Vérone, for her "vitality," energy, and willingness to risk arrest for feminist causes, all the more striking.[93] Clearly, assumptions about "national character" colored these relations as the Americans adopted an attitude of superiority toward the French and promoted their own tactics as the winning ones.

The Americans were not alone in their efforts to universalize their experience. Notions of national, cultural, and racial superiority were widespread within women's rights movements in this era. Indeed, many French feminists also universalized their own experiences and, with some important exceptions (notably Hubertine Auclert), were infrequently critical of the impact of European colonization.[94] As I have argued elsewhere, Vérone had complicated views of women's emancipation in the case of French colonies.[95] She acknowledged that European imperialism brought with it problems such as alcoholism, prostitution, derogatory representations in literature, and exploitation of child labor in the manufacturing of goods exported for the European market.[96] Vérone supported the growth of indigenous women's associations in French colonies but opined, from her encounters with the Kabyle (Berber) community in northern Algeria, that girls and women would be, in aggregate, better off under French secular laws and educated in secular schools than under religious law or in religious schools of any denomination. She insisted that the French legislature owed an equal number of schools to boys and girls of Algeria.[97] While she condemned the social costs of colonialism, she nevertheless maintained that secular, republican laws had potential protective and emancipatory power (e.g., over family abandonment, illegitimate children, and compulsory education). She argued that all women merited the rights of citizenship.[98] In other words, Vérone's feminist internationalism was rooted in the social rights legacy of French republicanism.

The International Feminist Agenda, the Equal Rights Treaty, and the League of Nations

In February 1928 Stevens pronounced the birth of "international feminism" and introduced the Equal Rights Treaty project in Havana before thousands of women at the Pan American Conference of Women: "If men can act internationally, we said, so can women. More and more the acts of humankind are being defined and determined globally. We have entered the international field to stay. Womankind admits no limits to her partnership with mankind. We mean to be citizens of the world together. No one shall fetter us or bind us to a tiny claim stake. Our homestead is the world."[99] Stevens returned to Europe (on Paul's instructions and Belmont's funds) to "confer" with feminist leaders, garner support for the international women's rights campaign, and launch the ERT in Paris.[100] In 1928, as head of the Inter-American Commission of Women (IACW), Stevens endeavored to see the imposition of women's equal rights from "above" while she also intended to mobilize grassroots activism. It was a risky and ambitious strategy.

1928: Protests at Rambouillet and the Debate over Militancy

The formal launch of the ERT in Europe by militant action occurred at Rambouillet in the summer of 1928. Stevens chose this moment in hopes of capitalizing on the international attention focused on the Kellogg-Briand antiwar negotiations. Yet neither Stevens nor her French allies, including UFSF activist Malaterre-Sellier, could secure a meeting with French President Aristide Briand during this historic political event.[101] Thus frustrated, Stevens and fellow activists from the NWP's Council on International Action pursued the Kellogg-Briand delegates to the forested town of Rambouillet, sixty-eight kilometers from Paris, in the hopes of a meeting.[102] The protesters, led by Stevens, included Americans Harriet Pickering and NWP treasurer Betty Gram Swing, the French artist Fanny Bunand-Sévastos, and two French representatives of the LFDF: the lawyer Yvonne Netter and treasurer Madame Auscaler.[103] On August 28, in a street protest outside the president's chateau, the activists displayed a large banner stating "Nous demandons un traité nous donnant des droits égaux" (We demand an equal rights treaty), waved national flags, and requested an audience with Briand (fig. 6).[104] Protesters hoped to present copies of the ERT to European delegates, each one tied with decorative ribbons in the color

6. An international delegation of women demonstrating for an Equal Rights Treaty in Rambouillet, France, on August 28, 1928. Copy at Schlesinger Library, Radcliffe Institute, Harvard University.

of each country's flag, a symbolic reminder that the nation remained the foundation of the world order.[105] Contrary to claims issued in press releases by the IACW, Vérone did not attend the demonstration. She publicized her support, apologetic for missing the event: "I strongly regret that my absence from Paris prevented me from accompanying these protesters."[106]

The exaggerated press accounts of the protest obscure its specific character. Perhaps the women "stormed the gates [of the] presidential palace" and "were borne off, struggling" with police.[107] Perhaps the women "threatened" the security of the plenipotentiaries' meeting as they formed a "well-organized 'advance.'"[108] Perhaps the French police "tore up their petition" (that requested a meeting with Briand).[109] Stevens's private recollections suggest that the demonstration was brief, peaceful, and never posed a danger to the ensconced officials.[110] In fact she wrote the following to her colleague: "Of course we did none of the things the press said—such as 'kicking & struggling, etc.' & such as 'crashing' the gate. . . . We merely asked to have our request for an audience sent in. The plain clothes man at the gate tore it & threw it to the ground without reading it. We then offered a copy & asked him if we might give it to the concierge in the lodge a hundred yards away. Thereupon he arrested us."[111] Gendarmes detained the non-French protesters, including Stevens, Pickering, and Swing, for lack of proper residency papers (*permis de séjour*).[112] Attorney Netter protested their six-hour-long detention.[113] Stevens was angered by the loss of their flags and disappointed that they were prevented from presenting officials with a copy of the treaty.[114]

Vérone, observing events from a distance, urged her readers to perceive the American women as powerful, influential figures on matters of international relations and policy.[115] She defended women's rights to exercise free speech, to assemble, and to appeal to political representatives for their rights. She posited that in this case, women's demonstrations in the international context validated their political power on the national level. Granted, this statement may have been a rhetorical tactic to dispel the impression that the Rambouillet action was ineffectual.[116] At Vérone's request, Prime Minister Raymond Poincaré defended these women's right to protest and thus validated them as political actors.[117] Vérone's ability to rouse Poincaré into action signals her own domestic political clout.

Vérone valued civil disobedience, and the Rambouillet events prompted her to call attention to the efficacy of bold political tactics.[118] She reassured Stevens of her solidarity, stating that she preferred to risk prison than to accept a compromise on women's rights.[119] In an interview she declared the need for direct action in the face of ongoing Senate intransigence: "We [French] were not agitators, nor cowards, it was from sentiment and reason that we claimed our rights. We lost ground. We now want to change the method. What do we have to lose?" Malaterre-Sellier endorsed Vérone's call for action, saying, "We must redouble our activity" in the face of Senate obstinacy; she favored "grandes manifestations" in the streets.[120] UFSF president Brunschvicg did not initially condemn or condone the militancy displayed at Rambouillet. Yet a few months later she announced that French women were "too timorous, too timid, too inert" and that the French suffrage movement suffered from a lack of direct political action.[121]

In the historiography, the Rambouillet protest was significant because, according to Leila Rupp, the event "rekindled the debate over militant tactics within the international women's movement."[122] We know that NWP benefactors and allies were alienated by the demonstration. Belmont was so irate about the arrests at Rambouillet that she threatened to withdraw her financial support from Stevens and the larger organization. The Welsh suffragist Rhondda (of the Six Points Group), hitherto an ally, admonished Stevens that militant action should be a last, not a first, resort.[123] Historians have not appreciated, however, that the French chose to applaud American militancy at Rambouillet and consequently they also reconsidered the effectiveness of direct action. Stevens was immediately reassured upon reading the French press reports that the Rambouillet protest "roused the sympathy of the French public, which is a great achievement. French . . . support to an international cause is the greatest thing that can be desired."[124] The demonstration illustrated how the "average" female citizen could assert her views on international relations, in this case proposing political change to authorities. The events reinforced an association between women's political action and the French tradition of human rights, diplomatic finesse, and cultural leadership.

The Rambouillet affair was also an opportunity to reinforce political messages about equality and women's political power.[125] In her widely circulating column in *L'Oeuvre*, Vérone publicly endorsed the Americans' Equal Rights Treaty because it called for "civil equality, political equality, economic equality, *voilà*, the cause to which intelligent, devoted, and generous women have committed themselves." She valued the NWP's strategy of appealing to world authority as a means of influencing reform on a national level: "The Americans, who have not yet conquered absolute equality, know the fight; they have decided to appeal to the entire world for [the cause] of women's liberation."[126] Here Vérone acknowledged both Americans' global ambition and the reality that they had not yet achieved the constitutional equality that they had proposed via the ERA.

The relationship between American and French feminists was characterized by a desire for cooperation and intense national competition in the pursuit of articulating a vision of women's "international citizenship." In October 1928 at a meeting of the LFDF, Stevens declared that international law was the best safeguard for women's rights as a form of "human liberty" to be enshrined "as a fundamental principle of international law."[127] International legal action, she argued, was "the only answer" to the worldwide subordination of women in an interdependent world.[128] This unifying message was undercut, however, by Blanche Baralt, a literature professor and NWP member, who predicted that "the last shall be first and perhaps we [women of the Americas] may receive complete liberty and justice sooner than the venerable nations of the old world whose women have had to struggle so long. . . . Women of France, you have for centuries held up high the torch of civilization and idealism, will you allow it to be so?"[129] Baralt's comments contrasted a conventional, static "old Europe" versus a dynamic "New World." Thus, ironically Baralt provoked national competition in the name of international progress. She also evoked notions of national hierarchical differences that placed the Americans above the French while ostensibly promoting global sisterhood.

Seemingly undeterred by such tensions, Vérone seized this moment to urge Stevens to partner on a tour to promote the ERT in France, Belgium, and Switzerland.[130] This would have been a unique collaboration to bring attention to equal rights for women in these Western European countries. Even though Stevens had come to France in 1928 specifically to campaign for the ERT, she declined Vérone's invitation and abruptly turned over control of the treaty campaign to a disinterested Rhondda in February 1929. Moreover, in the summer of 1929 Stevens temporarily suspended her political action on the grounds that she was not welcome, observing that she should "tend [her] own garden [in the Americas] and not try to join with European action."[131] Diane Hill suggests that Stevens was then concerned about potentially antagonizing her European allies.[132] Rhondda had warned Stevens away from participating in the imminent debate on the married women's nationality campaign in Europe out of fear that Stevens would "antagonize all the supporters of the old International Feminist bodies & [would] be accused of butting in & be regarded as the black sheep of the movement."[133] Nevertheless Belmont and Stevens were determined to secure American participation in The Hague Codification of International Law Conference (1930) of the League, where married women's rights would be debated, in part so they could test the potential of the ERT.[134] By doing so they intervened in an already decades-old campaign in which Chrystal Macmillan and Maria Vérone were veterans. The abrupt change of plans around the ERT and the strained relations over women's nationality that developed raise the question of whether these transatlantic alliances were grounded in mutual understanding and appreciation, or rather in expediency.

1930: Working Independently and
Collaboratively toward a Common Goal

The activists who campaigned for women's legal equality made a radical claim for the inherent personhood of women. If the legal subject, the "person," could be rendered a gender-neutral term, then this would permit women to claim all the rights and responsibilities of citizenship articulated for men.[135] The campaign for married women's independent nationality rights at The Hague Codification of International Law Conference provided an opportunity for legal experts to assert their vision of women as persons, equal to men, meriting equal treatment under national and international laws. Vérone (representing the ICW) appealed to The Hague conference delegates to respect women's autonomy in nationality: "to prove that woman is no longer a chattel which the owner may dispose of as he thinks best, but a human being who, like a man is entitled to justice, freedom, independence, and I would say, the primary right of the human being: the right to a fatherland."[136] In her statements to the League Vérone articulated a central claim of feminist internationalism: that women have fundamental rights based on their personhood.

The Hague conference responded to the fact that the status of women's independent nationality varied during the interwar years, when some countries reformed or abolished marital naturalization and expatriation while others retained it. From its founding year in 1916, the NWP opposed the 1907 U.S. law that differentiated male and female rights to citizenship after marriage to a foreigner and consequentially compelled women to relinquish their citizenship. This discriminatory law personally affected several members of the NWP.[137] Rather than drawing on these cases, however, Stevens made a literary argument, that the story of Dalila, as represented in Milton's seventeenth-century poem "Samson Agonistes," demonstrates the patriotism of a women who sacrificed her private love to benefit a public commitment to her own people. This interpretation depends on seeing Dalila as compelled to change her "nationality" by external forces.[138]

Ultimately the Codification Conference resolved to study the possibility of introducing the "principle of equality of the sexes in matters of nationality" while leaving intact the principle that the nationality of individuals within marriage should follow that of the male (where not already modified).[139] Vérone concluded that this nonbinding decision moved the international debate in the direction of equality, namely, an express wish that nations respect women's consent in nationality concerns, a proposal that each nation should study the feasibility of egalitarian nationality laws, and a plan to send the question to a future League commission. By contrast, Stevens and Paul refused to support any agreement that failed to advance equality for women across the board, and they badgered U.S. delegates with calls, telegrams, and visits to urge them not to ratify the codification agreement.[140] Vérone disliked the Americans' disruptive actions and she called publicly for all feminists to unite.[141] There is no doubt that the alliance of Vérone, Stevens, and Paul was sorely tested by their difference of opinions on how to proceed on married women's nationality rights.

Candice Lewis Bredbenner argues that the Codification Conference "was a pivotal event in the history of women's nationality rights" that challenged countries to define and defend their positions and "fostered the coalescence of an international feminist movement for independent citizenship."[142] Ellen DuBois and Catherine Jacques each conclude that the conference was important because the feminist analysis articulated at the time was the product of more than a decade of thought on the matter and underscored the centrality of marriage to the legal inequalities that women suffered.[143] Beatrice McKenzie asserts that the NWP itself gained credibility and influence as a result of Stevens's participation at The Hague event.[144] The ways the feminists behaved toward one another, however, did not benefit the trajectory of their otherwise shared transatlantic equal rights campaign. When Stevens (with the IACW) secured an endorsement for equal nationality at the 1933 Montevideo International Conference of American States, she flaunted the fact that the "New World" leaders endorsed gender equality in contrast to the perceived timidity and chauvinism of the "Old World" Europeans, a fulfillment of Baralt's predictions.[145]

Simultaneously, between 1930 and 1933 women's political action for equal nationality rights had moved forward in Europe. Women's activism led to the creation of the League of Nations' Consultative Committee on Nationality, composed of two delegates from each of eight international associations, including Vérone as ICW representative and Paul for the IACW. This committee met in Geneva beginning in the summer of 1931 to authorize these nonstate actors to advise the League on critical questions of women's rights.[146] Vérone, who was largely responsible for writing the committee's reports, urged that "the principle of equality must be laid down in international legislation."[147] Paul and Vérone worked together on the Consultative Committee reports in 1931 and 1932 and they pressured the League to create and commit funds to form the Commission of Experts on the Legal Status of Women in 1933.[148] This commission was charged with studying the legal condition of women worldwide and codifying women's legal rights.[149] The forerunner of the better-known United Nations' Committee on the Status of Women, it was among the most significant outcomes of this cooperation.[150] By 1935 the Alliance, among other organizations, supported the ERT "in principle," though questions on how to apply equality remained unresolved.[151] This historic trajectory of the ERT in Europe reveals the multiple channels through which civic engagement, political power, and, occasionally, national prejudice proceeded.[152]

The extended history of the ERT in the 1930s is beyond the scope of this chapter; suffice it to say that the campaign for gender equality launched by these activists remained tremendously rocky. Briefly stated, the ERT project was adopted by the Equal Rights International organization, headed by Rhondda and staffed by members from Britain, Holland, Australia, and the United States.[153] In 1934, however, the relationship between Rhondda and Paul ruptured, apparently due to frustrations on the American side that although they possessed the power of the purse this did not grant them authority over others' actions.[154] In 1935 the French and British coordinated their efforts to secure equality for working women through the Open Door International, an organization dedicated to the "emancipation of the woman worker."[155] Andrée Lehmann, a lawyer and Vérone's second at the LFDF, established a French branch of the organization and made Vérone the vice president.[156] Lehmann defended working women's rights in a climate of increasing hostility. She lamented that French women were "always being asked to serve" but were "denied independence and security." She insisted, "The struggle to ensure woman's right to earn will be a hard one, and women need to revise all their methods, or all that they have gained will be taken from them. The professional women must realize their solidarity with other women, and cease to look on themselves as brilliant exceptions."[157] Such themes of solidarity and suggestions of resolute methods spoken by a French feminist to an Anglo-American audience seem to echo the LFDF experience of the 1920s. Members of the Open Door International articulated their struggle to emancipate working women from discrimination and an oppressive system of gender inequality as simultaneously national and transnational. Their experiences in the early twentieth century had cemented the necessity of this multilevel approach.

Conclusion

This snapshot of French-American cross-fertilization among women's rights advocates confirms that the French suffrage movement, particularly the UFSF, benefited from American money and that political action within the French context provided the Americans with a modest increase in publicity and exposure. The support each offered, however, did not yield the intended results. Responding to suggestions that Anglo-American feminism had eclipsed the French version, Vérone would later insist that egalitarian feminism was "born in France" despite what "many misinformed people think." In a radio speech Vérone defined French feminism as "a philosophical doctrine based on the equality of all human beings, and its aim is to establish equality between the sexes in all spheres, civil, political, intellectual economic and social," which, she insisted, was not imported. This was the shared egalitarian ideology that she hoped would be applied in law worldwide through the League's actions.[158]

The history examined in this chapter underscores women's desire to participate in international decision-making and their capacity to engage in comprehensive legal and comparative research and advocacy on women's status through their associations. In turn, the activism among feminists to secure individual equal rights through international law at The Hague and in Geneva reveals the importance of women's voices in the emerging "international society" where interconnectivity contributed to "functioning internationalism," or the opportunity for associations and private actors to contribute to social and humanitarian needs.[159] French and American reformers pursued international law as a mechanism to improve women's sociopolitical roles and status, and they drafted the very proposals that provided language for the international agreements that eventually took effect. The kind of work these reformers undertook in the area of international law required collaborative research and coordination that was not sponsored by universities or governments but rather was performed by politically motivated and educated women operating mostly as volunteers within their associations. Such international networking was part of the modern movement of feminisms that has fostered a globally interconnected movement.

Alice Paul, Doris Stevens, Germaine Malaterre-Sellier, and Cécile Brunschvicg lived to see (though Alva Belmont and Maria Vérone would not) women's equal voting rights granted in France in 1944 and women's equality formally established in the 1946 Constitution of the

French Fourth Republic (1946–58) and in the Universal Declaration of Human Rights (1948). This history should draw our attention to the potential power of citizens to act despite their formal exclusion from political rights (in the French case) or international bodies (in the case of the Americans' absence from the League of Nations). Moreover, these early feminists valued international law as a means to redress the imbalance of power between men and women.[160]

Inequality in the twentieth century sustained multiple modern processes that differentiated between the rights of men and women, adults and children, the colonizers and the colonized, as well as along other lines, such as race and religion.[161] The Equal Rights Treaty was a blunt instrument to attempt to redraw the social and sexual contracts through the narrow notion of gender equality.[162] Its fate in Europe reveals the lack of a consensus on the application of equality to diverse human subjects, a problem currently relevant in controversies around gender *parité* in political representation and equal pay in employment.[163]

The debates on women's rights that engaged the French and Americans also illuminate the activists' commitment to opening political spaces for the reconsideration of rights. The emphasis on "women's rights" per se, however, exposes the assumption that the "person" was a gendered subject. The American insistence on equality under the law through the ERT attempted to de-gender the political subject but in so doing failed to address the material reality of intersectional human identity and experience. The debate itself signifies the importance of grappling with the definition of "equal citizenship" for these female activists who, though marginalized in their own nations, used international forums to articulate visions for a more gender-neutral body politic. By seeking international dialogue as the privileged site for legal change and subsequent enforcement, these feminist activists questioned the power of the nation-state as the final authority to resolve problems such as inequality in citizenship. Activists gained authority through their international engagements before they ultimately returned to separate nations to pursue specific reforms, a pattern that reveals the enduring significance of the nation and its laws in the context of emergent internationalism.

One purpose of this volume is to interrogate the relationship between the women portrayed in these pages and the nature of the gender system and gender inequality in the modern period in France. The feminists portrayed here regarded the law under which they lived as antiquated and out of step with modern women's capabilities, with international trends, and with the experiences of men and women in their private lives. Feminists assumed that equality was their birthright as humans in the Western liberal democratic tradition and their activism challenged the status quo of legal inequality. Such activism emerged from their conviction that women must participate in decision-making at all levels governing the contours of their lives. Undoubtedly, their ideology of international gender equality had limitations and blind spots, especially related to the differences regarding maternity, gender identity, and colonial subjectivity. Nevertheless, international law, their preferred vehicle for reform, reflected within it the potential to grant to citizens equal treatment under the law based on concepts rooted in the Enlightenment and French and American revolutionary traditions.

Notes

1. "Mrs. O. H. P. Belmont Dies at Paris Home," *New York Times*, January 26, 1933; Katheryn P. Viens, "Belmont, Alva Erskine Smith Vanderbilt," *American National Biography Online*, Oxford University Press, 2000.

2. In 1925 Alice Paul met with Elizabeth Robins, Viscountess Rhondda, Dr. Louisa Martindale, Virginia Crawford, Dorothy Evans, Emmeline Pethick-Lawrence, Alison Neilans, Florence Underwood, and Miss Barry. (See photograph at U.S. Library of Congress, http://hdl.loc.gov/loc.mss/mnwp.159031).

3. U.S. House of Representatives, Equal Rights Amendment [the Mott Amendment], H.J. Res. 75, 68th Congress, 1st session, December 13, 1923.

4. Alice Paul in *An International Parliament of Women: Resolutions Adopted at the National Conference of the Woman's Party, November 17, 1923* (Washington DC: National Woman's Party, 1923), 3.

5. Paul in *An International Parliament of Women*, 3–4; Jane Norman Smith, "For the Equal Rights Treaty" [address to Pan-American Conference], *Equal Rights*, February 25, 1928, 21–22.

6. Susan Becker, *The Origins of the Equal Rights Amendment: American Feminism between the Wars* (Westport CT: Greenwood Press, 1981), 164.

7. "1925. Main Events," Doris Stevens Papers (hereafter DSP), box 48, folder 2, Schlesinger Library, Radcliffe Institute, Harvard University (hereafter SL). See also *Equal Rights* 1925 issues: March 28, 51; June 20, 145; July 18, 177; August 15, 209, 211.

8. Mme. Anthippe Couchoud and Fanny Bunand-Sévastos in the National Woman's Party Photograph Collection, (Washington DC), catalog numbers 1910.001.174 and 1910.001.155.01.

9. "French Women and the Franchise," *Equal Rights* 1, no. 5 (1923): 34. Global feminist political plan adopted in 1923 in Paul, *An International Parliament of Women*, 4.

10. Vérone and Belmont may have met at the IWSA conference in 1913 (Budapest) or 1920 (Geneva). See International Woman Suffrage Alliance, *Report of Seventh Congress, Budapest, Hungary June 15-21, 1913* (Manchester, UK: Percy Brothers, 1913); International Woman Suffrage Alliance, *Report of Eighth Congress, Geneva, Switzerland, June 6-12, 1920* (Manchester, UK: Percy Brothers, 1920); Sara L. Kimble, "Emancipation through Secularization: French Feminist Views of Muslim Women's Condition in Interwar Algeria," *French Colonial History* 7 (2006): 109-28; Sara L. Kimble, "Popular Legal Journalism in the Writings of Maria Vérone," *Proceedings of the Western Society for French History* 39 (2011): 224-35.

11. Juliette Rennes, "Maria Vérone," in *Dictionnaire des féministes: France XVIIIe-XXIe siècle*, ed. Christine Bard and Sylvie Chaperon (Paris: PUF, 2017), 1513.

12. Maria Vérone was twenty-one and working as an *institutrice* when her first child, Antoinette, was born in Paris in 1896; Maurice Giès recognized (*connue et légitimé*) Antoinette with his marriage to Maria on March 21, 1900, according to the *acte de naissance* (vital records).

13. See Dossier Maria Vérone, Bibliothèque Marguerite Durand, Paris; Christine Bard, "Maria Vérone," in *Dictionnaire Biographique du Mouvement Ouvrier Français*, ed. Jean Maîtron (Paris: Editions Ouvrière, 1993), 162-63.

14. League of Nations, *Acts for the Conference for the Codification of International Law* (Geneva: League of Nations, 1930), 2:180.

15. On Paul: Amy E. Butler, *Two Paths to Equality: Alice Paul and Ethel M. Smith in the ERA Debate, 1921-1929* (Albany: State University of New York Press, 2002), chap. 2.

16. Vera Brittain, "The Struggle for Equal Rights," in *Lady into Woman: A History of Women from Victoria to Elizabeth II* (New York: Macmillan, 1953), 67.

17. Edith Houghton Hooker quoted in Becker, *The Origins of the Equal Rights Amendment*, 163-64.

18. Doris Stevens, "Le féminisme et les questions internationales," ms (hand-written in French) MC 546 DSP, box 40, folder 298, Speeches. French League for Women's Rights, October 30, 1928, SL, 5.

19. Rhondda letter to Paul, 1926, cited in Becker, *The Origins of the Equal Rights Amendment*, n. 28, 191.

20. Stevens, "Le féminisme," 6. Belmont directed Stevens's action through the NWP's international action committee. Stevens chaired the IACW from April 1928 until 1939.

21. Katherine M. Marino, "Popular Front Pan-American Feminism and Working Women's Rights in the 1930s," in *Gender, Imperialism and Global Exchanges*, ed. Stephan Miescher (Chichester, West Sussex, UK: Wiley Blackwell, 2015), 265. See also Leila Rupp and Verta Taylor, *Survival in Doldrums: The American Women's Rights Movement, 1945 to the 1960s* (New York: Oxford University Press, 1987), 102.

22. Becker, *The Origins of the Equal Rights Amendment*, 162–63.

23. Carol Miller, "'Geneva—the Key to Equality': Inter-War Feminists and the League of Nations," *Women's History Review* 3, no. 2 (1994): 238.

24. Darrow asked whether "the entry of women into multinational poli-tics has been contingent upon the recognition of women's rights as an international issue" or "the opposite argument: that it was the entry of women into multinational politics . . . that placed and has kept women's rights on the world's agenda." Margaret H. Darrow, review of *Femmes et diplomatie: France—XXe siècle*, ed. Yves Denéchère, *H-France Review* 5, no. 39 (2005), http://www.h-france.net/vol5reviews/vol5htmlreviews /darrow3.html.

25. See Susan Zimmermann, "Night Work for White Women and Bonded Labour for 'Native' Women? Contentious Traditions and the Globalization of Gender-Specific Labour Protection and Legal Equality Politics, 1926 to 1939," in *New Perspectives on European Women's Legal History*, ed. Sara L. Kimble and Marion Röwekamp (New York: Routledge, 2017), 394–427; Carol Susan Linskey, "Invisible Politics: Dorothy Kenyon and Women's Internationalism, 1930–1950," PhD dissertation, State University of New York at Binghamton, 2013.

26. Karen Offen, *European Feminisms, 1700–1950: A Political History* (Stanford CA: Stanford University Press, 2000), 151–53.

27. Karen Offen, "Women, Citizenship, and Suffrage with a French Twist, 1789–1993," in *Suffrage and Beyond: International Feminist Perspectives*, ed. Caroline Daley and Melanie Nolan (Auckland: Auckland University Press, 1994), 151–70.

28. Martin Thomas, *The French Empire between the Wars: Imperialism, Politics and Society* (Manchester, UK: Manchester University Press, 2005), 152.

29. Sîan Reynolds, *France between the Wars* (London: Routledge, 1996), 188.

30. In 1923 IWSA changed its name to the International Alliance of Women for Suffrage and Equal Citizenship.

31. U.S. Delegation to the International American Conference, *Report of the Delegates of the United States of America to the Fifth International Conference of American States Held at Santiago, Chile, March 25 to May 3, 1923* (Washington DC: Government Printing Office, 1924), 61, 209.

32. In *The Origins of the Equal Rights Amendment*, Becker notes that the NWP envied the USSR and Scandinavian countries for their constitutional equality of the sexes (162–63).

33. Francesca Miller, *Latin American Women and the Search for Social Justice* (Hanover NH: University Press of New England, 1991), 106–8.

34. Paul Smith, *Feminism and the Third Republic: Women's Political and Civil Rights in France, 1918–1945* (Oxford: Clarendon Press, 1996), 38. Nancy Cott placed the origins of the international efforts by the Americans in 1926 in "Feminist Politics in the 1920s: The National Woman's Party," *Journal of American History* 71, no. 1 (1984): 65.

35. The press and NWP press releases stated that Vérone attended, and this error was repeated in Leila J. Rupp, *Worlds of Women: The Making of an International Women's Movement* (Princeton NJ: Princeton University Press, 1997), 138–39; and Mary K. Trigg, *Feminism as Life's Work: Four Modern American Women through Two World Wars* (New Brunswick NJ: Rutgers University Press, 2014), 150–52.

36. Ann Taylor Allen, Anne Cova, and Jane Purvis, "International Feminism," *Women's History Review* 19 (2010): 492–501; Julie Carlier, "Forgotten Transnational Connections and National Contexts: An 'Entangled History' of the Political Transfers That Shaped Belgian Feminism, 1890–1914," *Women's History Review* 19, no. 4 (2010): 503–22; Karen Offen, "Overcoming Hierarchies through Internationalism: May Wright Sewall's Engagement with the International Council of Women (1888–1904)," in *Women's Activism: Global Perspectives from the 1890s to the Present*, ed. Francisca De Haan, Margaret Allen, June Purvis, and Krassimira Daskalova (New York: Routledge, 2012), 15–28.

37. Chandra Talpade Mohanty, "Under Western Eyes: Feminist Scholarship and Colonial Discourses," *boundary 2* 12, no. 3 (1984): 333–58; Chandra Talpade Mohanty, "'Under Western Eyes' Revisited: Feminist Solidarity through Anticapitalist Struggles," *Signs* 28, no. 2 (2003): 499–535.

38. See Accampo's afterword in this volume.

39. In 1923, for example, this occurred at the Fifth International Conference of the American States (Santiago, Chile) and the International Woman Suffrage Alliance conference (Rome, Italy).

40. Lynn Hunt, *Inventing Human Rights: A History* (New York: Norton, 2008), 25.

41. Lorraine Coons, "Gabrielle Duchêne: Feminist, Pacifist, Reluctant Bourgeoise," *Peace & Change* 24, no. 2 (1999): 121-47.

42. Reynolds, *France between the Wars*, 196-97.

43. Three French names on a list of International Feminist Committee members, undated typed mss., in Alice Paul Papers, Series V, box 120, folder 1623, SL.

44. James McMillan, *France and Women, 1789-1914: Gender, Society and Politics* (London: Routledge, 2000), 212.

45. "French Join in World Feminism," *Paris Times*, April 22, 1925, copy in Alice Paul Papers, box 120, folder 1623, SL.

46. Letter dated April 28, 1925, quoted in Simone Tery, "American Apostles to France," *Equal Rights*, June 20, 1925, 149-50.

47. Judith Coffin, *The Politics of Women's Work: The Paris Garment Trades, 1750-1915* (Princeton NJ: Princeton University Press), 231-34.

48. Diane Elizabeth Hill, "International Law for Women's Rights: The Equal Treaties Campaign of the National Women's Party and Reactions of the U.S. State Department and the National League of Women Voters (1928-1938)," PhD dissertation, University of California, Berkeley, 1999.

49. Elinor A. Accampo, Rachel G. Fuchs, and Mary Lynn Stewart, *Gender and the Politics of Social Reform in France, 1870-1914* (Baltimore: Johns Hopkins University Press, 1995).

50. In the United States, the NWP split from the League of Women Voters on gender-specific protections. Maternalism served to further women's civic involvement by exalting women's maternal capacity and their ability to extend to society the values of care, nurturance, and morality. See Ann Taylor Allen, *Feminism and Motherhood in Germany, 1800-1914* (New Brunswick NJ: Rutgers University Press, 1991); Ann Taylor Allen, *Feminism and Motherhood in Western Europe, 1890-1970: The Maternal Dilemma* (New York: Palgrave Macmillan, 2005); Marian van der Klein, Rebecca Jo Plant, Nichole Sanders, and Lori R. Weintrob, eds., *Maternalism Reconsidered: Motherhood, Welfare and Social Policy in the Twentieth Century* (New York: Berghahn Books, 2012); Seth Koven and Sonya Michel, "Womanly Duties: Maternalist Politics and the Origins of Welfare States in France, Germany, Great Britain, and the United States, 1880-1920," *American Historical Review* 95 (1990): 1079; Offen, *European Feminisms*.

51. Nancy Woloch, *A Class by Herself: Protective Laws for Women Workers, 1890s-1990s* (Princeton NJ: Princeton University Press, 2015), 173.

52. International Alliance of Women for Suffrage and Equal Citizenship, *Report of Tenth Congress, Paris, France May 30th to June 6th, 1926* (London: Caledonian Press, 1926), 107, 121.

53. On conflicts between the National Woman's Party and the League of Women Voters, see Hill, "International Law"; Sylvia D. Hoffert, *Alva Vanderbilt Belmont: Unlikely Champion of Women's Rights* (Bloomington: Indiana University Press, 2012), 156; Candice Bredbenner, *A Nationality of Her Own: Women, Marriage, and the Law of Citizenship* (Berkeley: University of California Press, 1998), 199.

54. Geo London (pseudonym of Georges Samuel), "Les suffragettes travaillent et commencent par éliminer les propositions extrémistes et les extrémistes elles mêmes," *Le Journal*, June 1, 1926.

55. Becker, *The Orgins of the Equal Rights Amendment*, 163.

56. Cott, "Feminist Politics in the 1920s," 65. Other uses of money in politics: Belmont became the benefactor to the American suffrage movement in 1909 and supported the Women's Trade Union League (1909-10); see Viens, "Belmont, Alva Erskine Smith Vanderbilt."

57. "La présidente du parti américain des femmes est arrivée en France," *Le Matin*, June 3, 1926; Becker, *The Orgins of the Equal Rights Amendment*, 163.

58. Stevens's typed note headed "1926" in DSP, box 48, folder 3, SL, 6-7.

59. Letter from Winsor to Stevens, June 22, 1926, in DSP, box 48, folder 3, SL.

60. Bray admired Hubertine Auclert and believed humor could attract attention and prompt public reflection. On Bray, see Reynolds, *France between the Wars*, 178; Florence Rochefort, "La citoyenneté interdite ou les enjeux du suffragisme," *Vingtième siècle: Revue d'histoire* 42 (April-June 1994): 45; Laurence Klejman and Florence Rochefort, *L'égalité en marche: Le féminisme sous la Troisième République* (Paris: Presses de Sciences Po, 1989), 294-95.

61. Correspondence from Winsor to Stevens, June 26, 1926, in DSP, box 48, folder 3, SL. See also Fonsèque's letter to Belmont, March 10, 1926, Fonds Bouglé, Bibliothèque Historique de la Ville de Paris (hereafter BHVP).

62. In September 1926 a dozen "action league" activists toured France by motorcar, promoting suffrage in more than twenty towns with humorous posters, placards, and leaflets. "Le départ des suffragettes pour leur randonnée de propagande," *Le Matin*, September 8, 1926. Fonsèque also headed the suffrage section of the CNFF; Bray was an LFDF member.

63. Marthe Bray, "Un bel exemple," *La Fronde*, June 23, 1926, copy in Fonds Bray, BHVP.

64. Letter from Winsor to Stevens, June 22, 1926, in DSP, box 48, folder 3, SL.

65. Katherine H. Adams and Michael L. Keene, *Alice Paul and the American Suffrage Campaign* (Urbana: University of Illinois Press, 2008). On the WSPU: June Purvis, *Emmeline Pankhurst: A Biography* (London: Routledge, 2002).

66. In 1897 she lectured on education in Orleans for the Cercle d'enseignement laïc, an organization she cofounded. She had worked as an *institutrice adjointe* in Paris with the LFDF from 1894. For her statement on the "costs" of political protest, see LFDF meeting, November 22, 1922, Dossier 1922, Rapports et notes concernant l'activité des divers groupements féministes, Archives Nationales de France (hereafter AN) F/7/13266.

67. AN F/7/13266.

68. Klejman and Rochefort, *L'égalité en marche*, 291.

69. Differing viewpoints on militancy: "Les Françaises veulent voter," *La Renaissance: Politique, littéraire et artistique*, December 15, 1928, 8–10.

70. Cécile Formaglio, *"Féministe d'abord": Cécile Brunschvicg (1877–1946)* (Rennes: Presses Universitaires de Rennes, 2014), 72; see Mary Louise Roberts, *Disruptive Acts: The New Woman in Fin-de-Siècle France* (Chicago: University of Chicago Press, 2002).

71. Christine Bard, *Les Filles De Marianne: Histoire des Féminisme 1914–1940* (Paris: Fayard, 1995), 155; Anne Cova, "French Feminism and Maternity: Theories and Policies, 1890–1918," in *Maternity and Gender Policies: Women and the Rise of the European Welfare*, ed. Gisela Bock and Pat Thane (Oxford: Routledge, 1991), 130.

72. Belmont, Stevens, and Paul spoke and read French. Winsor was educated at Drexel Institute and Bryn Mawr College and studied abroad.

73. Brunschvicg and Vérone had "frosty" relations, notes Smith, *Feminism and the Third Republic*, 38.

74. Emile Borel bill; Frances I. Clark, *The Position of Women in France* (London: King & Son, 1937), 244.

75. Alice L. Conklin, Sarah Fishman, and Robert Zaretsky, *France and Its Empire Since 1870*, 2nd ed. (New York: Oxford University Press, 2015), 63.

76. Charles Sowerwine, "Revising the Sexual Contract: Women's Citizenship and Republicanism in France, 1789–1944," in *Confronting Modernity in Fin-de-Siècle France: Bodies, Minds and Gender*, ed. Christopher Forth and Elinor Accampo (London: Palgrave Macmillan, 2010), 19–42.

77. Charles Sowerwine, *France Since 1870: Culture, Society and the Making of the Republic* (London: Palgrave Macmillan, 2009), 119; see Steven C. Hause, and Anne R. Kenney, *Women's Suffrage and Social Politics in the French Third Republic* (Princeton NJ: Princeton University Press, 1984).

78. Stevens's typed notes from 1926, in DSP, box 48, folder 3 ("Correspondence and notes re: Belmont, 1926–1928"), SL.

79. "Suffrage Congress Stirs French Women," *New York Times*, June 8, 1926. The 1926 exchange rate was highly variable; the 1927 franc was valued at 4 cents. Malaterre-Sellier to Belmont, November 12, 1926, in DSP, MC 546, SL. *La Française*, edited by Jane Misme until 1926, was one of the most successful and enduring feminist newspapers (1906–34). Control over *La Française* had just moved from the CNFF to the UFSF, but neither group could finance the paper despite their efforts to raise funds through appeals to readers and higher annual subscription rates. See Marguerite Pichon-Landry, "*La Française* doit vivre," *La Française*, October 24, 1925; "*La Française* doit vivre," *La Française*, May 15, 1926.

80. The UFSF established a receivership for the newspaper, reduced their publication schedule, and installed new editorial leadership. "A Nos Lectrices," *La Française*, July 16, 1926. My thanks to Karen Offen for this source. Editor Suzanne Babled was replaced by Cécile Brunschvicg. On feminist lawyers and journalism see Sara L. Kimble, "Feminist Lawyers and Political Change in Modern France, 1900–1940," in *Women in Law and Law-making in the Nineteenth and Twentieth Century Europe*, ed. Eva Schandevyl (Aldershot, UK: Ashgate, 2014), 45–73.

81. Political demonstrators ran increasing risks; beginning in 1927 a police circular prohibited all nonofficial and nonfuneral processions, demonstrations, and marches on public roads. Circular of August 14, 1927, in Danielle Tartakowsky, *Les manifestations de rue en France, 1918–1968* (Paris: Sorbonne, 1997), 145.

82. Other members included law professor Georges Renard; lawyer Andrée Lehmann, who spoke on labor regulation; and labor activist Charlotte Bonnin (Syndicat des Postes, Téléphones et Télégraphes), who pleaded for lifting the ban against women's night work.

83. "French Women Ask for Equality," *Times* (Paris), December 8, 1926, in DSP, box 46, folder 16, SL.

84. Letters from Alice Paul to Anita Pollitzer, June 21, 1926, and August 23, 1926, in series of letters from June to August 1926, Pollitzer Papers 24/44/6, South Carolina Historical Society, Charleston.

85. I reviewed *La Française* from 1927 to 1930 and found few references to American activism.

86. Martha F. Davis, "Not So Foreign after All: Alice Paul and International Women's Rights," *New England Journal of International and Comparative Law* 16 (2010): 6.

87. Antoinette M. Burton, "The White Woman's Burden. British Feminists and the Indian Woman, 1865-1915," *Women's Studies International Forum* 13, no. 4 (1990): 295-308.

88. Marie Sandell, *The Rise of Women's Transnational Activism: Identity and Sisterhood between the World Wars* (London: I. B. Tauris, 2015), 72.

89. Latin and Eastern European countries included in letter of Bertha Nordenson to Lady Aberdeen, quoted in Sandell, *Rise of Women's Transnational*, 62-63.

90. Belmont in Tery, "American Apostles to France," 150.

91. Katharine Anthony, "Feminism in Foreign Countries, *Suffragist* 1, no. 9 (1921): 357-58.

92. Katherine Ward Fisher, "La Revue de la Femme," *Equal Rights* no. 35, October 8, 1927, 275.

93. "French Women and the Franchise," *Equal Rights* no. 5, March 17, 1923, 34.

94. Carolyn Eichner, "*La Citoyenne* in the World: Hubertine Auclert and Feminist Imperialism," *French Historical Studies* 32, no. 1 (2009): 63-84.

95. Kimble, "Emancipation through Secularization," 109-28.

96. Maria Vérone, "Impressions d'algérie," *Le Droit des femmes*, May 1926, 433-35.

97. Séance du 29 Janvier 1932, *Bulletin de la Société de législation comparée*, May-June 1932, 182-84.

98. Vérone spoke on "*la femme Kabyle*" on occasion, including in Paris: *Annales africaines*, July 3, 1925; Maria Vérone, "Section de Législation," *Conseil national des femmes françaises*, 1926, 20-22.

99. Doris Stevens, "International Feminism Is Born," *Time and Tide*, April 13, 1928, 355. On Latin American feminism and its relation to the NWP women, see Katherine M. Marino, "Transnational Pan-American Feminism: The Friendship of Bertha Lutz and Mary Wilhelmine Williams, 1926-1944," *Journal of Women's History* 26, no. 2 (2014): 63-87. See also Miller, *Latin American Women*; Megan Threlkeld, *The Inter-American Commission of Women: Sources on Hemispheric Solidarity* (Alexandria VA: Alexander Street, 2012), https://search.alexanderstreet.com/view/work/bibliographic _entity%7Cbibliographic_details%7C2476951. Also Ellen Carol Dubois, "Internationalizing Married Women's Nationality: The Hague Campaign of 1930," in *Globalizing Feminisms, 1789-1945,* ed. Karen M. Offen (London: Routledge, 2010), 204-16.

100. The precise date in 1928 when Stevens received this instruction from Paul is unclear in Stevens's "Main Events" of 1928 typed notes in DSP, box 48, folder 3, SL. Stevens, "International Feminism Is Born," 353-56. In Europe, Stevens met with barrister Chrystal Macmillan (Scotland), suffragist Lady Margaret Rhondda (Wales), Maria Vérone (France), Marquesa del Ter

(Spain), Dr. Blanche Baralt (a Cuban living in Paris), Hélène Vacaresco (Romania), and International Federation of University Women leader Professor Ellen Gleditsch (Norway). Doris Stevens, "Feminist Victory . . . Women Plenipotentiaries to The Hague Codification Conference," press release by IACW, September 14, 1928, DSP, box 94, folder 7, SL. Alice Paul studied law at American University (Washington DC).

101. Typed note with list of supporters of the Committee on International Action of the NWP, no date, in DSP, box 87, folder 4, SL; "Le Comité d'action internationale des femmes et les plenipotentiaires de la paix," *Le Matin*, August 23, 1928; letter dated August 23, 1928, from office of Affaires Etrangères, cabinet du Ministre, indicating to Doris Stevens that President Briand was not available but a meeting with others was possible, in DSP, box 87, folder 4, SL.

102. The French term in use was Comité d'action internationale of the "Woman's Party."

103. Maria Vérone, "Les féministes à Rambouillet," *L'Oeuvre*, August 30, 1928; Doris Stevens to Maria Vérone (addendum to letter), February 11, 1929, DSP, box 68, folder 13, SL. Bunand-Sévastos was involved in the International Action Committee; Auscaler's first name has not been identified.

104. "10 Women Arrested at Dinner to Envoys," *New York Times*, August 29, 1928, 1; "Women, Seeking Equal Rights, Land in Prison," *St. Petersburg (FL) Times*, August 29, 1928.

105. Memorabilia 5, Rambouillet action, August 1928, in DSP, Series V, box 94, folder 6, SL.

106. Vérone, "Les féministes à Rambouillet." Catherine Anger, an archivist at the Bibliothèque Marguerite Durand, reported that she found no mention of "l'affaire Rambouillet" or of Doris Stevens or Alice Paul in the dossiers "Maria Vérone" and "Ligue française pour le droit des femmes" as of February 4, 2015.

107. "Women Storm Palace; Jailed," *Pittsburgh Press*, August 28, 1928.

108. "10 Women Arrested."

109. Trigg, *Feminism as Life's Work*, 150.

110. Stevens to Vérone, February 11, 1929, in DSP, Series V, box 87, folder 5, SL; "10 Women Arrested."

111. Stevens to Elsie Ross Shields, October 1, 1928, DSP, Series V 83.13, SL.

112. "International Work of the National Woman's Party," typed ms., p. 3, in DSP, box 46, folder 19, SL; "French Arrest Doris Stevens, Feminist Chief," *Miami Daily News*, August 28, 1928.

113. Vérone, "Les féministes à Rambouillet."

114. Stevens to Vérone, February 11, 1929, in DSP, Series V, box 85, folder 5, SL; "10 Women Arrested."

115. Maria Vérone article published in *L'Oeuvre*, August 20, 1928, cited in Vérone, "Le statut mondial des femmes," *Le Droit des femmes*, September 1928, copy in DSP, box 94, folder 5, SL.

116. See Smith, *Feminism and the Third Republic*, 37–38.

117. Telegram from Vérone to Stevens, date illegible (circa August 29 or 30, 1928), DSP, box 87, folder 5, Rambouillet, SL. *L'Oeuvre*'s circulation was more than 135,000 in 1919 (230,000 by 1936), according to Archives Nationales, "Fonds *l'Oeuvre*," *Les fonds d'archives de presse conservé aux Archives Nationales (site de Paris), série* AR (Paris: Archives Nationales de France, 2010), 9. Vérone article published in *L'Oeuvre*, August 20, 1928.

118. Maria Vérone, "L'élection présidentielle aux Etats-Unis," *L'Oeuvre*, November 21, 1928.

119. Vérone to Stevens references an article in *Le Temps* of August 17, 1928, in postcard dated September 3, 1928, in DSP, box 87, folder 4, SL.

120. "Les Françaises veulent voter," *La Renaissance: Politique, littéraire et artistique*, December 15, 1928, 8–10.

121. Cécile Brunschvicg, "Manifestation et discipline," *La Française*, May 8, 1929.

122. Rupp, *Worlds of Women*, 138, 139, 270n60.

123. Angela V. John, *Turning the Tide: The Life of Lady Rhondda* (Cardigan, Wales: Parthian Books, 2013), 398.

124. Correspondence from IACW office (Elsie Ross Shields) to Doris Stevens, August 30, 1928, in DSP, Series V, box 83, folder 13, SL.

125. Letter from Georges Lhermitte to Doris Stevens, October 7, 1928, discussing the October 30, 1928, event arrangements, DSP, box 87, folder 4, SL.

126. Maria Vérone, "Le féminisme et les questions internationales," *L'Oeuvre*, October 24, 1928.

127. Stevens, "Le féminisme," 6.

128. Stevens's note to Belmont on events of 1928 in DSP, box 48, folder 3, SL.

129. "Translation of Madame Baralt's address," October 30, 1928, typed manuscript copy in DSP, box 94, folder 5, SL.

130. Letter from Stevens to Vérone, December 12, 1928, and letter from Vérone to Stevens, January 12, 1929, in DSP, Series V, box 68, folder 13, SL.

131. Quoted in Hill, "International Law for Women's Rights," 120; originally Doris Stevens to Helen Archdale, August 29, 1929, in DSP, box 4, folder 78, SL. By contrast, Macmillan and Vérone had a long history of working together through their overlapping associations, notably the IWSA, from at least 1913.

132. Hill, "International Law," chap. 2, passim.

133. Rhondda to Stevens, June 24, 1928, quoted in Hill, "International Law," 112, originally from DSP, box 5, folder 154, SL.

134. Letter from Stevens to Vérone, February 11, 1929, DSP, Series V, box 68, folder 13, SL. No evidence of collaboration between Rhondda and Vérone has yet emerged. I also corresponded with Angela John, May 19, 2015, who knew of no sources. See John, *Turning the Tide*, chap. 12, esp. 396.

135. On personhood, see Nitza Berkovitch, *From Motherhood to Citizenship: Women's Rights and International Organizations* (Baltimore: Johns Hopkins University Press, 1999).

136. League of Nations, *Acts for the Conference for the Codification of International Law*, 2:180.

137. Davis, "Not So Foreign after All," 4–6.

138. League of Nations, *Acts for the Conference for the Codification of International Law*, 2:182–83. For the poem see John Milton *Complete Poems and Major Prose*, ed. Merritt Yerkes Hughes (1957; Indianapolis: Hackett, 2003), 531–94.

139. League of Nations, *Acts for the Conference for the Codification of International Law*, 2:253.

140. Dubois, "Internationalizing Married Women's Nationality"; Davis, "Not So Foreign after All," 4–5.

141. Carbon copy of E. A. van Veen's interview with Vérone, associated with letter dated December 21, 1932, in Records of the ICW, Liaison Committee (5ICW/F/02), Women's Library, London School of Economics, London University.

142. Bredbenner, *A Nationality of Her Own*, 195.

143. Dubois, "Internationalizing Married Women's Nationality." See also Catherine Jacques, "Tracking Feminist Interventions in International Law Issues at the League of Nations: From the Nationality of Married Women to Legal Equality in the Family, 1919–1970," in Kimble and Röwekamp, *New Perspectives*, 321–48.

144. Beatrice McKenzie, "The Power of International Positioning: The National Woman's Party, International Law and Diplomacy, 1928–34," *Gender and History* 23, no. 1 (2011): 137.

145. Miller, *Latin American Women*, 106–8.

146. Other committee leaders: Margery I. Corbett Ashby (England) and Betsy Bakker Nort (Holland) of the International Alliance of Women for Suffrage and Equal Citizenship. Bredbenner, *A Nationality of Her Own*, 219.

147. 1932 report, quoted in Louise C. A. van Eeghen, "Maria Vérone," *Equal Rights*, September 1, 1938, 318. For photographic evidence of the meeting, see photos from July 2–6, 1931, in Alice Paul Papers, Series V, folder 1408, League of Nations: Women's Consultative Committee on Nationality, Geneva, mostly July 1931, SL.

148. See Susan Zimmermann, "Liaison Committees of International Women's Organizations and the Changing Landscape of Women's Internationalism, 1920s to 1945," in Sklar and Dublin, *Women and Social Movements*.

149. Jaci Eisenberg, "The Status of Women: A Bridge from the League of Nations to the United Nations," *Journal of International Organizations Studies* 4, no. 2 (2013): 13.

150. Gender equality in nationality was secured through a 1958 UN Convention via Convention on the Nationality of Married Women, 309 U.N.T.S. 65. See Agathe Dyvrande-Thévenin, "La Fédération International des Femmes Magistrats et Avocats," *La Vie Judiciaire*, November 10, 1934; Marcelle Kraemer-Bach and Marcelle Renson, *Le Régime matrimonial des époux dont la nationalité est différente: Rapport présenté à la Fédération Internationale des Femmes Magistrats et Avocats en 1934 et 1935* (Paris: A. Pedone, 1939); Sophie Grinberg-Vinaver, "The Status of Women throughout the World," *Marriage and Family Living* 17, no. 3 (1955): 197–204.

151. Go. [Emilie Gourd], "Le Congrès d'Istamboul," *Le Mouvement féministe: Organe officiel des publications de l'Alliance nationale des sociétés féminines suisses* 23 (January 12, 1935): 55.

152. Laura Briggs, Gladys McCormick, and J. T. Way, "Transnationalism: A Category of Analysis," *American Quarterly* 60, no. 3 (2008): 625–48.

153. "Equal Rights International Organized," *Equal Rights*, September 27, 1930, 267; Alice Paul, "Women Demand Equality in World Code of Law," *Congressional Digest*, November 1930, 279.

154. Christine Bolt, *Sisterhood Questioned: Race, Class and Internationalism in the American and British Women's Movements c. 1880s–1970s* (New York: Routledge, 2004), 58–59.

155. Macmillan opposed the ERT; see Hill, "International Law," 347–48.

156. Susan Pedersen, *Family, Dependence, and the Origins of the Welfare State: Britain and France, 1914–1945* (Cambridge, UK: Cambridge University Press, 1993), 406.

157. *Open Door International for the Economic Emancipation of the Woman Worker: Report of the Fourth Conference in Copenhagen, 1935* (Brussels: Open Door International, 1935), 19, 56, 19.

158. "Maître Maria Vérone parle du féminisme," on *The Blaze of Day*, Polydor, 1996, compact disc, recorded circa 1936–37.

159. Daniel Gorman, *The Emergence of International Society in the 1920s* (Cambridge UK: Cambridge University Press, 2012), 12, 58.

160. On internationalism via student exchanges see Whitney Walton, *Internationalism, National Identities, and Study Abroad: France and the United States, 1890–1970* (Stanford CA: Stanford University Press, 2010).

161. On inequality as a category of analysis see Patrick Manning, "Inequality: Historical and Disciplinary Approaches," *American Historical Review*, February 2017: 1–22.

162. Carole Pateman, *The Sexual Contract* (Stanford CA: Stanford University Press, 1988).

163. Joan Wallach Scott, *Parité! Sexual Equality and the Crisis of French Universalism* (Chicago: University of Chicago Press, 2005). The EU is pressured to follow Iceland's lead: Associated Press, "In World First, Iceland to Require Firms to Prove Equal Pay," *New York Times*, March 8, 2017; "Women in Paris Go on Strike and Rally for Equal Pay," *Agence France-Presse*, March 8, 2017.

Afterword

ELINOR A. ACCAMPO

This collection of essays reopens the discussion begun more than two decades ago about the dynamic between gender and the rise of the welfare state; one of the works in which it intervenes is a volume Rachel Fuchs, Mary Lynn Stewart, and I coedited just over twenty years ago, *Gender and the Politics of Social Reform in France*. Our purpose was to demonstrate how concerns about women and gender played a role in the political and social reforms that laid the foundations for the welfare state between 1870 and 1914. It was, admittedly, a top-down approach, in which we sought to understand how, during an era that was so foundational to the Third Republic, men formulated policies that would both benefit and circumscribe the lives of French women. This current volume goes well beyond that approach by expanding the period under consideration back to the Enlightenment and the French Revolution and forward to Vichy. Most important, however, it examines women instead of men, not as *objects* of social and political reform but as its *agents* in their own right who took advantage of prevailing political ideologies, state, and administrative policies, and their own ingenious resources in order to appropriate various rights of citizenship before such rights were legally or explicitly conferred on their gender. Indeed these essays make a major contribution in clearly demonstrating how both extraordinary and ordinary women shaped and advanced social reform.

Because citizenship is a conceptual thread running through these essays, returning to its definition—or definitions—is a helpful way to tease out the important collective implications of this volume and to gain an understanding in broader terms of the significance of what women were able to achieve without its legal status. Nimisha Barton's and Richard Hopkins's introduction, as well as critics they cite, justifiably point to the inadequacies of T. H. Marshall's classic definition of citizenship, first articulated nearly seventy years ago in the form of lectures.[1] They fault Marshall for focusing exclusively on England and on nonminority men, and some have questioned the chronological framework in which national communities achieved citizenship rights. Collectively the research presented here challenges Marshall's notion that one needs a state to confer the legal status of citizenship in order to access rights and power. It may be useful nonetheless to revisit his conceptual framework before rethinking the meaning of citizenship in light of the experiences portrayed in these pages.

Marshall's fundamental aim was, in his own words, "to throw a little light on . . . the impact of a rapidly developing concept of the rights of citizenship on the structure of social inequality." His overriding concern regarded the real and potential contradictions between the premise of equal status in a democratic community and the social and economic inequality inherent in industrial capitalism.[2] With an eye to developing countries, he sought to understand how nations incorporated new social classes into the polity and how they overcame traditional elites' grip on power. England offered the only European example of relatively "peaceful" change in the industrializing process. While Marshall did not entirely ignore gender in his analysis of incorporation into the polity, he was blind to race and ethnicity, a glaring omission given that British industrialization hinged upon imperialism and its grim violation of human rights.

Marshall did, however, draw his typology from a long view of English history, which he used as a basis to link civil, political, and social forms of citizenship to specific institutions: respectively, courts, parliaments, and educational and welfare-granting agencies. In Marshall's words, the "civil" element of citizenship consists "of the rights necessary for individual freedom—liberty of person, freedom of speech, thought and faith, the right to own property and to conclude valid contracts, and the right to justice." The political element conferred the right "to participate in the exercise of political power, as a member of a body invested with political authority or as an elector of the members of such a body." Once this right became "universal" in granting suffrage to all men, the lower classes would be able, through political institutions, to establish "social rights," which Marshall defines as "the whole range from the right to a modicum of economic welfare and security to the right to share to the full in the social heritage and to live the life of a civilized being according to the standards prevailing in society. The institutions most closely connected with it are the educational system and the social services." He qualified his schema by conceding there was "considerable overlap" between political and social rights in the nineteenth and twentieth centuries. Although not the only mention of women in his essay, he essentially dismissed them because of their "difference" from men: "The story of civil rights in their formative period is one of the gradual addition of new rights to a status that already existed and was held to appertain to all adult members of the community—or perhaps one should say to all male members, since the status of women or at least married women, was in some important respects peculiar."[3] Though he explicitly and importantly tied women's lack of citizenship to marriage, he unfortunately did not elaborate on what he meant by "peculiar" and apparently did not think women of any status relevant to his broader schema. It would be easy to argue from his language that he was perpetuating the notion that women did not share "adult" status—a status he clearly identified as "male."

Contrary to Marshall's sociohistorical typology, the various individuals the essays in this volume present were generally not "granted" rights by institutions, but they instead exercised civil rights, demanded social rights, and participated in the polity by influencing policy and legislation. They did so in a wide array of spaces: on the street; through a large variety of institutions such as charities, courts, consulates, and other bureaucratic offices; in associations and private salons; in print media; and through visual representations. The variety of ways in which they exercised agency blurs the definitions, in particular, of civil and social citizenship. As noted in the introduction, the authors in this collection seek to locate within the subjective practice of social rights the seeds for women's citizenship broadly construed. In other words, one can have agency as a citizen regardless of legal status by participating in the affairs of the community and determining outcomes. What do the women portrayed in these pages tell us about the gender system and the nature of gender inequality in the modern period, particularly in the French historical context?

My effort to synthesize and extract conclusions from the diverse cases presented in this volume will draw both on Marshall's typology and on the far more open definition of citizenship offered here based on women's active participation and their own sense of political subjectivity. The first two contributions, by Katie Jarvis and Victoria Thompson, consider issues of gender and the family raised by the Enlightenment and the French Revolution; each depicts transgressions of feminine boundaries and the female body, family roles, and punishment. The Enlightenment, followed by the tumultuous events of the French Revolution, threw into question the nature of patriarchal power—both in ordinary families and in the symbolic power of the king—which in turn destabilized gender relations in ways that resonated throughout the modern era, and indeed persist in our own. At the same time, it is helpful for this analysis to recall how foundational the French Revolution and its Enlightenment underpinnings were for the enduring concept of citizenship, because we see in the legal and constitutional history of the Revolution a microcosm of Marshall's typology: the language of the 1789 Declaration of the Rights of Man and Citizen clearly established civil rights for all men and political rights for some, and the Declaration of 1793 and Constitution of 1793 established political and social citizenship for all men, with direct implications for women's rights as well. Even though the provisions in the 1793 documents were almost immediately suspended, their language demonstrates the link between civil, political, and social rights. Articles 21 and 22 of the 1793 Declaration stated, respectively, "Public relief is a sacred debt. Society owes maintenance to unfortunate citizens, either procuring work for them or in providing the means of existence for those who are unable to labor," and "Education is needed by all. Society ought to favor with all its power the advancement of the public reason and put education at the door of every citizen."[4]

Though women were not explicitly and legally included in the language of these declared rights and laws, and some of their civil liberties were denied with the closure of their clubs and their expulsion from the galleries in 1793, their assumption that this language pertained to them and their participation as *citizenesses* has been well documented, especially in Dominique Godineau's work.[5] Of considerable significance is their iconic march on Versailles. Their violent actions are remembered for their result: bringing the king and his family to Paris. But just as significant is what motivated their actions. The women marched to Versailles not only because of bread prices (the social right to security, i.e., food) but because of anger over evidence that the king would not accept the August decrees and the Declaration of the Rights of Man, as well as outrage over rumors that the king's soldiers had drunkenly stomped on the revolutionary cockade during a lavish banquet—a scene all the more offensive in times of scarce bread.[6] The context in which the women marched to Versailles demonstrates their sense of political subjectivity and engagement with power, a sensibility common to the women portrayed in the essays of this collection.

The incident of the nun spankings brought to light in the first chapter of this volume, one of apparently only two examples of women's collective violence toward other women during the Revolution, offers a most interesting example of women's appropriation of citizenship rights. Jarvis presents an astute, multilayered analysis in her account of these thrashings and their representation in print and in visual imagery. No doubt because of the nature of the sources, the focus here is how the public perceived women's actions rather than on the women themselves and what they thought they were doing. Her conclusion that male perceptions of female violence were "contingent" and depended on a specific cultural context is persuasive. But what is most interesting with regard to appropriation of citizenship is the motivation behind the women's actions: their claim to have a say in the content of their children's education and their desire to remove religious influence from it. Not only were the women not condemned for their violence, but they went unpunished even though they were technically violating the nuns' civil rights. The market women took "justice" into their own hands because the nuns supported nonjuring priests in their refusal to adapt their instructional material to the Civil Constitution of the Clergy. They thus assumed the role of the state—and political citizenship—in acting as judges and executioners of the law, as well as in physically applying a punishment of their own choice, and thereby violated the nuns' own civil right to due process. As Jarvis notes, revolutionaries considered the clergy to be a separate "nation within the nation"; the nuns therefore did not belong to the nation that conferred rights. By supporting nonjuring priests the nuns relinquished any protection the status of citizenship would have conferred.

Given this specific context, it is not surprising that the market women's violence toward other women received no condemnation from male revolutionaries; the women performed a service not only in punishing the nuns in the name of the Civil Constitution of the Clergy but in a public action that lent itself to an important and "entertaining" form of revolutionary propaganda. Once journalists represented their actions in the printed word and visual imagery, however, their meaning also became eroticized and multilayered. Market women's retribution for the nuns' lack of compliance with the revolutionary principles of education became transformed into multifarious representations of motherhood/bareness, lesbianism, husbands' disciplining of wives, and, I would suggest as well, sadomasochistic fantasies. Thanks to Lynn Hunt and other scholars, we know that politically motivated pornography played a large role in the Revolution, and even if the representations of spanking did not become technically pornographic, they were, as Jarvis says, suggestive.[7] Surely women laughed at the jokes alongside men.

While such representations may not have trivialized the market women's actions, they did not dignify them either, especially in the context of citizenship and political subjectivity. In fact they may have done the opposite by reinforcing a sexualized conception of womanhood for both the nuns and their female tormentors. While the market women advanced the cause of the Civil Constitution of the Clergy, once the printed word and very rich imagery retold the story, it was no longer their own. Might the symbolic representations, especially the *verges* used for spanking, and the implication that the market women stepped in as "husbands" to punish "wives," have also served as a reminder and reinforcement of patriarchal domination?

The incidence of the market women's violence against other women implicitly contrasts with the example two years later, when they brawled with radical revolutionary women. In that case the "Dames des Halles" were themselves the victims of targeted violence on the part of ardently politicized women—also practicing citizenship, albeit far more overtly—in wanting to force the market women to wear the revolutionary cockade. This second example of women-on-women violence unfolded, however, in a much different context: that of the dethroned, then beheaded king, and the increasingly radicalized First Republic. The radical revolutionary women wanted to bear arms to protect the Republic and had already helped eliminate moderates from the National Convention in the insurrection of May 31 and June 2. It was at this juncture—women quite explicitly intervening in "male" politics as well as engaging in violence against other women—that members of the National Convention made proclamations about women's "nature" as inappropriate for public affairs. But it is important to note that the market women who opposed the cockade for their sex claimed that "only whores and female Jacobins wear cockades" and that women "should be concerned only with their households and not with current events." They insisted only men should wear the cockade.[8] That the representations of the market women and nuns "played with the tenuous connection between female sexuality and patriotic motherhood," alluding to the Dames' maternal capacities and nuns' childlessness, demonstrates the primal connection between womanhood and motherhood in the minds of male revolutionaries.[9]

The skirmishes of 1793 were far more overtly political precisely because revolutionary women thrust themselves into the National Convention itself, helping oust Girondins and at the same time seeking the right to bear arms explicitly to defend the Republic. Despite the swift repression of their clubs, as has been well-recounted, the Revolution offered women many opportunities to exercise various forms of citizenship beyond legal sanction, and thus it became necessary to reinscribe gender boundaries, most especially in the Civil Code of 1804.

While Napoleon's reign codified many gains of the Revolution, it also reinforced the family and reinstated patriarchal hierarchy. Under the First Republic and First Empire, the idealized responsibilities of motherhood incorporated an enactment of civic duties. But the actual fragility of families across social classes combined with instability in the concept of citizenship opened the way for women to taken on a variety of civic roles. The Restoration monarchy, as Thompson demonstrates, needed once again to redefine the royal family (ideal and real) and its relations to politics. Chastened by revolutionary upheaval, the restored royal family combined Christian ideals with those of motherhood—a particular notion of motherhood associated with republican-Napoleonic patriarchal ideals of domesticity and distinction between the sexes at a time when feminine models for belonging to the nation remained diverse and the concept of citizenship in flux.

In this context Thompson's essay complicates the relationship between family, gender, and citizenship. Marie-Thérèse offered confusingly diverse models of femininity, womanhood, and motherhood. Her own actions, and the contradictory representations of persona, reflected the instability of gender expectations, as well as expectations of the royal family and its relationship to the national family/national body. Through the extraordinary power of text and images, the rehabilitation of Marie-Antoinette as good mother and good wife served as a crucial step in that process. The next step for the monarchy, with Louis XVIII as a childless widower, was to reconstruct his own representational royal "family," with himself as a "good father," which he did through his niece, Marie-Thérèse. To create a strong family image, Marie-Thérèse, childless herself, assumed maternal duties over the duchesse de Berry's children and took on other feminine functions, such as engagement in charity. But as Thompson shows, she also acquired political responsibilities similar to those of a queen. Though she served to consolidate the royal family at a key moment, her multiple familial and political roles apparently produced confusion and resulted in accusations uncannily similar to those that had been leveled against Marie-Antoinette, thereby unraveling the carefully constructed image of a loving and balanced family. The attacks against Marie-Thérèse resulted from irreconcilable differences in the broader family—the French nation—between ultraroyalists and liberals, especially on the issue of regicides who wanted to return from exile to France. Had Marie-Thérèse been a legitimate queen she might not have been subject to the confusions surrounding Louis XVIII's fictional family in which she appeared as both a "daughter" and a "wife," opening the way for detractors to speculate about incest and conjure fantasies about sexual misconduct. She might have been able to exercise legitimate power as a monarch, independent of her identities as daughter, wife, or niece. As was her fate, Marie-Thérèse, like Marie-Antoinette and the nun-spanking market women of 1791, is remembered through vivid images in print media and visual representations that were not of her own creation; they were eroticized products of presumably only men's fantasies. In the cases of both the nuns (unmarried, barren, presumed to have sexual relations with priests) and Marie-Thérèse, the transgression of gender norms served as an excuse to discipline and punish for political reasons. This tendency remains remarkably alive in our contemporary world.[10]

It is probably no coincidence that Jarvis's and Thompson's sources and analyses reveal the prevalence of the age-old tropes of woman as either good mother or sexual transgressor. The role of women, female sexuality, and motherhood, and the relationship these reified concepts had with politicians and state policy, became ever more important topics of concern throughout France's tumultuous political history from the Restoration through World War II. They continued to insert themselves stubbornly into the conceptualization of rights and the languages of citizenship. While the latter were certainly linked to specific political regimes, language also transcended regime change, especially with regard to the political subjectivity both men and women experienced.

Thus it is not surprising that the essays in this volume are not bound by legal definitions of citizenship or specific regimes. Several of them have in common what historians have termed "the rise of the 'social.'"[11]

Generally speaking, this notion refers to a turning point at which, for the broader good of society, the individual's right to life (or, in Marshall's terminology, "security") took precedence over the classic right to freedom, with profound implications for rights of citizenship, the family, and gender. François Ewald locates this transition toward the end of the nineteenth century, when industrialization increased the risk of bodily harm, resulting in the 1898 law on work accidents. The economic and social transformations of modernization had made individuals ever more interdependent, to the point at which society had to take responsibility for assuring survival. "The problematic of social rights," Ewald said, "supposes a universal objectification of the living person as wealth that the society must extract, develop and multiply for the well-being of all: the most important capital is the living person. This problematic is turned towards the maximization of life under all its forms."[12] The timing of this transition also coincided with the rise of "solidarism," a political movement whose proponents feature in several of this volume's essays, and of which more will be said below.

The "rise of the social" and its implications for gendered citizenship, as contributions to this volume suggest, began much earlier than Ewald claims. Joshua Cole attributes its origins to the collection of population data from censuses and the registers of births, deaths, and marriages, registers that became rationalized and more accurate as a result of the French Revolution. These records afforded "new tools of quantitative research" that "served to distinguish the 'social' realm from older conceptions of the 'political' or 'economic.'" Cole's analysis merits quoting at some length for its insights into the stake any nation had in realizing its resources:

> In postrevolutionary France, the political domain was articulated in terms of the opposition between (male) citizens and the state, between a body politic and a sovereign power, which together formed a nation. The economic domain, in contrast, was constituted by relations of exchange between rational (male) individuals, whose public behavior followed a logic of calculation, competition, and enterprise oriented toward the acquisition of wealth. The "social"

realm distinguished itself from the "political" and the "economic" by . . . encompassing both public *and* private spaces, the activities of men *and* women, the effects of politics *and* commerce, the activities of both institutions *and* individuals. The social realm thus became a primary arena for examining the relationship between private decisions and public good, collective will and individual responsibility, and the various obligations that members of each aggregate group owed to the community as a whole.[13]

Thus as early as the first half of the nineteenth century, the work of population researchers produced an epistemological shift that led to a new understanding: national health depended not only on individual behavior but on the health of families, in which women, the nucleus of family well-being, were key players. Political economists such as Thomas Malthus, Jean-Baptiste Say, and Jules Simon viewed female wage earners not as free agents in a market economy but instead as dependents in relation to other family members, whether or not they lived in family units.[14] They thus understood female poverty to result from women's abandoning those "natural" relationships rather than from restrictions on their basic civil rights—property rights, occupations they could practice, or the dual labor market that kept their wages low. As many historians have shown, the recognition that the population was an important resource for labor and the military inspired national and local governments to protect at-risk children, as well as mothers and potential mothers.[15] The Child Labor Law of 1874 was the first of several French laws that restricted certain forms of work for women and children. The same process, of course, occurred in England with the early factory acts. In an important nod to gender, Marshall noted that these acts "meticulously refrained from giving . . . protection directly to the adult male—the citizen par excellence. And they did so out of respect for his status as a citizen, on the grounds that enforced protective measures curtailed the civil right to conclude a free contract of employment. Protection was confined to women and children, and champions of women's rights were quick to detect the implied insult. Women were protected because they were not citizens."[16]

But recent historical scholarship, as this volume points out, suggests that state "protection," contrary to what Marshall claimed, offered women opportunities for "social" citizenship, precisely because of their growing importance to perceptions about national health. Nimisha Barton's and Stephanie McBride-Schreiner's essays turn the process of "protection" upside down by demonstrating, in the context of the "rise of the social," that women exercised individual agency by appropriating social rights for themselves. Both essays depict citizenship as individual practice rather than as an abstract concept or legal category.

The establishment of public assistance and hospitals for indigent children in the first half of the nineteenth century clearly signified a greater concern for the population as a national resource. In particular public assistance and children's hospitals in Paris provide an excellent example of social service institutions created in the context of increased public concern over the health and survivability of young people—perhaps more acutely so in the wake of the Napoleonic wars. In any case the institutionalization of public assistance took place in the context of the "rise of the social": France's future depended on the health of its children, and children needed protection. It is in this framework that McBride-Schreiner notes the French state's public assistance administration considered access to medical care a "right," and eligibility for this form of "social citizenship" rested on two key elements: residence in Paris, which evoked the original, fundamental conception of citizenship based on membership in a community, and on proof of indigence.

The underlying premise in this conception of citizenship, which McBride-Schreiner challenges, is that indigent families taking advantage of charity, like protected workers, relinquished certain civil rights to autonomy and, in this case, control over their children once they entered the hospital. Historians and social scientists such as Marshall, Donzelot, Ewald, and Cole perceive the "rise of the social" as a top-down government response to poverty. McBride-Schreiner demonstrates that this particular form of "citizenship" amounted to a subjective sense of "right" among recipients of charity, so much so that they not only exercised agency in demanding and receiving aid beyond the rules of eligibility, but they challenged professional authority once their children entered the hospitals. One important point McBride-Schreiner makes has to do with maternal authority: mothers featured prominently in parental interventions regarding hospital care, "demonstrating that female agency and strong maternal bonds extended beyond the family unit and into the domain of public welfare institutions. . . . As primary caregivers, mothers were gatekeepers to their children's health and therefore played a crucial role in children's medical care." Not only did mothers have agency in their children's care; the implication here is that they influenced the development of public welfare policy.

Barton's essay on immigration and citizenship addresses issues on a similar register: disenfranchised women on the margins exploited the paternalist ideology and patriarchal state apparatus to their own ends. Also implicitly challenging Marshall's typology, Barton takes us to the interwar period of the twentieth century in the context of population instability caused by migration patterns and low birthrates. It was also a time in which the possibility for women's, especially migrant women's, economic autonomy was declining. On the basis of the case studies she analyzes, Barton claims French and immigrant women in twentieth-century France were able to acquire a gendered form of social citizenship on their own behalf. Her essay demonstrates how these women used the concept of citizenship founded on republican motherhood to engage the polity through their reproductive service to the nation.

In contrast to the revolutionary and Restoration eras, in which concepts of the family and womanhood seemed to be in flux, in the twentieth century it appears the Third Republican state had settled on motherhood as the core of female identity. Fear of "depopulation" intensified the paternalist determination to defend and protect motherhood, and the state extended this protection through its bureaucracy to French women—but largely because of female agency, the state also increased its surveillance of male sexual morality and marital and paternal responsibility. The case histories here challenge the definitions of "social citizenship" in multiple ways. They demonstrate that women, sometimes ingeniously, exploited the prevailing gender system that emphasized women's roles as mothers and limited their access to labor that would provide a living wage. In addition to tracking down men who had abandoned them, in at least one case the system allowed women, rightly or wrongly, to use state powers against men.

But here the definition of "citizenship" becomes murky. One of Barton's most important points is that the women who sought help from consulates, the police, and other administrative institutions, such as the League for the Protection of Abandoned Mothers or the North African Brigade, clearly felt entitled to their services, and in this regard "citizenship" amounted to a sense of entitlement that inhabited their psyches. This sense returns us to the premodern definition of the concept in which citizenship derives from habitation of a city or town.[17] Even in this very basic definition, not only are rights "endowed" with recognition of membership in the community, but duties are expected as well. Women in the cases Barton explores felt themselves to be members of a community whose regulations conveyed a message that such membership conferred a right to have the state intervene in their private relations when husbands or boyfriends did not live up to their "duties." Barton notes that French and immigrant women "co-opted a wide network of overlapping regulatory systems" to achieve their ends. If their ends were a measure of "social security," then they indeed actively established social citizenship for themselves; they were not passive recipients of a state "endowment."

This demonstration of feminine agency is particularly interesting given that immigrant women, unless married to French men, were not technically citizens of France. Did these women actually think of themselves as "citizens" performing the duties of republican motherhood, or were they simply trying to survive as desperate individuals? Did their actions have any influence on the system itself?[18] Certainly some of these cases suggest that even though women exploited the French national rhetoric of "protection" to use state and police powers, they did so for their own self-serving ends, with little consciousness of any French national identity whose basis would confer "universal" rights. Could it be they were simply "working the system" without any consciousness of a national citizenship based on the concept of universal rights? Did the manipulation of state and police powers, with (or without) knowledge of ideology that informed policy, constitute a form of citizenship? Clearly the cases Barton presents suggest these women were quite savvy in manipulating the official paternalist policies that framed their status, one from which they benefited because they inhabited the French nation. We cannot know, however, whether their demands for redress reflected a subjective sense of social citizenship connected to a national identity or simply reflected the extension of anonymous bureaucratic functions into private lives.

While McBride-Schreiner's and Barton's essays demonstrate economically marginalized women's abilities to practice a form of citizenship by taking advantage of social services and state institutions, the remaining essays in this volume address middle- and upper-class women's implicit or explicit claims to citizenship through various forms of civic engagement. These women acted as self-conscious "citizens" in their efforts at social reform, especially with regard to women's and children's vulnerabilities to the economic, social, and cultural vicissitudes of modernization. Emblematic of the "rise of the social," the authors to whom Jean Pedersen devotes her essay reflect this civic engagement. Her research unveils yet another ingenious way women asserted themselves into a male-dominated public sphere of print culture. Similar to how women in Barton's chapter appropriated a system of regulation to their own ends, Pedersen shows how the school inspector Pauline Kergomard, the consumer activist Elise Chalamet, and the feminist journalist Louise Compain appropriated the facts of social statistics and reproduced them in forms more compelling than those of social scientists. Through their respective professions and activism, as well as through their fictional publications, these three women contributed to the establishment of social service institutions that helped fulfill the right to security for women and children. Indeed the documentation in this essay demonstrates that the impetus behind social reform and its concrete results had major input from women in the realms of child protection and education, housing for domestic servants, and issues regarding women's social and legal conditions. Just as the work of the Union française pour le sauvetage de l'enfance continues to this day, so do many of the social problems these women identified. Most poignantly, perhaps, is the cheap, slave-like female sweated labor that continues to produce inexpensive clothing for fashion-conscious middle-class women. The character's plea in Compain's novel that there be a campaign to convince women not to purchase clothes that did not provide living wages for the women who produced them has been made in our own time on behalf of migrants to the United States and workers in foreign countries who enjoy no citizenship rights of any sort.[19]

Pedersen rightly emphasizes the power of these women's words, especially in newspaper articles, serialized novels, and books that were widely consumed. That Compain received such a positive review from the solidarist Charles Gide indicates further the influence she and other writers had on the social reform movement known as "solidarism" in the early Third Republic. Gide was a leading proponent of this reformist political ideology, who wanted to use the "facts" of social science to reconcile the working class and the bourgeoisie and thereby ward off socialism; Pedersen highlights her authors' implicit and sometimes explicit contributions to the social project of solidarism by noting that they encouraged readers to empathize across class lines in their effort to harness support for social reform.

The women featured in Eliza Ferguson's essay on the white slave trade also demonstrate the power of female voices in solidarism and other reform movements across the political spectrum. Similar to the efforts of the authors Pedersen analyzes, these reformers also targeted female vulnerability, but in this case they were concerned with the dangers sexual predators posed. While Barton's essay suggests that female sexuality (leading to pregnancy) made women economically vulnerable and in need of state-sponsored protection, Ferguson writes that women's economic vulnerability was equated with sexual, and thus moral vulnerability. The assumption that women, single or otherwise, could not earn a living wage clearly links the two essays, as does the premise that women were not supposed to achieve economic independence even if their need to work went unquestioned.

This realm of philanthropy also opened new spaces for bourgeois women to become actively involved in social reform. As Ferguson shows, the orphanages, schools, shelters, and placement agencies gave women reformers the opportunity to train young girls in proper domestic duties that would help "regenerate" the nation; memberships in organizations and associations and attendance at national and international conferences allowed middle-class women to engage publicly with men, contribute to the formulation of social reform policies, and develop their own careers in public speaking, organizing, administration, and journalism. Preserving these girls and young women from predators was not the only goal of these philanthropists; they also targeted more generally the social inequities of low-paid work and bad housing and recognized the importance of helping young women acquire lucrative skills. Even more significant for the themes in this volume, through their charitable organizations these women philanthropists participated institutionally in not only assisting victims but in actively contributing to the prosecution of criminals through surveillance, data collection, presentation of reports, and the formulation of government policy itself.

The women reformers became empowered in part because of the common purpose so many agencies shared. The government initiatives and the private Protestant, Catholic, Jewish, and secular charities that would have otherwise had competing goals, all shared the same ideas about "the status of girls and why they merited protection," writes Ferguson. Their goal was not to eliminate prostitution but to preserve young French women from it, particularly in foreign countries. In this case of investigating human trafficking, however, the reformist agendas appear to be somewhat ambiguous. The actual "social facts" regarding *blanches* being traded as sexual slaves seem less clear than interest in the *jeunes filles* as a demographic category—a category that had potential for either good or ill—in motivating concern about their vulnerability. A higher proportion of girls and women working for wages outside the home, in addition to increased geographic mobility made possible by trains across Europe and trams in large cities, gave rise to what we might call a "New Girl," who generated anxieties parallel to those over the "New Woman" just around 1900, when the impacts of secular education became palpable.[20] With her comment "Rather than being lost to international sex work, girls' productive and reproductive capacities were essential to revitalizing the French nation and race," Ferguson implies that reformers primarily hoped to channel young working-class women into proper female roles and harness their reproductive potential for France more than protect civil and social rights.

Nonetheless these women reformers exercised civil rights in their public activism, created social rights by establishing educational and welfare institutions, and practiced political agency and subjectivity by influencing government policy. The women philanthropists who intervened in the "white slave trade" demonstrated a subjective sense of membership in the national and even international polity and through their own practices intervened in the relationship between the state and citizens. Pedersen's and Ferguson's essays both highlight the importance of social reform efforts coming from women, especially how the philanthropic networks and strategies among women ultimately influenced national and international policies.

Another common theme is that middle-class women central to each essay were participating in the body politic, influencing the male world of state politics, by seeking to protect and improve the conditions of others rather than seeking civil, social, or political rights for themselves as individuals. Although women successfully brought attention to and proposed remedies for the white slave trade—and shaped the policies that men instituted—their activities fit traditional notions of womanhood defined as self-sacrificing and nurturing. Even this account of powerful elite women philanthropists helping prostitutes or potential prostitutes once again illustrates the sexualized tropes based on woman as either angelic mother or whore in need of salvation, in this case the former being the antidote to the latter. This observation is not at all intended to denigrate the work many of these women performed: not only did they clearly participate with words and actions in civil society, but they took the issue of the white slave trade to the international level. Acknowledging what they did is all the more important given that, like the continued international exploitation of workers today, human trafficking persists; the actions these women took to address the exploitation of girls and young women not only merit the acknowledgment made here but provide models for intervention in a problem too readily ignored.

Cheryl Koos's essay also presents a case of women's political subjectivity and active engagement in the public realm, as well as a process of integration into male associations in ways remarkably similar to those presented in Ferguson's and Pedersen's chapters. Koos demonstrates clearly the strong influence on social policy that the Catholic activist Vérine (Marguerite Lebrun) and her associates, such as G. Jean Camus, exerted through the Ecole des parents and the Union féminine civique et sociale, and in their association with the Alliance Nationale and other natalist-familialist groups. Moreover the ideology these women (and the men with whom they associated) advocated bears some resemblance to solidarism in its focus on gender hierarchy and class reconciliation, particularly through the family. Similar to solidarists, Vérine and her associates believed the strength of the lower-class families was key to national health and that family well-being depended entirely on women, though unlike President Georges Risler of Musée Social, she did not blame the creation of slums on poor housekeeping.[21] Several factors distinguished Vérine and her fellow social reformers from their predecessors: the economic, physical, cultural, and emotional upheavals of the Great War and the perception of moral weakness and degeneration—especially in the wake of the movement that had tried to popularize birth control. The war and the massive population losses and dislocations it incurred brought increased attention to the ongoing demographic crisis of "depopulation" and the perception of weakened family life as birth rates continued to be anemic.

Similar to other women in this volume, Vérine succeeded in becoming a political fixture in a predominantly male world and thus "practiced citizenship" as broadly defined in these essays. Her rhetoric, however, goes much further than those of solidarists in seeking to define the social rights and duties of women by saying that "the wife, the mother is . . . a person who only finds her real identity in the most total and complete self-abnegation" and that "woman is . . . made for man, for the child, for the home."²² Her iterations not only reflect the traditional Catholic doctrine of female self-sacrifice but of course also manifest her desire to reverse the historical course of the family—and of human rights—that in the previous two hundred years resulted in pernicious individualism and civil rights of citizenship for women. If Vérine had simply been one marginal voice in this movement, perhaps her words could be taken less seriously; instead her explicit admiration of youth education in Nazi Germany and fascist Italy, her contributions to the manifesto of the National Revolution of Vichy, and the path she and the natalist-familialists helped pave toward the Vichy regime and its family policies are testimony to her power as a "citizen." These testimonies also provide another example of how such power could be turned against the rights of women as human beings with inherent personhood.

Sara Kimble's contribution to this volume is the only one that discusses women who explicitly sought equal rights of citizenship in a legal sense. Like Koos's activists, Kimble's pursued their agenda in the tumultuous wake of World War I, but also in the important international context of women in most democracies having achieved political citizenship. Since France was the exception with regard to winning the vote, it made sense that French feminists would reach out to their enfranchised sisters in other countries; unlike the nonfeminist or antifeminist reformers portrayed above, the feminists in this chapter overtly engaged in politics for the benefit of all women, not just those deemed in need of rescue or protection. But crossing national boundaries also raised the issue of women's rights beyond specifically national citizenship and highlighted in particular the legal inequalities marriage caused. Kimble argues that international feminists' activism ultimately provided substance to international agreements and in turn helped advance French women's equal voting rights in 1944, the establishment of women's equality in the French Constitution of 1946, and the United Nations' Universal Declaration of Human Rights in 1948. The debate generated by the collaboration of French and American feminists not only helped advance these measures but demonstrates once again that French women could achieve political change without having legal political citizenship.

Despite positive (though unfinished) results, the disagreements over tactics, strategies, and goals in these debates have much in common with issues highlighted in other chapters. One of them was married women's right to their own nationality, so important to the core of personhood. The other was the persistent conflict between the quest for equality and the insistence on the importance of biological difference. Both issues point to the bane of feminism: women, as a gender, do not share common interests even with regard to marriage itself. Why would women oppose a law allowing them to choose their nationality? Did they think it would undermine paternal authority, weaken the national fabric, or leave women unprotected if they lived in a country that was not of their own nationality? Unlike other women discussed in this volume who practiced citizenship through their varied forms of activism, the feminists in Kimble's essay addressed head-on the intractable issues of women's personhood, raised in only negative terms by Vérine, who denied women any inherent personhood. Through their courageous words and actions the American and French feminists of the interwar years ultimately, if not immediately, succeeded in using international law as a mechanism to shape international agreements resulting in women's improved status.

The enduring and intractable paradox of "equality versus difference" has prevented full equal rights for women and has always caused well-known divisions among feminists.[23] It is also an issue implicit in in this volume's essays. Many of the women who practiced citizenship without its full legal benefits did so as subordinates taking advantage of the need for "protection" either for themselves or for other women, girls, or children. While they broke the restraints of gender normativity in their practices, many of them also reinforced it. Bourgeois women's participation in solidarism is particularly interesting in this regard because while defending and seeking to stabilize the Third Republic and republicanism in general, solidarism was also grounded in gender inequality and restrictive definitions of womanhood. At the height of his own and his fellow solidarists' influence, for example, Emile Cheysson noted the centrality of woman in the home; she was the "keystone of the family" whose responsibility was keeping order and stability in domestic life. The universality of these female obligations, he said, "brings together all the women of the world, those of the bourgeoisie and those of the people."[24]

Although not all solidarists shared views on gender roles quite that rigid (Cheysson did not think women should participate in reform movements), his words do reflect the general solidarist position that social order depended on class and gender cooperation, collaboration, and, perhaps most important for the purposes of this collection, hierarchy. It goes without saying that women cannot be reduced to a single biological and cultural identity that knows neither class nor national boundaries. Several decades of women's history, and many of the women depicted in this volume, give the lie to Cheysson's reductive, naïve, and self-serving vision. Wives and mothers have very different interests from lifelong single women who, whether or not by choice, do not have children, and of course gender interests vary along lines of race, class, sexual orientation, national/cultural/ethnic identity, and sexual/gender identity—which is not to say that gender is no longer a useful category of analysis.

Each chapter in this book demonstrates a diversity of women who sought to establish human rights and dignity for themselves and for others in their own historical eras and contexts. From the market women of Paris during the Revolution to the likes of Marie-Thérèse during the Restoration, migrant and working women of Paris, and bourgeois social reformers, women conducted themselves in a manner suggesting they subjectively felt membership in the polity despite the fact that they were categorically excluded from full citizenship. They also appropriated republican language and law for their own purposes and took advantage of concerns about population health and fears of decline and "degeneration" to demand in some cases medical care and in others protection from errant partners who contributed to family pathology. Middle-class women led full lives and found fulfilling careers as they engaged in reform movements to redress issues of family degeneration and female vulnerability caused by disruptions of modernization.

Although Cheysson erred in his ideal vision of a "universal" womanhood, the common thread that runs through these chapters is revelatory: in one way or another each essay includes commentary on women as mothers or potential mothers, even if that theme is not the primary focus. And indeed it is thanks to France's population crisis and the natalist-familialist movement that mothers and children in that country have comparatively more support and benefits than in many others, especially the United States; through the twentieth century these benefits improved quality of life and afforded mothers, children, and families a measure of security they would not otherwise have had. Perhaps because of the repeated revolution and consequent destabilization of gender roles, and because of the important context of "republican motherhood" and maternalism, feminist movements to establish full equality in France were more divided, weaker, and more reticent than in other modernizing countries in the nineteenth and twentieth centuries. A large faction of French feminists, moreover, helped advance and took great advantage of the maternalist vision, which in turn helped reinforce gender difference.[25] The starting premise of this book is that it "demonstrates how gender normativity and the constraints placed on women as a result nevertheless created opportunities for a renegotiation of the social—and sexual—contract."[26] It is possible indeed that the ability to practice "social citizenship" undermined the need to insist on full political citizenship, and thus undermined feminism itself.

It was not just French feminism that was weak, however; what this volume also demonstrates is an implicit and surprising link between the rhetoric of solidarists and that of the far-right natalist-familialists. The same maternalist vision, as Koos's chapter demonstrates, paved the way for a darker, more oppressive vision of the family and its relationship to the state, one that restricted women's roles and especially restricted reproductive rights and the ability of women to be fully autonomous individuals.[27] It is no accident that birth control remained illegal in France until 1967. While this volume clearly demonstrates women's ability to practice citizenship, the outcomes of these women's actions did not always advance the interests of women as a category, nor, with the important exception of activists for the Equal Rights Treaty, did they advance the interests of women as autonomous human beings who have inherent personhood.

Notes

1. T. H. Marshall, *Class, Citizenship, and Social Development: Essays by T. H. Marshall*, with an introduction by Seymour Martin Lipset (New York: Doubleday, 1965), chap. 4, "Citizenship and Social Class."
2. Marshall, *Class, Citizenship, and Social Development*, 134, xii.
3. Marshall, *Class, Citizenship, and Social Development*, 78–79, 21, 18.
4. "Declaration of the Rights of Man and Citizen from the Constitution of the Year I (1793)," in *The Constitutions and Other Select Documents Illustrative of the History of France 1789-1901*, ed. Frank Maloy Anderson (Minneapolis: H. W. Wilson, 1904), 170–74, reprinted in *Liberty, Equality, Fraternity: Exploring the French Revolution*, ed. Jack R. Censer and Lynn Hunt, American Social History Productions, 2001, http://www.columbia.edu/~iw6/docs/dec1793.html.
5. Dominique Godineau, *The Women of Paris and Their Revolution*, trans. Katherin Streip (Berkeley: University of California Press, 1998), 53, 299.
6. William Doyle, *The Oxford History of the French Revolution* (New York: Oxford University Press, 1989), 120; Jeremy Popkin, *A Short History of the French Revolution*, 5th edition (Boston: Prentice Hall), 42.
7. Lynn Hunt, "The Many Bodies of Marie Antoinette: Political Pornography and the Problem of the Feminine in the French Revolution," in *Eroticism and the Body Politic*, ed. Lynn Hunt (Baltimore: Johns Hopkins University Press, 1991), 108–30; Lynn Hunt, "Pornography in the French Revolution," in *The Invention of Pornography: Obscenity and the Origins of Modernity, 1500-1800* (New York: Zone Books, 1993), 301–9. Politically motivated pornography, Hunt shows, reached its height in the 1790s.
8. Godineau, *The Women of Paris*, 159–62.
9. The quote is from Jarvis in this volume.
10. Parallels might be made to social commentary on the confusing, conflicted roles of the "first ladies" and "first daughters" contemporary to our own times.
11. For example, Jacques Donzelot, *L'invention du social, essai sur le déclin des passions politiques* (Paris: Seuil, 1994); François Ewald, *L'Etat providence* (Paris: Grasset, 1986); Donzelot, "The Promotion of the Social," *Economy and Society* 17 (August 1988): 404.
12. Ewald, *L'Etat providence*, 25.

13. Joshua Cole, *The Power of Large Numbers: Population, Politics, and Gender in Nineteenth-Century France* (Ithaca NY: Cornell University Press, 2000), 12. See also Mary Poovey, *Making a Social Body: British Cultural Formation, 1830-1864* (Chicago: University of Chicago Press, 1995), on which Cole said he bases his argument.

14. In addition to Cole, see also Joan Wallach Scott, "'L'ouvrière! Mot impie, sordide . . .': Women Workers in the discourse of French Political Economy, 1840-1860," in *Gender and the Politics of History* (New York: Columbia University Press, 1988). In summarizing Say, Scott notes, "A woman's labor in childbirth and her activities caring for children did not figure in . . . [wage] calculations. Childbirth and childrearing were rather the raw materials on which economic forces acted, the elements of nature with which human societies were built" (144).

15. Elinor Accampo, "Gender, Social Policy, and the Formation of the Third Republic," in *Gender and the Politics of Social Reform in France, 1870-1914,* ed. Elinor A. Accampo, Rachel G. Fuchs, and Mary Lynn Stewart (Baltimore: Johns Hopkins University Press, 1995), 1-27.

16. Marshall, *Class, Citizenship, and Social Development*, 89.

17. See any dictionary definition, such as in the OED. Marshall, for example, states, "Citizenship is a status bestowed on those who are full members of a community. All who possess the status are equal with respect to the rights and duties with which the status is endowed" (*Class, Citizenship, and Social Development*, 92).

18. For another assessment of migrant women and issues of citizenship in France—in this case mostly (but not all) upper-class Americans—see Nancy L. Green, *The Other Americans in Paris: Businessmen, Countesses, Wayward Youth, 1880-1941* (Chicago: University of Chicago Press, 2014), esp. 77-112.

19. Contemporary examples, while invisible to consumers, are pervasive. One poignant case is the Rana Plaza complex in Bangladesh, one of the major suppliers of highly popular cheap European and American clothing brands such as H&M, Gap, Tommy Hilfiger, and many others. It was known for terrible working conditions prior to the building's collapse in 2013. The demand for cheap clothing from Europe and the United States and competition with low-cost producers in other countries makes it impossible for factories to improve working conditions or raise wages. "Building Collapse in Bangladesh Leaves Scores Dead," *New York Times*, April 24, 2013.

20. For the cultural impacts of secular education, especially on women, see Patricia A. Tilburg, *Colette's Republic: Work, Gender, and Popular Culture in France, 1870-1914* (New York: Berghahn Books, 2009).

21. For example, the solidarist Emile Cheysson wrote that women "held the secret of the alleviation of misery, of the well-being of the worker, of the reconciliation of the classes, of social peace, and of the moral unity and greatness of the nation." He strongly believed that qualities essential to womanhood—nurturing, modesty, and the ability to maintain a household—would make good citizens of workers. See Sanford Elwitt, *The Third Republic Defended: Bourgeois Reform in France, 1880–1914* (Baton Rouge: Louisiana State University Press, 1986), 73.

22. See Koos, this volume. It is perhaps worth mentioning that it was precisely this image, *l'éternelle sacrifiée* (eternally sacrificing woman), against which the feminist and birth control advocate Nelly Roussel (1878–1922) bitterly fought during the entirety of her brief adult life. Her ideology had little purchase, even among mainstream feminists, but she certainly incurred the wrath of pronatalists and Senator René Berenger and the likes of people such as Vérine. Elinor A. Accampo, *Blessed Motherhood, Bitter Fruit: Nelly Roussel and the Politics of Female Pain in Third Republic France* (Baltimore: Johns Hopkins University Press, 2006).

23. The classic example is Joan Wallach Scott, *Only Paradoxes to Offer: French Feminists and the Rights of Man* (Cambridge MA: Harvard University Press, 1996).

24. Emile Cheysson, *Les Ouvriers et les réformes nécessaires* (Paris: Dentu, 1877), 12–14, 27–33; *Revue de la Solidarité Sociale* (1906): 433–34, as quoted in Elwitt, *Third Republic Defended*, 73 (specific source of quote not cited). Elwitt goes on to say, "[Cheysson] did not expect bourgeois women to play active public roles in social reform—he looked for no French Jane Addams—but he did expect them to acquit their social responsibilities as members of a ruling class" (75).

25. See especially Anna Cova, *Maternité et droits des femmes en France: XIXe–XXe siècles* (Paris: Anthropos, 1997); Anna Cova, *"Au service de l'église, de la patrie et de la famille": Femmes catholiques et maternité sous la IIIe République* (Paris: L'Harmattan, 2000).

26. Barton and Hopkins, this volume.

27. The birth control, or neo-Malthusian, movement was increasingly persecuted after 1910 and was completely repressed and prosecuted during World War I. All forms of female birth control were made illegal in 1920 (Accampo, *Blessed Motherhood, Bitter Fruit*). For women in Vichy, see Amanda Pollard, *Reign of Virtue: Mobilizing Gender in Vichy* (Chicago: University of Chicago Press, 1998).

Contributors

Elinor A. Accampo is a professor of history at the University of Southern California. She specializes in modern French social and cultural history. She has focused her research on gender and family issues, nineteenth- and twentieth-century France, and European social and cultural history. Her books include *Blessed Motherhood, Bitter Fruit: Nelly Roussel and the Politics of Female Pain in Third Republic France* (2006) and *Industrialization, Family and Class Relations: Saint Chamond, 1815-1914* (1989), as well as several co-authored and edited books, including *Gender and the Politics of Social Reform in France, 1870-1914*, with Rachel Ginnis Fuchs and Mary Lynn Stewart (1995) and *Confronting Modernity in Fin-de-Siècle France: Bodies, Minds and Gender*, with Christopher E. Forth (2010). She is currently doing a project on the 1918 influenza pandemic.

Nimisha Barton is a diversity consultant in higher education. Her scholarly work centers on gender and sexuality studies, migration and diaspora, and modern French and European political, social, and cultural history. Her publications have appeared in *Journal of Women's History* and *French Politics, Culture and Society* as well as edited volumes such as *A History of Work in the Twentieth Century*. Her book manuscript is entitled "Reproductive Citizens: Gender, Immigration, and the State in France, 1900-1945."

Eliza Earle Ferguson is a visiting scholar in Duke University's Department of History. Her research focuses on French social, cultural and gender history. She has published in the *Journal of Social History*, the *Journal of Women's History,* and the *Journal of Urban History*. Her book, *Gender and Justice: Violence, Intimacy,* *and Community in Fin-de-Siècle Paris* (2010), analyzes the practices of violence in intimate relationships among the working poor of Paris at the end of the nineteenth century.

Richard S. Hopkins is an assistant professor of history at Widener University and affiliate faculty in the Gender, Women's and Sexuality Studies Program. His research and teaching focus on modern French and European social, cultural, urban, and gender history. He is the author of *Planning the Greenspaces of Nineteenth-Century Paris* (2015), which explores, in part, women's active role in shaping urban space. From 2011 to 2014 he served as managing editor for the journal *French Historical Studies*.

Katie Jarvis is an assistant professor of history at the University of Notre Dame. Her research focuses on popular politics and the intersection of social and cultural history during the French Revolution. Her articles have appeared in the *Journal of Social History* and *French Historical Studies*. She is the author of *Politics in the Marketplace: Work, Gender, and Citizenship in Revolutionary France* (forthcoming).

Sara L. Kimble is an associate professor at DePaul University. Her research focuses on the history of gender, society, and law in modern France and transnationally. Her publications have appeared in journals such as *French Historical Studies* and *French Colonial History*, as well as anthologies such as *Law and Lawmaking in Nineteenth and Twentieth Century Europe* (2014). With Marion Röwekamp she published a chapter in and co-edited *New Perspectives in European Women's Legal History* (2017). She recently published "Transatlantic Networks for Legal Feminism, 1888–1912," in "Forging Bonds across Borders: Transatlantic Collaborations for Women's Rights and Social Justice in the Long Nineteenth Century," special issue of *German Historical Institute Bulletin Supplement*, edited by Britta Waldschmidt-Nelson and Anja Schüler, 13 (2017): 55–73. Her book manuscript, entitled "Women, Feminism, and the Law in Modern France: Justice Redressed," is under contract with Routledge.

Cheryl A. Koos is a professor of history and California State University, Los Angeles. She has written extensively on the topic of women, the family, and the extreme right in twentieth-century France. She is a co-editor with Cora Granata of *The Human Tradition in Modern Europe* (2007) and has contributed to anthologies such as *The French Right between the Wars: Political and Intellectual Movements from Conservatism to Fascism* (2014) and *Women, Gender, and the Extreme Right in Europe, 1919-1945* (2003). She has published articles in journals such as *French Historical Studies*, the *Journal of Family History*, and *Modern and Contemporary France*.

Jean Elisabeth Pedersen is an associate professor of history at the Eastman School of Music of the University of Rochester. Her research interests include modern French history, comparative French and American history, European and American intellectual history, the social and cultural history of knowledge, and the national and international history of feminism. She is the author of *Legislating the French Family: Feminism, Theater, and Republican Politics, 1870-1920* (2003), and her articles have appeared in a range of journals that includes *French Historical Studies*, *Gender and History*, *Historical Reflections/Réflexions historiques*, the *Journal of the History of the Behavioral Sciences*, and *SIGNS: Journal of Women in Culture and Society*.

Stephanie McBride-Schreiner earned her PhD in history and graduate certificate in scholarly publishing from the School of Historical, Philosophical Religious Studies at Arizona State University. She is the publications manager for the Mary Lou Fulton Teachers College at ASU, where she oversees the college's open access scholarly journals of education. Her background is in nineteenth-century European social history, and her primary research interests include the histories of childhood, women and gender, social institutions, and medicine. Her current project is a comparative study of two nineteenth-century children's hospitals in London and Paris that examines the transcultural flows of pediatric knowledge and practices between these medical institutions.

Victoria E. Thompson is an associate professor of history at Arizona State University. Her work combines cultural and social history approaches, focusing on the interplay between representation and experience. Her research interests include the history of urban space, travel and travel writing, and the history of women, gender, and sexuality. She is the author of *The Virtuous Marketplace: Women and Men, Money and Politics in Paris, 1830–1870* (2000) and, with Rachel G. Fuchs, *Women in European History* (2004). She is currently completing a book manuscript entitled "Inventing Public Space: Paris, 1748–1790."

Johnson Kent Wright is an associate professor in the School of Civil and Economic Thought at Arizona State University. A specialist in European intellectual history in the era of the Enlightenment and the French Revolution, he is the author of *A Classical Republican in Eighteenth-Century France: The Political Thought of Mably* (1997) and a forthcoming book, "The Revolutionary Atlantic, 1763–1830," as well articles and essays on Montesquieu, Rousseau, and modern historiography. From 2011 to 2014 he was a co-editor, with Rachel Fuchs, of the journal *French Historical Studies*.

Index

Mayer, Arno, 48n96
McBride-Schreiner, Stephanie, 10, 268–69
McKenzie, Beatrice, 239
medical care. *See* health care
militancy, of women's movement, 235
Miller, Carol, 220–21
monarchy. *See* royal family
Monod, Sarah, 167, 183n44
Monod, Wilfred, 143
Monsaingeon, Maurice, 195
Montenach, baronne de, 170
moral education. *See* Ecole des Parents
Morgenstern, Mira, 55, 71n21
Morsier, Emilie de, 167–68, 184n48
motherhood: agency in children's health care, 110–16, 117–19; and childbearing obligations, 79, 192, 193; as form of civic participation, 55–56, 282n21; of Marie-Thérèse, 62–63; patriotic, 32–34, *33*. *See also* Ecole des Parents; family

Napoleon Bonaparte, 60, 63
natalism and familialism: and concern for depopulation, 191–92; and nationalism, 198–202, 204–5; opposition to, 282n22; organizations promoting, 192–98; and women's childbearing obligations, 79, 192, 193
nationalism and patriotism: and moral education, 198–202, 204–5; and patriotic motherhood, 32–34, *33*
nationality rights, 237–39
Netter, Yvonne, 232, 234
Nolin, Louise, 118
North African Brigade, 90–91

novels. *See* social novels
nuns: caricatures of, 27–29, *29*, 32–36, *33*, *35*; as counterrevolutionaries, 19, 24–25; satires on, 30–32, 36–39; spanking of, 19–20, 25–27; vindicating violence against, 39–41
NWP (National Woman's Party): expansion into France, 217–18, 223–24, 226–31; international equality campaigns, 219–21, 231–36, *233*, 238–39; strict definition of equality, 225–26, 247n50

Oeuvre des libérées de Saint-Lazare, 168
Oeuvre international de la protection de la jeune fille, 169–70, 174
Offen, Karen M., 5, 95n8
Oster, Madame, 171

Pange, Jean de, 204
Parti Social Français (PSF), 205–6
Passmore, Kevin, 205
Pateman, Carole, 1, 20
paternal authority, 3–4, 54–55, 57–58, 66
paternity suits, 139
patriotism and nationalism: and moral education, 198–202, 204–5; and patriotic motherhood, 32–34, *33*
Paul, Alice, *216*; as activist, 219; expands NWP, 217–18, 224; promotes international equality, 220, 238, 239
Pedersen, Jean Elisabeth, 10–11, 96n17, 271–72
Péguy, Charlès, 204
Pernot, Georges, 198, 199
Perreau, Bruno, 17n24
Pethick-Lawrence, Emmeline, 217

CPSIA information can be obtained
at www.ICGtesting.com
Printed in the USA
LVHW091515051218
599364LV00001B/136/P